Green Energy and Technology

Climate change, environmental impact and the limited natural resources urge scientific research and novel technical solutions. The monograph series Green Energy and Technology serves as a publishing platform for scientific and technological approaches to “green”—i.e. environmentally friendly and sustainable—technologies. While a focus lies on energy and power supply, it also covers “green” solutions in industrial engineering and engineering design. Green Energy and Technology addresses researchers, advanced students, technical consultants as well as decision makers in industries and politics. Hence, the level of presentation spans from instructional to highly technical.

Indexed in Scopus.

Indexed in Ei Compendex.

Alessandra Battisti · Maurizio Marceca ·
Giuseppe Ricotta · Silvia Iorio
Editors

Equity in Health and Health Promotion in Urban Areas

Multidisciplinary Interventions at International and National Level

Springer

Editors
Alessandra Battisti
PDTA—Department of Planning, Design and Technology of Architecture
Sapienza University of Rome
Rome, Italy

Maurizio Marceca
DSPMI—Department of Public Health and Infectious Diseases
Sapienza University of Rome
Rome, Italy

Giuseppe Ricotta
DISSE—Department of Social Sciences and Economics
Sapienza University of Rome
Rome, Italy

Silvia Iorio
Department of Medical-Surgical Sciences and Biotechnologies, Unit of the History of Medicine and Bioethics
Sapienza University of Rome
Rome, Italy

ISSN 1865-3529 ISSN 1865-3537 (electronic)
Green Energy and Technology
ISBN 978-3-031-16181-0 ISBN 978-3-031-16182-7 (eBook)
https://doi.org/10.1007/978-3-031-16182-7

This Springer imprint is published by the registered company Springer Nature Switzerland AG
The registered company address is: Gewerbestrasse 11, 6330 Cham, Switzerland

Preface

In international scientific thinking, the urban context is today the meeting ground between different disciplines and areas of study. The inherent complexity of this subject of study requires highly complex responses, which must also take into consideration the peculiarities and characteristics of *urbs*—that is, understood as a physical city. At the same time, this is also *civitas*—understood as urban society, the community. In order to stay within these multiple levels of thought, it is necessary to adopt knowledge and tools from numerous areas of study from the field of social sciences as well as technical sciences.

Some proposals of the World Health Organization go in this direction. Starting from the knowledge acquired in the last decade from the approach based on Social Determinants, these proposals aim to integrate, in a single toolkit, qualitative–quantitative, epidemiological and urban-architectural tools, for the evaluation of urban interventions, with the aim of identifying and responding to social inequalities in the urban environment. To date, more than half of the world's population lives in an urbanized environment—an estimated 70% by 2050. Based on these findings, it was decided to build the path of this volume that guarantees priority of scientific attention and new strength to the field of health in urban environment, or 'urban health'. By bringing together multidisciplinary contributions of international experts, the volume aims to become an opportunity for a meeting ground and discussion between leaders from different areas of studies and disciplines (architecture, urban planning, public health, sociology and anthropology).

The varying and complex relationships that occur among the individual, the community and the urban dwelling—understood in a very broad sense as a space in which the different activities of people take place (work, social and recreational)—significantly affect the quality of our existence, which is determined by the level of our physical, mental and social health. For these reasons, reflecting today on the role of health within our lifestyles and on the organization of cities requires a multi-voice evaluation as well as a debate on broader issues that closely connect a number of different issues: climate change and urban models of sustainable development, social inequalities and public policies, access to services and quality of infrastructure, questioning the future of the territories, in particular the most fragile and vulnerable ones, and the social dynamics of the populations living there. Faced with an interest in achieving meaningful, fair and lasting solutions in order to contrast and reduce health inequalities, we have worked to implement the formulation of new multidisciplinary approaches, oriented to the quality of life within an ecological model of health. This scientific initiative—which arises from the interest of the Working Group on Equity in Health, inside Sapienza University of Rome—was built with a solid multidisciplinary approach. There is a growing awareness that facing the complexity that today's world increasingly presents us, requires a convergence of viewpoints and experiences, as well as the study and sharing of objectives and approaches. In this regard, we need to draw on the philosophy of SDGs, the Sustainable Development Goals of the United Nations. More specifically, we should highlight the interdependence of the Goals, and therefore, the need for coordination of the sectors concerned has launched its very important challenge. At first glance, it could therefore be said that the volume considers the interaction between Goal 3—*Health and Wellbeing*—and Goal 11—*Sustainable Cities and Communities*. This is certainly true, however, if we look closer we can see the need to consider how much the promotion of health in urban areas, or the focus chosen for this meeting, is also closely linked to Objective 16—*Peace, Justice and Solid Institutions*—, as well as to Objectives 6—*Clean water and sanitation*—, 7—*Clean and accessible energy*—, 9—*Enterprises, innovation and infrastructure*—, 12—*Responsible consumption and production*—, 13—*Fight against climate change*—. And how can we fail to invoke the more classic objectives, which in the medical-scientific literature take the name of 'determinants of health'? That is, the 4th—*Quality education*—, the 8th—*Decent work and economic growth*, the 1st—*Defeating poverty*—and the 2nd—*Defeating hunger*. And last but certainly not least, Objective 5—*Gender equality* (and opportunities like this represent not only an exchange of knowledge between different areas of study and disciplines, but also lay the foundations for creating an increasingly complex network of scientific culture and operational collaboration. We therefore believe that these initiatives have the potential to transfer knowledge and also gain the attention of public opinion, influencing decision-makers through advocacy. In addition, given the key to the general understanding of 'urban health' as the quality of life and well-being in the urban and residential space that characterizes the conditions of the community to which the Sapienza research group has allocated its action-research, it is our hope that the result will also be the promotion of health protection initiatives and participation in the formulation of public interest programmes (policy-making).

Rome, Italy

Silvia Iorio
Alessandra Battisti
Giuseppe Ricotta
Maurizio Marceca

Contents

Integrated Approaches to Urban Health

Urban Regeneration between Well-Being, Social Determinants and Sustainable Development Goals

Alessandra Battisti

Abstract From the beginning, the concept of public health is deeply connected to the social development of mankind, focusing on housing and now, during COVID-19 pandemic and the POST-COVID transition, we are witnessing the exacerbation of all those phenomena of social inequality that have clearly highlighted the structural lack of public spaces and services in the most disadvantaged areas of cities. It is therefore necessary to contribute to the improvement of the living conditions of the beneficiary populations not only to ensure the satisfaction of the primary needs for development, but also to make communities less vulnerable to the climate-environmental emergency. Actions outlined by the major international institutions, which through the UN 2030 Agenda provides for the integration of three dimensions of sustainable development—environmental, social and economic.

Keywords Healthy housing · Social equity · AIQ · Water quality · Spatial quality

1 Introduction

In the last twenty years, processes of metropolization have seen an uncontrollable increase, registering a rate of global urbanization that—according to the "World Urbanization Prospects 2018" of the United Nations—will reach almost 70% in 2050 [1]. These data, with a global vision, underline the dynamics of the growth of settlements and cities in quantitative, qualitative, historical and social evolution. In poor countries, this growth continues to take place following models of urban aggregation that has been unchanged over the years and inadequate to guarantee minimum conditions of health and sanitation. This situation continues to generate a proliferation of informal areas in conditions of extreme poverty and environmental vulnerability. According to a recent UN-Habitat report, which reports how more than a billion people are forced to live in informal settlements and estimates that this number will double by 2030, slums represent a phenomenon destined to define the near future

A. Battisti (✉)
Department of Planning, Design and Technology of Architecture, Sapienza University of Rome, Rome, Italy
e-mail: alessandra.battisti@uniroma1.it

A. Battisti et al. (eds.), *Equity in Health and Health Promotion in Urban Areas*, Green Energy and Technology, https://doi.org/10.1007/978-3-031-16182-7_1

of our metropolises, where about 18% of all housing units, numbering about 125 million, are made up of non-permanent structures and more than 30% of temporary dwellings will be in areas subject to noteworthy phenomena of environmental risks [2].

In Europe and in the OECD countries, the same process of human concentration in large urban agglomerations shows models of densely populated cities, with high rates of air pollution and land consumption, with an increasing number of social groups that are subject to socio-economic marginality and consequent housing and health problems [3]. From the beginning, the concept of public health is deeply connected to the social development of mankind within the housing environment, focusing on housing as a problem of primary urgency [4]. In literature, a healthy habitat is tightly connected to the importance of the physical and social environment as a determining factor for health and social equity [5, 6], and is currently characterized by the COVID-19 pandemic and the POST-COVID transition. Consequently, we are witnessing the exacerbation of all those phenomena of social inequality that have clearly highlighted the structural lack of public spaces and services in the most disadvantaged areas of cities [7]. Due to the fact that this problem affects a quarter of the world's population, it is clear that it is no longer elusive and that it requires a coordinated and multidisciplinary response. This response must contribute to the improvement of the living conditions of the beneficiary populations not only to ensure the satisfaction of the primary needs for development, but also to make communities less vulnerable to the climate-environmental emergency. In addition, these actions should move in the direction outlined by the major international institutions, which through the Sustainable Development Goals of the UN 2030 Agenda provides for the integration of three dimensions of sustainable development—environmental, social and economic [8]—as a prerequisite for eradicating poverty in all its forms and for ensuring health for all and guaranteeing sustainable cities. Moreover, this approach should be in line with those SDGs among the 17 objectives set out in the Agenda [9] that focus more on these problems, such as the third on the need to ensure health and well-being for all, which focuses on different areas of intervention, including specifically: fighting against epidemics of viral diseases in the world; countering communicable diseases as well as chronic diseases; and, promoting well-being and mental health. Over time, the spread of improved global hygiene had been making significant improvements, especially in the most disadvantaged parts of the world. More generally, attention to environmental factors was the necessary prerequisite for these advances, especially in the reduction of communicable diseases, a process that came partially to a halt during the recent pandemic. Furthermore, by focusing on solving the problems mentioned above, we find the sixth goal concerning the availability of water, with the aim of making water accessible and safe for the population and for ecosystems as a guarantee of survival and good human and natural health. The thirteenth goal promotes actions to combat climate change, and the fifteenth is aimed at protecting and restoring a sustainable use of the terrestrial ecosystem and the eleventh focused on cities with the aim of making them inclusive, safe, resilient and sustainable. In this perspective, cooperation, solidarity and sustainability are the three dimensions of a synergistic approach to the sustainable development of marginalized communities in Europe and the rest of the world [10].

2 Public Health: From the Ethical Value to Social Determinants

Already in 2010, Michael Marmot together with the UCL Institute of Health Equity research group—in the post-2010 Strategic review of health inequalities in England report entitled "Fair Society, Healthy Lives", also known as the Marmot review—had highlighted how social determinants, (i.e. the conditions in which people are born, grow up, work, live and age and their access to power, money and resources), are the main factors that determine unfair, avoidable and remediable health inequalities among different social groups. The specific social determinants produced and continue to be produce these inequalities include: poverty and deprivation; mobility imposed on precarious low-wage workers; lack of social protection; overcrowded housing; poor protection at work and low standards of health at work; inequality of legal status or residence; stigmatization; inequality of access to acceptable information on public health; inequality of access to economic care, prevention and vaccination [11].

The report certainly marked a new way of thinking about health, and specifically urban health. No longer can it be considered as a collateral issue to social housing policies, shifting the focus beyond actions strictly focused on social welfare, making the issue of public health one of the cornerstones of practices that concern local development, urban regeneration, housing policies, security policies, education, services and employment opportunities [12].

The same concept had already been highlighted by Didier Fassin in Critique de la santé publique, when he wrote how public health was characterized by a conviction, necessarily shared among those who claim it, in a common value: health as a public good or asset. This definition—which in the writing of the French anthropologist—should allow us to understand, among the values that a society possesses, how health is the most important among all values. Moreover, in principle, this value is systematically in favor of the collective interest towards a healthy city, or an abstract universe in which the common principle of public health would be realized as a question of ethics and values that must be defended by other values, in particular by economic aspects or values [13].

Working in this direction also means considering urban regeneration actions as a response to the rights of citizens and residents, specifically the weakest and most vulnerable groups, as well as the growing need for social cohesion and an acceptable quality of life. To this end, the WHO, in redefining the concept of health, has also adapted the new focus from a biomedical model, focused on the individual and limited to the health sector, to a bio-psycho-anthropo-social model [14]. Here, health is conceived as the result of different political, socio-economic, cultural and environmental factors, in other words the aforementioned "determinants". The premises of this change of thought were also evident in the Charter of Healthy Cities of Belfast of 2008, which clearly states that "the well-being, health and happiness of our citizens depend on our willingness to give priority to the political choices that shape and address the determinants of health and well-being throughout life [...]" [15], issues that are now confirmed once again in the United Nations 2030 Agenda for Sustainable Development Goals [16].

3 Post Covid19 Living Needs: A Question of Quality

The pandemic, from a housing and social point of view, has often led urban communities to dissociate themselves from their primary needs related to housing. Consequently, it has removed the individual from the possibilities of personal fulfillment and esteem [17].

Therefore, the first question to ask is how it is possible to solve the psychological problems and respond to the needs of the inhabitants who gradually transformed after the spread of the COVID 19 pandemic [18]. Consequently, how it is possible to regenerate the forms of living to adapt to these changes that have changed the way we live, relate to others, work and study. Even back in 1928, Alexander Klein in Grundrissbildung und Raumgestaltung von Kleinwohnungen und neue Auswertungsmethoden represented in the formulation of the existenzminimum housing as the place of physical, spiritual and social needs, designed and dimensioned according to biological, psychological and social measures [19], in order to guarantee protection, well-being and productivity for the inhabitants [20]. However, when addressing these needs today, it is necessary to add at least those of connectivity, flexibility and environmental sustainability, while also asking ourselves how and to what extent can we regenerate our cities and places of living according to a correct concept of public health. Moreover, we need to address how we can rethink our urban spaces of collective life according to new models to live together the future. Paraphrasing Engels[1] of "The Housing Question" [21] the individual who lives must be able to perform those specific actions required by the mode of a tangible and intangible function and, all this must happen in a specific place in time, able to contain the movements of the human body and the mind, therefore, the entire extension of the gestural and virtual plane of the actions that the individual must be able to perform in order to be satisfied precisely that need that solves that functional component [22].

[1] "The individual who lives [there] must be able to perform those specific actions required by the mode of a function and, all this must happen in a specific place, which contains the movements of the human body and, therefore, contains the entire extension of the gestural plane of the behaviors that the individual must be able to perform so that the need that that functional component solves is met". Friedrich Engels "The Housing Question", Editori Riuniti, Rome [Italian publication], 1974, pp. 25–26.

From some behavior implemented during the pandemic and the lockdowns connected to it, innovative housing forms adapted to the changed needs [23, 24] have been deduced according to a rational system of "fundamental measures for the living space" based on the satisfaction of contingent needs such as:

1. Measures referring to the virtual space necessary for the performance of the functions necessary for the daily life of man in the changed intangible way that is superimposed on the real and tangible [25].
2. Measures referring to the flexible space for the use of the tools necessary to perform new productive-home functions such as teleworking [26], e-learning, or health functions such as tele-medicine.
3. Measures relating to a healthy and sustainable space more accessible to all inhabitants, capable of fostering social cohesion while ensuring environmental sustainability and energy efficiency [27].

In this direction, it is possible to enucleate three possible main macro-approaches[2] to the issue of housing that intervene strongly in the definition of urban regeneration, according to a diversified implementation gradient, technological solution, and the ability to reconsider space according to uses also based on management methods [28, 29]:

- Technological-spatial solutions, designed specifically for accommodation, perfectly designed around the people who live there, allowing even in very little space different solutions and additions of open spaces, gardens, balconies, terraces, greenhouses that can allow buildings to function as ecosystems and inhabitants to become self-sufficient [30]. Places configured and created as real filters of dialogue and transition between interior and exterior, susceptible to host innovative functions neither strictly urban nor domestic, yet also suitable to accommodate a series of innovative functions and programs or traditional functions and programs that vice versa are slowly disappearing from our cities such as: conviviality and social aggregation, urban production (gardens| traditional and/or hydroponic greenhouses | aeroponics, traditional or innovative laboratories), sports, culture and events [31]. Private, semi-private semi-public spaces that constitute "proximity units", sized in proportion to the building and assembled in order to stimulate interaction, able to animate from the inside and from the outside the building envelopes to guarantee the recovery of nature in the city [32] through surfaces for the collection of water, for the self-production of clean energy, green spaces introduced through acupuncture intervention processes to be linked to the connective tissue of the city for microclimatic mitigation and the production of oxygen [33]. Through interdisciplinary design groups, we have the opportunity to rethink internal and external environments not only to be more comfortable and healthy, but also to link them to the culture of contexts often to restore identity to the places and the surrounding natural environment.

[2] In addition to these, we could add many others, however due to the specificity of the discussion we chose to present only those that were considered the most relevant for urban regeneration.

This approach requires us to grasp a broader vision of the aesthetics of buildings, going beyond the standards related to dimensional and statistical metrics and embracing an experiential and multi-sensory perspective [34]. An architecture and a socio-cultural design process that helps settled communities reconnect with nature, live sustainably and integrate the use of renewable energies, carefully taking into account all phases of the building's life cycle and understanding the implications of each design choice, reducing harmful emissions by up to 75% compared to traditional homes and using the circular economy as a means to prolong the life of the building and reduce maintenance, labor and waste management costs [35].

- Technological-spatial solutions, which through a modular and modular architecture, include the variable time in the configuration of the accommodation [36] allowing the enlargement or reduction of a space using lightweight, dry, easily assembled and disassembled technologies that integrate ICT technology distribution, configuring and adapting to a search attentive to the innovative styles of: living, working, studying, comparing with others in a technology-assisted manner, an operation that allows an overlap of uses in the functional variation of the space, without the need for dimensional compromises. Specifically, the introduction of the metaverse in architecture will imply the convergence of important technological trends (AR, VR, MR and AI) [37], all potentially capable of having an impact on our approach to housing. Within the metaverse, these innovative technologies can collectively improve individuals' outcomes in terms of learning, care and work, reduce healthcare costs and create entirely new channels for the provision of healthcare and education worldwide [38]. In order to revolutionize the global healthcare sector, the metaverse can create unlimited new opportunities, including telepresence (i.e. the ability to be together virtually even when you are physically far away) [39], digital twinning (i.e. the creation of models based on real-world data that can be used to simulate any system or process) and blockchain technologies (using them as an integral part of the metaverse to protect users' personal data and digital assets in virtual reality).
- Technological-management solutions that enhance the concept of quality and in particular "air quality", "water quality" and "spatial quality". The new models of Indoor Air Quality currently seek to achieve high levels of indoor air quality for all buildings for the entire duration of the building throughout its life cycle [40]. New pilot projects through digital twin modelling tend to monitor key air quality parameters through on-site tests or sensors and meet certain performance thresholds [41]. By monitoring indoor air quality, research studies can be conducted on the actual exploitation of space and the degree of human crowding and displacement to estimate how to adapt these phenomena according to lifestyles, to sharing or to private life to feel safe and to ensure that spaces are highly performing and to use data to guide maintenance strategies, as well as for design interventions and human behavior [42].

"Water quality" is tightly linked to universal access to water, sanitation and hygiene, often grouped in approaches to public health [43]. The Earth has enough drinking water, although in many parts of the world millions of people die from diseases due to the supply of unsafe water, and this is compounded by inadequate sanitation and hygiene. Climate change and the pandemic have also exacerbated the problem of water availability and made created the urgency to demand adequate hygiene for all. However, forecasts for the future are far from favorable.

Designing water quality means increasing the rate of adequate water supply in building users, reducing health risks due to contaminated water and excessive humidity inside buildings and providing adequate sanitation. All or this should be accompanied by better infrastructure management, combined with the awareness that water is a necessary resource to be consumed carefully and managed with care. Along these lines, there are many intervention projects for the reduction of water consumption through IoT and monitoring processes able to carry out tests to ensure adequate performance thresholds.

The "Quality of spaces", on the other hand, involves in particular the strategy of selecting materials and construction products. A great deal is being done in this sense, especially through certification processes that allow the evaluation and optimization of the composition of products in order to minimize the impacts on human and environmental health.

4 Conclusions

SDGs, together with the problems of our time—namely climate change and pandemics—will lead us to new unified models for living that may no longer refer to only numerical standards. Above all, these models will be based on qualitative conditions that relate to the needs and requirements of the individual in relation to their real and virtual behavioral model. The debate on the recognition of new standards is still open, tending to emphasize the need to formalize the needs of a man placed before "limit objectives" that go beyond the human body and physicality and therefore beyond a rational anthropometric of housing and city spaces or ergonomics. In order to ensure the maximum comfort of physical and virtual spaces, it will therefore also be necessary to start from parameters that generate adaptability, flexibility and sociality. These aspects are always the result of a process of contextualization with respect to changing urban conditions that face the climate and energy crisis, even in difficult situations of environmental and social context—the result of an interaction dialogue where the mixtures between public and private spaces, internal and external, allow for the introduction of innovative types of places to meet and use, as well as high levels of ecological, energy, microclimatic and psycho-perceptive performance. Furthermore, in order to assess the suitability and success of these solutions, it will be necessary to resort to types of performance-based metrics that allow for an objective measurement of the effect of the surrounding environment on users through physiological and psychological measures of well-being.

The reliability of the results can only be obtained by adopting a multimodal approach that can combine two or more methods of physiological and psychological detection of tests with on-site measurements. Moreover, this must be carried out through data collected with sensors and change scenarios, verified through digital models and simulations and surveys with webcams and on-site photographs in order to note in space and time how and in what matter users move in spaces. Questionnaires should also be used. However, the use of these methods is relatively new in the field of construction and climate engineering, where it is necessary to establish solid theoretical bases and unified language protocols before being used in design.

References

1. United Nations (2019) Department of economic and social affairs, population division. World urbanization prospects 2018: highlights
2. UN-HABITAT (2021) Cities and pandemics: towards a more just, green and healthy future
3. World health organization (2013) Environmental burden of disease associated with inadequate housing. Methods for quantifying health impacts of selected housing risks in the WHO European Region
4. World health organization (1946) In: Preamble to the constitution of the world health organization as adapted by the international health conference, New York
5. World health organization (1986) In: Division of health promotion, and international WHO-conference on health promotion. Ottawa Charter for Health Promotion. Ottawa
6. World Health Organization (2011) Burden of disease from environmental noise: quantification of healthy life years lost in Europe. World Health Organization Regional Office for Europe, Copenhagen
7. Capolongo S, Rebecchi A, Buffali M, Appolloni L, Signorelli C, Fara GM, D'Alessandro D (2020) COVID-19 and Cities: from urban health strategies to the pandemie challenge. A decalogue of public health opportunities. Acta Biomed 91(2):13–22. https://doi.org/10.23750/abm.v91i2.9615
8. UN (2020) The sustainable development goals report 2020
9. Van de Ven P (2019) Measuring economic well-being and sustainability: a practical agenda for the present and the future. Eurona
10. EU (2018). Europe moving towards a sustainable future Contribution of the SDG multi-stakeholder platform to the reflection Paper. Towards a sustainable Europe by 2030
11. Strategic review of health inequalities in England post-2010 (2010) Fair society, healthier lives: The Marmot review. Retrieved from. https://www.instituteofhealthequity.org/resources-reports/fair-society-healthy-lives-the-marmot-review/fair-society-healthy-lives-full-report-pdf.pdf
12. Barton H, Thompson S, Burgess S, Grant M (eds) (2015) The routledge handbook of planning for health and well-being. Routledge Taylor & Francis, Oxfordshire, UK, New York, USA pp 37–47
13. Dozon JP, Fassin D (eds) (2001) Critique de la santé publique. Une approche anthropologique. Éditions Balland, Paris
14. World health organisation (2012). Health 2020: a European policy framework supporting action across government and society for health and well-being. WHO Regional Committee for Europe, sixty-second session. WHO Regional Office for Europe. Copenhagen
15. World health organization (2008) Millennium development goals
16. UN-Habitat (2017) New urban agenda, united nations conference on housing and sustainable urban development (Habitat III), United Nations, General Assembly, A/RES/71/256, New York
17. Dipartimento cooperazione, solidarietà e protezione civile del Consiglio nazionale architetti, pianificatori, paesaggisti e conservatori in collaborazione con il Dipartimento ambiente, energia e sostenibilità (eds) (2020) Lo spazio morale

18. UN-Habitat (2020) Guidance on COVID-19 and Public Space. United Nations Human Settlement Programme (UN Habitat), Nairobi
19. Klein A (1928) Grundrissibildung und Raumgestaltung von Kleinwohnungen und neue Auswertungsmethoden. Zentralblatt der Bauverwaltung 48, Berlin.
20. Gropius W (1959) Die soziologischen Grundlagen de Minimal Wohnung in W. Gropius, Die Wohnung für das Existenzminimum, Francoforte 1930. Traduzione italiana in Walter Gropius, Architettura integrata, Mondatori, Milano.
21. Engels F (1971) La questione delle abitazioni. Editori Riuniti, Roma
22. Croci E, Bagaini A, Lucchitta B, Molteni T, Monfardini M (2021) SUR lab position paper 2021 new living and working models after the COVID-19 pandemic. SUR Lab Bocconi, Milano
23. Eurofound (2020) Living, working and COVID-19. COVID-19 series, Publications Office of the European Union, Luxembourg
24. D'alessandro D, Gola M, Appolloni L, Dettori M, Maria G, Fara AR, Settimo G, Capolongo S (2020). COVID-19 and Living space challenge. Well-being and Public Health recommendations for a healthy, safe, and sustainable housing. Acta Biomed 91(9-S):61–75. doi: https://doi.org/10.23750/abm.v91i9-S.10115. PMID: 32701918; PMCID: PMC8023091
25. UN-Habitat (United Nations Human Settlements Programme) (2021). Cities and pandemics: towards a more just, green and healthy future. Unispace (July 30, 2020). Office downsizing and cost savings—the legacy of COVID-19. Available at: https://www.unispace.com/news/office-downsizing-and-cost-savings-the-legacy-of-covid-19
26. ARUP (2020) Future of offices in a post-pandemic world
27. Urban Design (2021) Future neighourhoods. Urban Des Group J 160 (Autumn 2021). ISSN 1750 712X
28. World health organization (2018) Housing and health guidelines
29. OECD, IEA (2018) Global energy & CO2 status report 2017
30. Guallart V (2014) The self-sufficient city. Actar, New York
31. Palumbo M (ed) (2012) Architettura produttiva: principi di progettazione ecologica. Maggioli Santarcangelo di Romagna
32. Kellert SR (2018) Nature by design. Yale University Press, The practice of Biophilic design
33. AA.VV (2021) L'approccio urban health nella valutazione dei piani urbanistici. manuale per l'applicazione di uno strumento di valutazione multicriteriale per la definizione delle implicazioni di salute negli interventi urbani, - Pubblicazione realizzata nell'ambito del Progetto CCM 2017 "Urban Health: buone pratiche per la valutazione di impatto sulla salute degli interventi di riqualificazione e rigenerazione urbana e ambientale".
34. Edwards AR, McKibben B (2010) Thriving beyond sustainability: pathways to a resilient society, New Society Publishers
35. Tucci F (2019) Green building and dwelling approaches, strategies, experimentation for an environmental technological design. Altralinea, Firenze
36. Martí Arís C (1994) Le variazioni dell'identità: il tipo in architettura, CittàStudi. Milano
37. Trivedi M, Mishra K (eds) (2018) Ambient communications and computer systems. In: Advances in intelligent systems and computing, vol.696. Springer
38. Gurov O, Konkova T (2022) Metaverses for human or human for metaverses. Artif Soc 17(1)
39. Morina N, Ijntema H, Meyerbröker K, Emmelkamp P (2015) Can virtual reality exposure therapy gains be generalised to real-life? A meta-analysis of studies applying behavioural assessments. Behav Res Ther 74:18–24, Rev Measure scales Eur J Pub Health 25:731–740
40. WSC POLICY #02-430 (2002) Indoor air sampling and evaluation guide; commonwealth of massachusetts executive office of environmental affairs. Dept Environ Prot. Boston, MA, USA
41. Ali N, Islam F (2020) The effects of air pollution on COVID-19 infection and mortality—a review on recent evidence. Frontiers Publ Health. https://doi.org/10.3389/fpubh.2020.580057
42. Lindert J, Bain PA, Kubzansky LD, Stein C (2015) Well-being measurement and the WHO health policy health 2010: systematic
43. Conte G (2008) Nuvole e sciacquoni come us are meglio l'acqua, in casa e in città, Edizioni Ambiente, Milano

Public Health Approach to Outdoor Urban Health

Maurizio Marceca, Marise Sabato, Igor Aloise, Nicolò Baiocchi, and Giancosimo Mancini

Abstract Recent years of the Covid-19 pandemic have seen a proportional increase in the amount of time we spend in our homes each day. In spite of this, urban dwellers continue to spend-although varying from area to area of the world-many hours outside their homes for work, daily needs, recreation, and social relationships. This implies that the urban environment, both tangible and intangible, has several factors that can be both protective and risky for health. As highlighted in the 2016 Quito Conference, health can be the pulse of the new urban agenda for sustainable urban development [1]. It is not easy to take stock of where we are. On a global scale, there still seems to be a limited ethical-cultural awareness, a lack of political attention and thus of resource allocation, an insufficient capacity to use innovative choices and technologies and to actively involve local communities in decision-making processes and in the implementation of possible interventions. On the other hand, there are numerous positive experiences of urban realities that have produced convincing efforts in recent decades to make our cities more livable and healthy. Let us hope that the 2030 agenda proposed by the United Nations on the Sustainable Development Goals can really exert a driving role in this direction. A real willingness to set in motion virtuous processes to guarantee us a better quality of urban life, including by agreeing to revise our development and consumption patterns, will make all the difference.

Keywords Public health · Outdoor urban health · Sustainable development goals · Health promotion

---

M. Marceca (✉) · M. Sabato · I. Aloise · N. Baiocchi · G. Mancini
Department of Public Health and Infectious Diseases, Sapienza University of Rome, Rome, Italy
e-mail: maurizio.marceca@uniroma1.it

A. Battisti et al. (eds.), *Equity in Health and Health Promotion in Urban Areas*, Green Energy and Technology, https://doi.org/10.1007/978-3-031-16182-7_2

1 Introduction: The Impact of Urbanization on Our Mental, Social and Physical Health

In these years, according to the United Nations, more than 4 billion people live in an urban setting and, due to rapidly increasing urbanization, the World Urbanization Prospects 2018 estimated that more than two-thirds of our world population will be living in urban areas by 2050 [2].

Rapid urban growth can bring both positive factors (economic growth, financial services, education and other services) and negative factors (increased pollution, reduced outdoor green areas, excessive strain on transport, housing and health care, and an increase in socio-economic inequalities), which must be all taken into account [3]. The impact of rapid urban growth is seen in the rising number of chronic Non-Communicable Diseases (NCDs), such as cardiovascular diseases, chronic respiratory diseases, cancer and diabetes, which according to WHO kill 41 million people each year (71% of the global population mortality) [4].

As is well known, in 1948, the WHO (World Health Organization) Constitution defined Health as "*a state of complete physical, mental and social well-being and not merely the absence of disease or infirmity.*" [5].

The global Covid-19 pandemic has taken a great toll on our physical, mental and social health underlining and amplifying all the previous difficulties and increasing inequalities in our society. The disruption of our day-to-day life has once again proved what are the most important pillars of a healthy lifestyle and the importance of both the indoor and, especially, the outdoor surroundings from an urban and Public health point of view.

The decline of mental, physical and social health due to lockdown measures, linked with big changes in lifestyle such as a lack of physical activity, an increasingly housebound life, stress eating and lack of social interaction has shown the need for good physical surroundings and good healthy habits.

The relationship between Public health and Urban Planning plays a decisive role in the promotion of healthy lifestyles and healthy environments. Creating healthy environments requires good urban planning, good infrastructure, redeveloping degraded areas and the creation of suitable public spaces that promote community living; such as social community centers, the creation of designated green areas and pedestrian and cycle paths to encourage a healthy lifestyle. Moreover, it also requires a focus on different measures to reduce air, light and noise pollution.

The Public Health perspective in reading the city therefore adopts a systematic perspective, which sees the urban built environment as an important structural determinant of health, strongly interconnected with all other determinants [6]. A fundamental reference in the cultural and scientific pathway related to these interests is the WHO 'Healthy Cities Network', instituted in 1988 [7].

This perspective can be found in the approach given to the United Nations Programme on the Sustainable Development Goals (SDGs), which is the largest and most ambitious one currently underway. Following the Millennium Development Goals (MDGs), in 2015, the 193 countries of the UN General Assembly developed

"Transforming our World: The 2030 Agenda for Sustainable Development". With its 17 Sustainable Development Goals (SDGs), it aims to achieve prosperity, equality, a healthy environment and to end poverty and hunger worldwide through partnership and global teamwork in order to achieve these SDGs by 2030. It should be noted that Goal 11 is dedicated to 'Making cities and human settlements inclusive, safe, resilient and sustainable' [8].

In this chapter, an attempt has therefore been made to address schematically the main—interrelated—dimensions that influence physical, mental and social health in the urban environment outside the home, namely: environmental pollution; urban mobility/transport; physical activity and nutrition as main behaviours/lifestyles; and the community dimension (understood as a network of social relations).

As emphasised in one of our previous contributions, Health Promotion in the urban context therefore necessarily requires a multidisciplinary approach and actions [9].

2 The Environmental Pollution

"Environmental pollution is an incurable disease.

It can only be prevented".

(Barry Commoner)

The Global Burden of Disease Study ranked Environmental Pollution as the 4th in the top five global causes of death, rising rapidly in the ranks of global causes of mortality in recent years. The urban environment is an aggregation point for many environmental exposures that are important determinants of health: air pollution, toxic chemicals in the soil, noise and light pollution, as well as being a primary source of both economic and psychological stress. Most deaths from air pollution are cardiovascular accidents [10].

Chronic exposure to high levels of fine particulates impairs vascular function: this increases the risk of myocardial infarction, high blood pressure, stroke and heart failure. The predominant sources of fine particulates are the combustion of fossil fuels and biomass, industrial pollutants, agricultural pollutants and windblown dust particles. Although scientific evidence correlates chronic exposure to PM2.5 with increased cardiovascular risk, the pathogenetic mechanism is still not entirely clear. The mechanism should be based on the induction of chronic inflammation by PM2.5 that produces oxidative stress, as well as vascular and endothelial dysfunction. These in turn facilitate the onset of pathologies such as hypertension, diabetes and atherosclerosis, which can obviously lead to much higher health risks such as heart attacks, strokes, acute heart failure and venous thromboembolism. A recent study estimated an excess mortality in Europe due to air pollution of approximately 790,000 people per year; it is estimated that between 15 and 28% of the annual cardiovascular mortality rate is due to air pollution, so it may even exceed the risk due to tobacco smoke [11].

Outdoor physical activity in polluted cities increases the risk of exposure to harmful agents (so physical activity—discussed below—should also be done in a healthier city or environment). Additionally, it has been shown that the occupants of cars in city traffic have the greatest exposure to pollutants, and are even more exposed than cyclists passing through the same environment [12].

Noise pollution ranks second among environmental causes of health loss in Western Europe, preceded only by particulate air pollution. The WHO describes 'environmental noise' as any noise from any source other than noise from the workplace. Among the various adverse health effects of prolonged exposure to urban noise when it reaches harmful intensity levels are cardiovascular effects that manifest with the risk of developing hypertension, metabolic effects with an increased risk of diabetes, deterioration of cognitive abilities especially in the age of development, psychological stress and sleep disorders. A recent study estimated that more than 20% of the world's population lives in areas where noise pollution from urban transport reaches levels that are hazardous to an individual's health (> 55 decibels). Reducing urban traffic would not produce a significant reduction in noise since the decibel scale has a logarithmic basis, hence a 50% reduction in traffic would lead to a mere 3 dB reduction on the noise scale. Even the widespread adoption of electric cars would not solve the problem since most noise pollution from urban transport is due to tyres rolling on asphalt (at an average speed of > 30/40 km/h). Exposure to noise pollution has been found to cause hypertension and has a negative effect on the cardiovascular system in general [13].

Light pollution, despite an increasing body of alarming data, has received very little attention from environmental scientists until now. Light pollution has detrimental effects on the health of the individual, altering hormone levels and thus also the circadian rhythm, pressure regulation, etc. It also affects the circadian rhythm of insects and birds, causing their premature death and, consequently, a significant alteration of biodiversity [14].

Urbanisation has become more rapid in recent decades since globalisation allowed technologies and industrial innovations to be shared across the globe. Physical urban spaces have grown disproportionately to population growth over the last 40 years (2.5 times physical growth compared to 1.8 times numerical population growth); London took 130 years to grow its population from 1 to 8 million, Bangkok 45 and Seoul only 25 years. This process has seen the haphazard growth of urban agglomerations on the outskirts of large cities, growth driven by the lower cost of renting or building in more peripheral areas; however, this has led to an increase in the time it takes to get to work, has led to unequal access to essential services that are much more lacking in peripheral areas, and has also led to a reduction in green or even cultivable areas. Cities, especially the healthier ones, have contributed largely to climate change on the planet. In fact, cities alone are responsible for about 75% of the world's energy consumption and about the same percentage of global waste production, and they are also responsible for about 60 per cent of greenhouse gases. Ironically, city areas are also the most affected by climate change, especially by rising water levels (spotlight on cities vulnerable to rising waters: Cotonou, Alexandria, Dhaka, Venice) [15].

Homes also have a non-negligible impact on environmental pollution due to their high energy consumption, which increases PM2.5 emissions and also plays a role in the exposure time to such emissions. This creates a vicious circle whereby climate change induces more and more consecutive days with extreme heat, which leads to an increase in energy consumption for air conditioning in homes and offices/ urban environments. [14].

Domestic pollution—which is discussed in more detail in another chapter of this volume—continues to be significant in parts of Africa and Central and Eastern Europe. Meanwhile, in parts of India, fumes from the burning of wood for cooking and for strictly social and religious activities contribute largely to air pollution, as does the burning of biofuels for the purpose of producing bricks [14].

Individuals living in urban poverty are the most affected by climate change. This is because they live in substandard housing, which has little resilience to new climate extremes. In contrast, cities may have great potential to reduce global pollution and moderate climate change. As urbanisation grows, so will the problems arising from climate change, as floods, tornadoes and hurricanes will become more frequent, and as we have seen recently, urban areas in developed countries are also susceptible to the more rapid spread of infectious diseases, given their population density. Rising temperatures will lead to increasingly frequent heat waves in densely urbanised areas, which will not be mitigated by the presence of vegetation. This will also lead to a change in the availability of water in cities and a deterioration in water quality, both of which will also lead to changes in hygiene conditions and in the availability and quality of food, which in extreme cases could lead to famine. Climate change will contribute to a spread of diseases with insects as vectors, as the warmer global climate will bring about a change in the life cycles of insect vectors and facilitate their spread to areas with environments that were previously hostile to them [16].

In addition, the change in temperature promotes an increase in air pollution: it has been calculated that a 1° Celsius increase in temperature leads to an increase in deaths due to air pollution of about 20,000 people per year, mostly due to cardiovascular accidents and lung disease [17].

Children in urban areas often make the street their playground, exposing themselves to the environmental dangers of cities, both in terms of pollution and safety. A city with an efficient and sustainable transport network drastically reduces these dangers. The WHO estimates the deaths from air pollution in 2004 at around 1.1 million people. Obviously, more economically disadvantaged people find themselves living in city areas that are more exposed to urban pollution, such as flats near busy roads or basements, which maximise the negative effects of urban pollution on health [15].

In 2016, the Third United Nations Conference on Sustainable Housing and Urban Development (Habitat III) was held in Quito; many points and projects emerged from the Conference, including an Agenda for the Sustainable Development of Cities by 2030. In fact, the world population is expected to double by 2050, making urbanisation one of the most significant events of the twenty-first century. Paragraph 54 of the New Urban Agenda, drafted by the UN during the congress, states that UN member states commit to generate and use renewable and affordable energy, as well as to use sustainable and efficient means of transport (where possible), thus reducing costs in terms of public expenditure, increasing global health benefits by decreasing air pollution, decreasing urban heat island effects and reducing noise pollution. Paragraph 66 of the Agenda commits to the 'smart-city' approach, which looks at integrating new technologies, both in public infrastructure, transport and energy. Urban greenery is an important resource, as it increases the resilience of cities to increasing climate change and disasters by introducing and implementing local risk reduction and disaster response plans, including strategic evacuation and emergency plans [18].

Concerning the goals of the UN New Urban Agenda, there is a tool that shows the progress made by the various member countries in achieving the goals of the agenda. This tool shows that many countries are lagging far behind in the pursuit of the 2030 goals [19].

As far as Western Europe is concerned, only Germany has published an updated report highlighting the concrete objectives on which its policies have focused: for example, in the field of combating climate change, a systematic review of all existing municipal measures with regard to their impact on climate change has been proposed. A large number of German municipalities have won national prizes for implementing exemplary projects against local climate change. For the time being, the main act of climate protection remains the implementation of more or less radical measures to reduce CO2 emissions, although energy refurbishment of existing buildings and the adoption of renewable energy sources for the air-conditioning of newly constructed buildings are also increasingly gaining ground. Educating citizens on the virtuous behaviours to follow in order to fight climate change is part of the tools available to nations in order to combat climate change [20].

Measures to counter climate change at the local level are still difficult to record or even quantify, thus there's a need to have specific local climate and public health control bodies, organised in operational units as for any other health area, which deal with the challenges and protocols to be followed in an interdisciplinary manner.

The energy transition from fossil fuels to renewable energies is one of the key points on the agendas of all world governments. This is a thorny issue because so far the use of fossil fuels has not only been widely maintained, but also promoted, through incentives and tax breaks. The shift to green energy is seen by world economies as potentially disastrous, as it would lead to the loss of thousands of jobs. The concern of member states of large international coalitions, such as the European Union, is that the costs of transition will not be fairly distributed, as well as the international funding allocated precisely to incentivise the transition to renewable energy. The energy taxation system of most countries in the world still shows a rejection of increased taxation for the use of fossil energy sources, while there is still an almost total lack of tax incentives for technologies such as electric engines/vehicles, which are facing an uphill battle to gain a significant foothold in the transport sector [17].

The European Climate Act, introduced in 2021, enshrines the commitment of EU member states to achieve climate neutrality by 2050 with an intermediate goal of decreasing greenhouse gas (GHG) emissions by 55% from 1990 levels by 2030. The Paris Climate Accords held in April 2021 also saw the return of the United States, which is among the world's largest GHG producers, to the global target agenda (cooperation had been abandoned during the Trump administration). The goal of achieving climate neutrality by 2050 is an ambitious challenge for any country, requiring a series of substantial transformations in energy governance, infrastructure and technological adoptions. In 2020, due to the pandemic, the world witnessed a drastic reduction in pollutants followed by a negative rebound effect as early as 2021, but the extensive economic and governmental structure crisis that unfolded during the pandemic led to many countries having to provide economic support packages that represent an unprecedented opportunity to boost the energy transition. It must be said that despite the fact that the price of producing and supplying energy from renewable sources has been on a continually decreasing trend in recent years, this alone is not enough to promote a concrete transition to green energy, as there is still no way to integrate renewable energy into viable local and international market proposals and models [21].

This is why renewable energy in 2018 provided only 4% of the world's total energy supply. Even some countries, such as India, aim to invest again in coal in the coming years, because they have large national reserves of it. Moreover, the maintenance costs for the production of some types of renewable energy are still high (e.g. in Italy) [22].

Unfortunately, to greatly slow down these desirable energy conversion processes, first the Covid-19 pandemic and, more recently, the war in Ukraine intervened in an unforeseen and dramatic way, resulting—through the sanctions taken against Russia, a strong gas exporter—in a worldwide upheaval of available energy sources and their costs.

A key resource for the goal of emission neutrality and combating climate change is certainly the assumption of the concepts of 'energy sufficiency' and 'energy efficiency', i.e. energy models that favour those services and activities that naturally use less energy (sufficiency), or renovate existing activities and businesses so that they consume less energy (efficiency). Since the sectors to be decarbonised are mostly those of transport, air conditioning and agriculture, the use of clean electricity in these sectors should be implemented, coping with the obvious growth in demand for electricity by producing it through renewable sources. A key role in this turnaround could be played by the use of hydrogen as a source of electricity with near-zero environmental impact in the case of the use of so-called 'green hydrogen', i.e. when the production of hydrogen is achieved using renewable energy sources, such as solar or wind power [22].

The energy transition will have to be fair, in order to leave no country behind and not create or worsen social and, consequently, public health inequalities. Since the concept of energy poverty was introduced to refer to those sections of the population that cannot access or afford energy, and for whom standards of living and health are inevitably lower than for the privileged sections, it has been seen that some 7% of the European population is, to date, in energy poverty [22].

Therefore, the energy transition will have to be accompanied by a legislative groundwork that gives due consideration to the most vulnerable and underrepresented groups in society, so that it can be an opportunity to level out some of the most serious social inequalities. Last but not least, there is a need to create a strong and incisive narrative about the energy transition that engages people and creates what is termed 'energy citizenship', whose motto should be 'emissions avoided are emissions reduced'. Increased public awareness of energy issues is a key step to reduce waste and foster accountability of institutions as well.

Urban transport—which is discussed below—is among the largest causes of air pollution in cities around the world.

3 The Public Transport

> "If we're going to talk about transport, I would say that the great city is not the one that has highways, but one where a child on a tricycle or bicycle can go safely everywhere".
>
> (Enrique Penalosa)

As mentioned, in recent years we are witnessing a gradual abandonment of the countryside, provinces and small towns in favour of moving to the urban agglomerations of large cities, which are richer in services, recreational activities and, above all, job opportunities. Today, it is estimated that about 75% of individuals in Europe have chosen an urban area as their place of residence and that by 2050 this share will reach about 80% [23].

In the face of ever-increasing population growth, large urban centres continually redefine their boundaries and structure. However, while ever larger and more densely populated cities represent a great social and employment opportunity, the risk of a reduction in the efficiency of urban mobility—i.e. of all modes of transport available to citizens within an urban area—is equally great. The means of transport are manifold and are implemented and used in an extremely heterogeneous manner, depending on the urban architecture of the city in question. The aspects of mobility and city transport constitute an element of great impact on public health, as they are able to significantly influence the daily life of those who live in the city. For this reason, the management of the urban transport infrastructure and network is an element that must be taken seriously not only by urban planners and related professionals (e.g. traffic engineers), but also by local health authorities. There are many levels of interaction between the urban planning of the city and all that this entails in terms of urban transport and the health outcomes of the resident population.

The car is the most widely used means of transport for the population today; it is estimated that in the United States 75% of the population use their cars independently to get to work [24].

The environmental impact, and thus indirectly the health of citizens, of the use of autonomous vehicles is very significant. The use of private cars is not only responsible for the increase of CO_2 emissions into the atmosphere; it is also directly and indirectly involved in the increase of temperature within the urban space, contributing significantly to the formation of the Urban Heat Island (the so-called 'island effect'). The island effect consists of a consistent temperature difference between the urban area and the surrounding area, caused by the massive presence of heat-absorbing materials (buildings, asphalt, vehicles, etc.) within cities. The area with the highest temperature tends to be located in the centre of the city, at ground level. Generally, the air tends to establish convective motion, whereby the warmer air at ground level tends to rise and, once cooled, returns to ground level. Adding these convective motions to area shifts from the countryside to the conurbation produces a 'dome' effect that tends to thermally isolate the city and keep pollutants inside. An urban strategy aimed at favouring the use of private vehicles as the preferred mode of transport will lead to a progressive consumption of land, due to the enlargement of spaces dedicated to roads and parking and at the expense of green city areas, further fuelling the problem [25]. Several authors recommend some fundamental measures to achieve the reduction of the island effect and the consequent lowering of temperatures within urban areas, such as encouraging the implementation of urban greenery and the use of public transport and active transport (cycling, walking…) [26].

In addition to having a significant environmental impact, urban and intercity travel by citizens also has a direct impact on the health of individuals. The ever-increasing urbanisation and the continuous extension of city boundaries increase the duration and distance of journeys citizens have to make to their places of daily living. In particular, many citizens have to travel long distances to reach their workplace. The scientific community has repeatedly affirmed the relationship between health, both physical and mental, and commuting. Even when the commute takes place within the same city, taking a long time to get to work leads to a reduction in the time normally devoted to exercise—which will be discussed in more detail below—or other healthy activities, including social relationships.

Spending much of one's time driving a car, especially if this activity is combined with performing a sedentary job, is an important predictor of mortality from cardiovascular accidents. In particular, a 2010 study found a 50 per cent increased risk of mortality from cardiovascular accidents in individuals who report driving a car for more than 10 h per week compared to individuals who report driving for less than 4 h [27]. Another 2012 study found a significant association between the distance travelled daily to work and a reduction in individuals' moderate to vigorous physical activity and cardio-respiratory fitness. Furthermore, commuting itself constitutes a sedentary activity, especially when the distance to work is travelled while driving a car; indeed, there is a significant association between distance travelled, increased Body Mass Index (BMI)[1] and abdominal circumference. The tendency towards obesity is in turn associated with the presence of the so-called Metabolic Syndrome[2] and increased risk of mortality from cardiovascular complications. The increases in adiposity indices are largely attributable to the reduction in daily physical activity secondary to time spent commuting, but the study suggests that commuting

[1] The body mass index is a biometric data, expressed as the ratio between the weight in kilograms and the height in centimeters squared and is used as an indicator of the state of an individual's healthy weight. Its normal value (normal weight) is between 18.5 and 24.99.

[2] 'Metabolic Syndrome' is a medical term that, schematically, is used to refer to a combination of diabetes, high blood pressure and obesity; these are all three cardiovascular risk factors, but when present at the same time, the risk is even higher than for the individual conditions.

also has an independent effect on the increase in adiposity caused by an overall reduction in the individual's energy metabolism. Another factor contributing to increased adiposity in commuters is the fact that on many occasions workers who are forced to travel long distances by car to work come from suburban districts where public transport connections in the city are poorer. This in turn implies greater difficulty in accessing essential services and reaching recreational or 'salutogenic' places, leading to a more sedentary lifestyle [28].

The consequences of commuting are also reflected in the mental health of workers. An interesting Australian study from 2017 relates perceived stress levels to the time spent commuting to work, especially when commuting by car. Specifically, in this work, the 5-item Mental Health Inventory (MHI-5), a validated scale that assesses symptoms of depression and anxiety (nervousness, low mood) and positive aspects of mental health (feeling calm, happiness) was used as a method of measuring mental health outcome. The study showed that the mental health score worsened significantly in commuters who took longer (overall more than 6 h per week) to commute to work. Moreover, the association between the duration of commuting and mental health is even stronger if one considers the type of work performed: the same study shows that mental health worsens even more among commuters who reported having less control over their work (less flexible working hours, less predictable and plannable tasks at work, and so on). For these reasons, the study highlights how the time taken to travel to work should be included more frequently among the aspects that are evaluated to determine the job satisfaction of individuals, an element that is often given little weight in the literature [29].

While spending a lot of time in a car is detrimental to the physical and mental health of workers, physically active commuting to work, such as walking or cycling, is a definite factor in improving worker well-being.

A 2013 study correlates multiple health outcomes in relation to active commuting. To determine the health perceptions of commuters, the Short Form Health Survey 36 (SF-36) was used in this study. This is a validated questionnaire consisting of 36 questions designed to investigate eight basic aspects of physical and mental health status: physical functioning, limitations due to physical health, limitations due to emotional problems, energy and fatigability, emotional well-being, social activities, pain, and perception of general health. Two summary scales were then derived from this questionnaire to investigate the individual's physical health (PCS) and mental health (MSC). The study found that commuting to work in a physically active way, such as walking or cycling, is strongly associated with improved physical well-being independent of other forms of daily physical activity; however, in this study, there was no significant association with workers' mental well-being. The study population, comprised of workers resident in the Cambridge (UK) area, is embedded in a socio-economic fabric that is sufficiently affluent to be able to afford to travel to work by car. This underlines how the choice of these individuals to walk or cycle to work is also motivated in part by a better perception of health and well-being that they derive from this type of travel; indeed, the study suggests that the association between well-being and active commuting may appear less markedly favourable when studying a population made up of individuals with less economic capacity, who are forced to renounce to the car or public transport to travel to the places of daily activity [30].

A systematic literature review published in 2015 also shows that the benefits of active transport (walking or cycling) are manifold. While improvements in physical health are also evident here, other important associations were noted. For example, it is emphasised that an increase in the use of bicycles as a means of transport within the city can lead to an increase in traffic accidents, an effect that can only be mitigated if the significant increase in bicycle use is matched by an equally significant decrease in car traffic; therefore, it is evident that *urban design* and the provision of safe cycling and walking routes should be considered a priority [31].

In the light of this data, it is clear that it is essential to implement an urban design that facilitates citizens' travel to work and places of interest, as well as distributing work opportunities and essential services in a widespread and homogeneous manner within the city. It is also evident how efficient and optimised city mobility mechanisms need to be implemented in the area. While traditional mixed public transport (bus, metro, tram and so forth) is of great importance in connecting the city's possible destinations and reducing air pollution, efforts should be made to formulate an infrastructure design that can also provide citizens with green transport alternatives that can implement physical activity and reduce sedentariness, such as the ever-growing *bike-sharing* services.

In this regard, a model for redefining the city's mobility plan has been implemented based on eight measures that can be implemented at urban level [32]:

- *Accessibility of destinations*: most workplaces, public services and recreational places should always be accessible by public transport. In particular, these places should always be reached within 30 min using public transport.
- *Distribution of work*: employment opportunities and workplaces should be effectively distributed in the city area so that the workplace is always well accessible to all citizens.
- *Interventions on the supply of public parking spaces*: the reduction of parking spaces and the increase of parking prices, in addition to reducing land consumption, may discourage the use of private means of transport in favour of alternative methods.
- *Revisiting urban design*: implementation of urban design solutions to minimise distances between homes and the destinations of daily activities, reducing exposure to traffic, creating preferential routes for pedestrians and cyclists, and organising blocks to increase residential density and promote green space. In this respect, a virtuous model called '*superblock*' has been implemented in Example (Barcelona) [33]. The superblock constitutes an urban cell that, when repeated, creates a mosaic stretching across the city. In the case of Barcelona, each superblock consists of a block of 3 × 3 buildings, 400 m long, bordered by city arteries that connect services and destinations throughout the city. While much of the city's traffic is channelled onto the arteries delimiting the superblock, within the superblock, limited traffic, bicycle lanes, urban greenery and pedestrian areas are promoted.

- *Increased density of residential areas*: while an increase in residential density may be critical in the control and spread of infectious diseases, adopting such an urban design may increase the efficiency of the local economy by favouring the presence of essential services, entertainment venues and public transport stations within each residential area of the city.
- *Reducing the distance to public transport*: increasing the frequency of public transport and thus reducing the walking distance between the house and it; ideally, bus stops should be less than 400 m from the house and train/metro stops less than 800 m.
- *Housing diversity*: residential areas built with different types of housing mixed with commercial, public and recreational activities, available near or integrated with services necessary for daily life.
- *Increasing the desirability of residential neighbourhoods*: this is done through strategies aimed at reducing local crime (such as improved urban lighting), optimising traffic and green areas, the presence of recreational activities and essential services [32].

4 Urban Environment and Individual Lifestyles

Recognizing the importance of reducing risk factors for premature death due to an unhealthy diet and lack of physical activity as a response to the 'World Health Report in 2002', the WHO adopted a "*Global Strategy on Diet, Physical Activity and Health*", in 2004. This report highlights the fact that physical inactivity and unhealthy diets are two of the major risk factors, of premature death due to NCDs, along with tobacco use, obesity, high cholesterol and heavy alcohol consumption [34].

The objectives of this Global Strategy were to reduce risk factors for NCDs by means of health promotion and preventive measures in order to increase awareness and understanding of healthy habits, to encourage the development and implementation of global, national and regional policies that consisted of action plans to facilitate a sustainable healthy lifestyle. National strategies have been implemented following dietary and physical activity guidelines, globally, in collaboration with other intergovernmental bodies including FAO, UNESCO, the UN and others promoting research in these fields. Since 2006, several papers have been published regarding the link between physical activity, obesity and health issues, especially in Europe. Subsequently, the WHO has promoted 'Physical Activity' by creating active campaigns and guidelines to help local governments in creating "Healthy Cities" through policy-making and a joint effort in making a difference globally. In 2008, thanks to the "Healthy Cities Network" a planning guide was published: "*A Healthy City is an Active City*" together with different guidelines which enable local governments worldwide to create a plan for encouraging physical activity, active living and sport in their cities/communities through different approaches [35]. In 2018, a Global Action Plan entitled "*More Active People for a Healthier World*" was published by the WHO in order to achieve the goals set out in the Sustainable

Development Agenda 2030. This framework for action 's main mission is to create safe and enabling environments to allow people to be physically active every day, thus improving individual and community health [36].

4.1 Physical Activity

"Mens Sana in Corpore Sano".

(Giovenale)

It is well known that Physical Activity (PA) is significant in the promotion of a healthy and sustainable lifestyle, as it encourages both socialization and improvement of mental health but is also known to help in reducing the risk of NCDs which account for around 75% of the health-care costs globally.

Physical Activity (PA) is defined by the WHO as "*any bodily movement produced by skeletal muscles that requires energy expenditure*" which includes all types of movements such as walking, running, cycling; and any sport activity done during leisure times.

Having seen all the benefits of PA across all age cohorts, many different countries internationally, as part of their National programs and government-led initiatives, have encouraged PA starting at a young age, including PA in school curriculums and promoting different health campaigns. For example, Ireland with "*Healthy Ireland*", United States with "*Let's Move Active Schools*", Canada with "*Passport for Life*", Finland with "*Finnish Schools on the Move*" and many more.

In 2010, Finland started a new health program "*Finnish Schools on the Move*" with a pilot scheme. Seeing the great benefits and results of this program, in 2015–2018, the Government of Finland, along with the Finnish National Agency of Education and the Ministry of Education and Culture made this program one of the key projects in the field of knowledge and education in their "Government Program of Finland" [37].

A program "*Passport for Life*" started in Canada in 2013, has shown significant improvement in participation and interest were recorded in children who participate in the program, along with better coordination and control, growing confidence and relationships that all benefit healthy development [38].

"*Healthy Ireland*", launched in Ireland in 2017, supports evidence-based initiatives for the implementation of strategies and policies within the Republic of Ireland such as "*Get Ireland Active*", "*The National Sport Policy 2018–2027*" and "*The Healthy Ireland Strategic Plan 2021–2025*" and different awareness campaigns organized by the Health Service Executive (HSE) in Ireland such as the "*Let's Get Set*" campaign that gives tips and advice in order to stimulate the population to follow a healthy and more sustainable lifestyle [39, 40]. In Ireland, PA is mandatory in both primary and secondary schools for at least 1–2 h weekly and the vast majority of the schools also include extra-curricular activities such as football, basketball, rugby, tennis or hockey on a voluntary basis. About 70% of young primary school children and about 63% of secondary school children participate in these extra-curricular activities at least once a week. An "*Active School Flag*", started in 2009, is awarded to schools that self-promote and commit to an "*Active School Week*" in their yearly calendar. They follow national guidelines by getting children to be as active as they can. A "*Safe Route Program*" was launched in March 2021 to encourage young pupils to walk and cycle to school. Each Junior school participates in inculcating an interest in PA from a very young age by weekly "*Walk to School on Wednesday*" for example. National Guidance Programs provide different schemes to encourage more sustainable commuting and travel, promoting walking, cycling, the use of public transport and car-sharing [41]. It doesn't stop here. The Irish government also has programs such as "*Go for Life: more older people, more active, more often*" encouraging older adults to remain active at home or close to home in the different parks and green spaces available in the community. Reports have shown good cognitive mental health and a great reduction in disabling and chronic diseases in the elderly thanks to a more active lifestyle [40]. The influence of the media has proved to be a very effective tool in promoting a healthy, active lifestyle. For example, Healthy Ireland sponsors an Irish television program on RTE called "*Operation Transformation*" which is a health and fitness program, based in Ireland, where the participants are monitored and guided daily by different experts. Since its debut, in 2008, it has captured the interest of numerous viewers and has inspired Irish people to focus on healthy wellbeing. As viewing has skyrocketed in the last decade, Operational Transformation collaborated with different Local and National associations and universities (Dublin City University, Sports Ireland, Get Ireland Walking, GAA clubs, etc.) in organizing national campaigns and Nationwide walks—mini marathons 'Operation Transformation 5 k' with great turnouts. This program, available across all social media, on radio and TV, has proved very successful in promoting personal and community involvement in PA nationwide. The participants become inspirational role models and leaders in the communities as stories, diets, healthy recipes and fitness programs are also shared on their websites. People follow their progress and the expert panel's advice on healthy nutrition, mental health and wellness strategies and tailored programs of PA. Operation Transformation has caught the attention of two other European television stations such as RTL in Holland and VTM in Belgium which have then bought rights from RTE and have now adapted versions of the program.[3] These different programs have proven to have many positive effects on learning outcomes and mental health across all age groups.

With regards to the "*Sustainable Development Agenda 2030*", PA can contribute in reaching 6/7 SDGs *(SDG 3 "Good Health and Well-Being"; SDG 4 "Quality Education"; SDG5 "Gender Equality"; SDG7 "Affordable and Clean Energy"; Awareness of air pollution. SDG8 "Decent Work and Economic Growth"; SDG10 "Reduced Inequalities"; SDG11 "Sustainable cities and communities")* [8].

[3] Operation Transformation—https://ot.rte.ie/

In order to ensure healthy lives and promote well-being for all at all ages, SDG 3, several studies have shown that PA is fundamental in this goal as it has been demonstrated that regular PA helps to reduce stress and the risk of premature death due to NCDs [42–44]. Benefits are also psychological and social and PA has, furthermore, been shown to be very important in maintaining good mental health (SDG 3.4). Promoting a suitably healthy lifestyle through 'sports and a good diet' can help reduce alcohol and drug abuse [42] (SDG 3.5). Through global promotion and campaigns for sports, healthy diets and daily activities, can help increase the prevention of NCDs, thus reducing the cost of healthcare globally, as studies have shown [45, 46].

Moreover, participation in PA has other, important, personal and social benefits. Firstly, it can help to contribute to prioritize a holistic quality of education in order to "*ensure inclusive and equitable quality education and to promote life-long learning opportunities for all*" (SDG 4). It has been proven that sports/physical education in schools help in the child's development by giving children life-long skills such as social, emotional and cognitive capabilities. Involvement in sports reinforces fundamental personal and social values such as goal setting, self-discipline, teamwork, fair play and the respect for rules and others (SDG 4.1, 4.2, 4.4). At a personal level, PA improves mental health. It reduces anxiety, it improves mood, self-esteem and cognitive functions [47, 48].

Implementing the teaching of sports in schools can also give young children and adolescents a growing awareness of the significance of Sustainable Development and the importance of a healthy and active sustainable lifestyle. It increases awareness of the environment, communities and surroundings. Sports is all-inclusive and the inclusion of vulnerable and marginalized groups, such as the disabled, the socially disadvantaged and immigrants, in the community can also be achieved through sports. Sports provides a safe learning environment and helps to create more cohesive communities by reducing or helping to eliminate inequalities. Involvement in sports provides a "level playing pitch" for all where inequality and social disadvantaged recede. All are allowed to shine and to reach their potential regardless of their background (SDG 4.7). Furthermore, sporting prowess and the opportunity to gain a "Sport Scholarship" allowing access to University/Third level education can be particularly relevant in socio-economically disadvantaged situations (SDG 4.3). Moreover, good PA programs and global campaigns can reinforce the promotion of gender equality and thus helps "*to end all forms of discrimination against all women and girls everywhere*", as positive role models are formed which create leadership within the community encouraging future generations to follow in their steps.

From an urban planning perspective, the requalification of parks and abandoned or derelict urban spaces, not only enhances the physical environment, but can also promote greater social pride and cohesion in communities and improve social interactions between individuals. In the last decade, the increase in sports tourism and sports events have contributed to economic growth in cities by creating job opportunities as well as bringing communities together to organize the hosting and organization of sporting events.

Again, from an urban planning point of view, the provision of many more designated bicycle lanes in our cities and suburbs, as has happened in Ireland, Holland, Denmark and many other European countries), has a twofold benefit. It promotes a healthy lifestyle where people can cycle to work, school or social events. It also reduces reliance on cars and public transport and thus contributes to cleaner air, less noise pollution and the creation of greener and more attractive cities.

Therefore, careful urban planning and the creation of green areas or small parks in urban areas and the provision of public sport facilities such as soccer pitches, basketball and tennis courts can help in motivating PA as a mean to release stress and as an inspiration in meeting wellness goals. One example would be the "Walkways of the Heart" in Viano (Reggio-Emilia Province) in Italy, which like many other towns promote 5 km walks in beautiful nature surroundings conducive to cardiovascular health and prevention of cardiovascular disease [49].

4.2 Diet and Nutrition

> "Let food be thy medicine and medicine be thy food". (Hippocrates)

Diet and nutrition are core elements of a healthy, active lifestyle.

Obesity and other diet-related, disabling, NCDs such as type 2 diabetes, hypertension, and common cancers are still highly prevalent worldwide. Different dynamics including an increasingly sedentary lifestyle, altered dietary habits and the increasing consumption of unhealthy 'junk food' have all contributed to creating this secondary "pandemic" which is predominantly a burden on the health system but, also, an economic one from the increased 'work absences' due to these preventable illnesses.

In addressing the question of nutrition at a global level, many aspects must be looked at: the socio-economic context, industrialization, globalization, cultural aspects and nutritional values.

In many places of Africa, South America, India and Vietnam globalization has destroyed natural habitats and, now, food access for the local native communities living on the forest frontier is scarce [50]. One example would be the current deforestation in Brazil. Along with the international global effect of deforestation, a research has proved that this alarming topical subject had a huge impact on the reduction in the consumption of fruit and vegetables, causing vitamin deficiency and malnutrition, and the reduction of the soya production used for animal food [51]. This caused an increased use of Genetically Modified Organisms (GMOs) that subsequently end up in our food chain [52]. Amazonian deforestation has also led to the loss of many medicinal herbs and plants used in the pharmaceutical industries.

The fast-paced urban lifestyle has transformed our lives in many different ways. New technologies, new manufacturing techniques and economic shifts have collectively contributed to the change in our diet, the quality of food and our food intake as Popkin & coll. have demonstrated [53]. New technology has been invented in order to make lives easier but, at the same time, it can make people lazier thus contributing to a higher sedentary life and physical inactivity. This leads to an increase in BMI which then becomes a risk factor for NCDs. Manufacturing techniques have created ready to use, durable and highly palatable ultra-processed foods. Their increased shelf life, ease of transport and low-cost Ultra-Processed Food (UPF) are now part of global household diets.

Monteiro & coll. in 2018 analyzed household consumption in 17 different European countries and has demonstrated that the "easy access" to ultra-processed food which is rich in salt, sugars and saturated fat has contributed to the increased obesity risk [54]. As we try to find ways to navigate our increasingly busy lives, the availability of large multinational supermarket chains and the parallel growth of the fast food industry in urban settings unfortunately become attractive alternatives to traditional home-cooking and slow-cooking. They increase the consumption of UPFs and so-called 'junk food' in our daily diets. UPF, however, are characterized by low nutritional quality and high energy density products, which contain a higher sugar and sodium quantity and also lower fibre and protein contents compared to non-ultra-processed foods according to the NOVA Classification System [55].

Unfortunately, the quality of our food is not the same as it was 40 years ago. Global trends have shown the economic shift in the nutritional transition following an expansion of the world's raw sugar production and how the food market has changed over the last century. Many studies have demonstrated that the nutritional value of the food available nowadays is about 30% compared to the food that was available in the earlier twentieth century, showcasing how the manufacturing process has also deteriorated the quality of food.

In the past 30 years, there has been a boom of GMOs with the introduction of different genetically engineered crop varieties, especially in America. Canada, for example, grows wheat all year around because they have identified the problem where new strains of grains were needed to be developed to withstand harsher climatic conditions. Agricultural conditions have changed drastically over the last few centuries due to global warming and the high use of pesticides is damaging from a health perspective, as pesticides have also been linked to a higher risk of cancer. Nowadays, many people are attracted to the market of the Non-GMOs but, unfortunately, their higher cost can't be afforded by all. This creates larger inequality in different socio-economic classes as people buy what they can afford.

Healthy eating is linked demographically to our socio-economic status as many studies have shown. Evidence would suggest that nutritional choices at the lower end groupings are driven by economic concerns, while those at middle-higher level in society are not limited in their choice. For people living in the lower socio-economic grouping, their choices are mainly monetary and not nutritionally based: the value of our food is based on what is affordable rather than what is needed. This is due to the switch to 'survival mode': less money means that people can usually only afford cheap processed foods as "*any food is better than nothing*".

In many cases, this can also be influenced by being less informed about healthy food choices. Having a lower education means not being able to see the long-term health impact of an inadequate diet of low nutritional levels. On the other hand, Middle to Higher socioeconomic groups are better educated and can also afford a more balanced organic diet. Therefore, they can make the choice to eat healthier foods, they tend to look for gym membership/access to sport clubs and exercise more due to peer pressure to conform to a healthier appearance and lifestyle.

In the past decade, extensive research has shown the link between ultra-processed food (UPF), nutritionally unbalanced diets and the increasing worldwide obesity pandemic. Systematic reviews have shown that different types of cancers, mood changes like depression, NCDs and many more diseases are associated with the higher consumption of UPFs, due to the processing methods and 'obesogenic' components found in them [56, 57].

Quarantine and restrictions during the COVID-19 pandemic have had negative influence on the household consumption of a good healthy diet too. Studies have demonstrated that the COVID-19 pandemic has changed the dietary habits by increasing the consumption of UPF due to the limited access to fresh food. Moreover, it also led to increased mental distress, as anxiety and stress increased due to physical and social confinement. These combined with a lower PA has led to a rise in obesity and higher BMI globally. US consumer surveys have shown an increase in harmful eating habits (60% of the respondents have declared they snack continuously and 64% admitted to eating more junk food and more UPF) during the pandemic years. In order to combat this the US government has increased mass media campaigns advertising healthy habits and physical activity. It is noteworthy that a subsequent study from Harvard Department of Nutrition has demonstrated a decrease of these bad dietary habits as a result [58].

Healthy eating is becoming difficult in many respects, so as part of the 2030 Agenda for Sustainable Development, the SDG 2 aims to end worldwide hunger, to achieve better food security and to improve nutrition. On the 1st April 2016 the United Nations proclaimed the UN Decade of Action on Nutrition for the years 2016–2025 and its implementation is led both by the FAO and WHO [59]. With this Agenda many countries have implemented different campaigns and action plans to educate about what constitutes a healthy diet. In some countries, the results of these campaigns were school and workplace policies with mandatory 'healthy lunches' and where 'junk food' is not allowed. Countries like Italy, Ireland, Canada, Sweden and Denmark, for example, also promote all good eating habits as part of government-led programs.

In this regard, the Irish government—as part of the "Healthy Ireland" initiative framework—gives guidelines, tips and advice on healthy eating and it also avails of the use of all media platforms to encourage everyone to be inspired to eat healthily and live a more active lifestyle, as mentioned earlier through 'Operation Transformation' [39].

A good diet is linked also to Physical Activity and a lot of campaigns/action plans are being implemented globally. A responsible and active use of media platforms such as Facebook, Twitter and Instagram to convey the message about the importance of healthy eating and exercise to as wide an audience as possible is underway.

5 The Community Approach

"Alone, we can do so little; together, we can do so much".
(Helen Keller)

Referring to the 2003 WHO model of health determinants, a key role is played by the social sphere, which alone is estimated to contribute to premature death for around 15% [60].

This fundamental impact on health sees the city and the urban context as key players since it is the privileged theatre in which human relations take place.

The social environment describes the structure and characteristics of relations between people within a community. The components of the social environment now include both real interpersonal interactions and those through social networks, social capital and interpersonal interactions.

Based on the above, individual and group behaviour influence health by acting as amplifiers or attenuators of stressors. Health outcomes are improved if there is easier access to goods and services such as food, health services and housing.

Adopting 'salutogenic' strategies in the urban dimension means increasing social support and the presence of associations and organisations dealing with the social sphere with the aim of improving the quality of life in the community. Certain social problems such as organised crime and substance abuse are correlated with high levels of social stress. This translates into social isolation, violence and extreme poverty. This vicious cycle impoverishes the community by decreasing the availability of social support and access to social and health services, thus weakening social cohesion [61].

The Urban Health model proposed by the WHO 'Healthy Cities' sees the city space declined in exactly this way: pro-social, aggregative and inclusive. Of the 6 'P's that decline it (People, Participation, Prosperity, Planet, Place and Peace), 3 refer directly to people and their relationships (People, Participation, Peace) [62].

This translates into a vast presence of places where communities can meet together, confront each other and carry out activities for individual and collective growth. This virtuous process tends towards a simultaneous consolidation of both the identity of the individual and the community of which he or she is part, in a game of mirrors in which the two entities are intimately connected.

What has been described so far triggers in the urban context a process whose complexity requires a multidisciplinary approach, and there are now several scientific evidences emerging in the literature to support this perspective [63].

Antonovsky's model pursues precisely the idea of flanking the study of aetiological pathogenesis with that of salutogenesis by defining the concept of HOPE (Healing Oriented Practices and Environments). It is precisely this intuition of imagining a health-promoting urban and social environment that is in full synergy with the horizons of Urban Health [64].

Civil society with community-based organisations such as neighbourhood associations and tenants' groups represent the living fabric that actively promotes an environment of social empowerment throughout the community.

The role of religious organisations is also relevant in terms of social support and advocacy, as they provide safe spaces and political leadership. The role of minorities such as slum dwellers, the poor or marginalised groups can bring new voices into the political space and mobilise as a community for better living conditions.

A crucial aspect is the possibility of intercepting the health needs of the population, understood in the holistic interpretation of Alma Ata of 1978, and engaging in dialogue between the 'grossroots stakeholders' and the institutions responsible for responding to these needs.

The role of social movements is crucial for political and social change. The vitality of civil society in a community significantly influences the ability to protect the health of citizens. The reasons for this are to promote social cohesion and combat marginalisation and stigma. The primary objective for researchers in the field of urban health is to find tools to measure the well-being of society and to analyse the impact of various social factors on the determinants of health. Among the factors to be considered are both national phenomena such as urbanisation and international ones such as immigration and globalisation.

A key asset for the intersectoral promotion of urban health is the social and human resources and social capital available to citizens. This allows, even with limited resources, the intersectoral promotion of urban health. An effective public health programme must move along these lines both to intervene effectively in a specific urban context and to reduce the need for external resources. Those working in urban health address this challenge by finding the appropriate resources, mobilising them and ensuring the long-term sustainability of the intervention. Providing adequate external support is also an ongoing objective for international organisations.

In the urban context, however, there are also barriers in the interlocution between bottom-up initiatives and institutions, which become evident when it comes to the implementation and realisation of any agreed actions. Critical issues that emerge are: the frequent absence of a plan to monitor and report on the implementation of the intervention, and the lack of accountability to stakeholders following the deliberative process.

There is a problem of accountability and the paradox that the time, money and effort invested in the creation of the consensus planning process is not proportionate as weight in monitoring the implementation of the consensus-based plan.

The literature today shows us that the most successful negotiations that enabled the achievement of real goals took place outside formal procedures, often when community leaders took the initiative and threatened or implemented actions through protest.

From the analysis carried out, it appears that firstly, participatory planning processes in the implementation phase see the interruption of the participatory process. Secondly, where processes have produced benefits from the perspective of grassroots stakeholders, these have occurred with independent grassroots action.

These two aspects are interrelated and demonstrate the existence of a tension motivated by existing power relations.

It is possible to identify in some participatory processes and their lexicon, an attempt to both implement and mitigate neoliberal economic practices. The result of this process is "*a riot of dissonance*". Notions with undefined definitions such as 'inclusion' and 'social capital' inherently have the capacity to address social and economic issues generated by overlapping power structures such as neoliberalism and colonialism [65].

It is interesting to delve into what leads a community to activate and mobilise. According to the literature, the key actor is the sense of community, which has proven to be the main catalyst. The methodology of 'participatory action-research', increasingly used by researchers, plays a fundamental role in this type of research [66].

Let's look at some experiences in Italy.

According to a quantitative survey of this kind conducted in a neighbourhood of the city of Milan (Italy), it was possible to identify the predictors of the inhabitants' civic participation, considering the sense of community as an overall index and its factors individually. Using appropriate questionnaires with participation scales, a civic participation index was also constructed by assigning a score from 1 to 8 with respect to the degree of commitment required by different forms of participation, at least occasionally. A two-stage analysis of civic participation was then carried out. In step 1, variables related to the perception of problems were included, in step 2 psychosocial variables. The final results showed that problem perception seems to play a role in motivating community members to get active, as does the relevance of people's perception of being able to make a contribution to their community [67].

Acting in terms of Urban Health on the ability to amplify the sense of community must therefore be a priority objective for the public interest, as this triggers a virtuous circle in which the health outcomes of the population improve as well as in parallel the attractiveness of the urban space itself increases.

The Milanese social housing estates as an action-study intervention follow this urban health philosophy. These structures represent realities in which there is often a confrontation with different ways of interpreting the sense of community. Cohabitation and living lend themselves to different interpretations for those who work or reside there. The dimension of this experience is seen in different ways: for some it is the confrontation with memories of the past, for others it is the fostering of ties and for others still the search for personal space.

Neighbours and operators of social housing estates are seen in two antithetical ways: on the one hand as a valuable element of emotional and material support, on the other hand as a pivot on which frustration and conflict episodes are triggered. The action-research involved 10 doormen and 8 tenants of different genders and ages. It was set up as a project to develop effective ways of living together. Central to this was the organisation and implementation of training courses aimed at promoting the quality of living through neighbourhood networks and cohabitation rules, as well as the possibility of regenerating the bond between subjects. The points addressed concerned the individual condition perceived in the blocks of flats: present conflicts, emerging needs and the management of problems. The action-research path made it possible to overcome a recriminatory attitude, fostering the possibility of activating people in a community context and enabling the free sharing of good practices and experiences by strengthening the community bond. The intervention thus realised is part of a long-term project on community mediation [68].

The experience of the street neighbourhoods in Bologna (Italy) is also part of the direction of nurturing a collective urban imagination in which the social fabric is self-sustaining in a salutogenic process. The idea of experimenting with pedestrian resting places was born in Bologna in 2010 as an action-research project. The main objective was to create places capable of acting harmoniously and self-organising. By means of urban planning tools, the project facilitated the emergence of moments of coexistence in common spaces. The emergence of these networks of small squares-workshops in the form of neighbourhoods has brought about changes in shared spaces, even on a permanent basis, facilitating casual encounters between inhabitants of neighbourhoods. In this action-research project, the neighbourhood becomes a micro-reality with shared meeting facilities, which facilitates activation and social initiative as well as participation of the inhabitants. This creates a space-instrument that facilitates cooperation, community project planning as well as contextual knowledge. During the three years in which the project has been field-tested, there has been a noticeable change in the approach to neighbourhood problems from a predominantly urbanistic approach to a more social one. The balance of this project sees a collective empowerment in living in a neighbourhood context. This is evident in the fact that as a result of the project, new and different street neighbourhoods have sprung up. This project emphasised how fundamental it is for the activation of neighbourhood realities to act on neighbourhoods and how this process leads to an urban and social regeneration of sense and care for places as well as social cohesion [69].

Strengthening the sense of community and creating empowerment dynamics are in these contexts a priority for the community in terms of public safety as well, since potential social conflicts are mitigated. Investigating what underlies the sense of community is a complex operation for which one must consider affective, emotional and motivational aspects that are part of a feeling of belonging, influence, emotional connection and needs. The concept of empowerment, on the other hand, is expressed in the increase on the part of people, of their ability to actively control their own lives. This process is therefore necessarily individual but strongly influenced by the community. Sense of community and empowerment are the two cornerstones of individual well-being and social integration of young people as they underpin the development of personal skills, increase self-esteem and trust in the community. It has been shown that the more effectively young people are involved in community life, the more developed their propensity as adults to take an interest in public affairs and socio-political development will be.

Turning to a purely foreign framework, an effective model on how to set up a health-promoting action in synergy with increasing social cohesion is provided by the 'Well communities' programme developed in England since 2017. The programme aims to act in two main directions: (1) promoting and deploying community capacity building activities and resources for all neighbourhoods; (2) to intervene on specific local needs and issues through a portfolio of themed activities and projects determined by the needs and problems identified by each community; some programme activities and projects address specific health outcomes through traditional behaviour change activities (e.g. exercise and cooking and nutrition classes), while others specifically encourage a community approach to health, i.e. participation, volunteering, capacity building, community networks and community cohesion.

First, socio-demographic and individual well-being data were analysed to identify neighbourhoods for action. The action-research approach is universalistic with a focus on the health gap in deprived areas within a vulnerable community. The action research initiative was developed in an urban area with approximately 5,500 residents. The programme had no ethnic, age or gender barriers and was open to the entire neighbourhood [70].

Asset-based health creation approaches underpin Well Communities and are used to ensure a participatory, community-wide governance approach. The extensive community involvement process is carried out through CEAD (Community Engagement, Assessment and Design). Applying this methodology leads the target population to feel actively involved in both the identification of present community needs and the strategies implemented.

The CEAD process comprises a series of activities:

- Street interviews and door-to-door contacts;
- Community cafés. Inspired by the 'World Café' model, it allows small groups to discuss issues of interest to the community in an informal setting that encourages active participation in the conversation;
- Information from Community Cafés and street interviews is combined with information from datasets and resource maps and presented at community action workshops. These are attended by both residents and local stakeholders. The use of workshops involves reflections in the community on what is good and what can be improved.

One of the most striking aspects is the high interest and participation recorded. In phase 2, it was possible to see important improvements in terms of preventive medicine outcomes such as: increased physical activity (total MET minutes of physical activity per week), healthy diet (increased consumption of fruit and vegetables) and mental health.

Specifically:

- 82% did more physical activity at follow-up increasing their MET values compared to baseline. 54% decreased their sedentary lifestyle;
- about 50% ate healthier with 19% reported eating 5 fruits or vegetables per day;
- 54% reported improved mental wellbeing according to the Warwick Edinburgh Mental Wellbeing Scale (WEMWBS). More noticeable outcomes occurred with the Adult Hope scale and the General Health questionnaire 12-item scale (GHQ12);
- for social connectedness, 31% reported a positive change according to the questionnaires;

- for volunteering, 60% reported increased active participation in these initiatives.

The results of this project on a qualitative and quantitative basis simultaneously include increased networks and connections within the local community, in the form of increased widespread participation in voluntary organisations and an increase in the human and economic resources of the neighbourhood at a disadvantaged start.

The idea of giving the inhabitants of the neighbourhood a central role in developing inclusive and socially propulsive public spaces is reflected in the project 'Jämställda platser I Malmö' (in English, 'Equal Opportunities in Malmö'). This initiative aims to implement a set of activities for a socially sustainable Malmö with the overall aim of creating greater involvement of the younger generation in the city and public spaces.

The Environmental Administration and 'Girls in association' collaborated on the project, also involving the three site owners chosen to implement the project.

In the project there was the active involvement of 25 young people who, in different phases of the project, acquired more knowledge and skills in acting in the direction of gender equity, sustainable urban development and against any kind of discrimination.

The first phase of the project saw as its main actors the three owners of the site to be redeveloped and 'Girls in association' who, working with the young people, organised workshops and events on the designated sites with the aim of involving local residents in the various projects. On an operational level, the young people collected ideas and desires, proposed new inputs, and fed a common reflection on public places and spaces.

The second phase of the project involved the collaboration of the architects who, on the basis of the ideas and proposals that emerged, took care of the implementation by applying their skills and knowledge based on the latest theories on gender equality in public urban design.

The opening of the sites took place in June 2016. During the implementation work, the 15 young people involved together with 'Girls in association' took care of the launch and organisation of the events. Specifically, the planning involved the opening ceremony and ongoing activities at the three designated sites. The objective of involving residents was achieved as well as the possibility of creating public spaces where young people could develop their ideas in the public interest.

The 'Gender Equal Places in Malmö' project was developed from the city's own desire to adopt new methods to improve gender equality in urban development processes and in the use of public spaces in order to overcome the critical issues identified by the various associations in the area. One avant-garde project in the city was 'Rosens Röda Matta', implemented in an area in the Rosengård district whose design and management is by young women. It was precisely this reality that functioned as a 'fil rouge' in the realisation and follow-up of 'Gender Equal Places in Malmö'.

Among the outcomes of the project is the effective implementation of three new meeting places that are permanently active in the city. The increase in the human and social capital of the 25 young participants as well as the residents who embraced the project also led to greater knowledge and competence to act in terms of gender equality, anti-discrimination and sustainable urban development. In conclusion, 'Girls in association' documented the entire work experience in the book 'Gender equal urban development' [71].

In conclusion, the community approach in Urban Health appears to have important potential in enhancing a lively and pro-active social fabric that directly counteracts the various external stressors on the community and at the same time also leads to forms of community self-advocacy. What has been said with a view to a future Health System increasingly centred at the territorial level would make it easier to reach even hard-to-reach communities with a vigilant and agile proximity medicine that would allow more effective and compliant preventive medicine interventions for the entire community with also in the long term obvious savings in terms of cost-effectiveness.

6 Brief Concluding Remarks

> "And that we are all responsible to all for all, apart from our own sins, you were quite right in thinking that, and it is wonderful how you could comprehend it in all its significance at once. And in very truth, so soon as men understand that, the Kingdom of Heaven will be for them not a dream, but a living reality".
>
> (Fyodor Dostoyevsky)

We are aware that we have only addressed a part of the issues related to our Urban Health in this chapter (e.g. the albeit important issues of urban waste and urban safety in their impact on citizens' health have not been dealt with except fleetingly).

Virtually all of the various critical issues we have tried to illustrate can be traced back to human beings and their choices (including the ongoing Pandemic).

This appears both comforting and worrying.

As long as our health—understood as the quality of our lives—and the possibility of all of us achieving a satisfactory existential quality is not perceived as a priority value and is therefore not placed at the top of the international, national and local political agenda, Urban Health will continue to present unacceptable contradictions.

We now have virtually all the knowledge we need to take action. In the context of health promotion, the strategies and actions that seem necessary to better qualify Urban Health have already been discussed and proposed [72, 73].

With reference to the oft-mentioned Sustainable Development Goals, every year, the UN Secretary General presents an annual SDG Progress report, which is developed in cooperation with the UN System, and based on the global indicator framework and data produced by national statistical systems and information collected at the regional level.

In the latest available report on Goal 11 'Making cities and human settlements inclusive, safe, resilient and sustainable', the following considerations can be read:

109. As epicentres of the COVID-19 crisis, many cities have suffered from insufficient public health systems, inadequate basic services, a lack of well-developed and integrated public transport systems and inadequate open public spaces, as well as the economic consequences of lockdowns. As a result, the pandemic is likely to further increase the number of slum dwellers. To improve the lives of over one billion slum-dwellers, there is an urgent need to focus on policies to improve health, affordable housing, basic services, sustainable mobility and connectivity.

110. Over the years, the number of slum dwellers continues to grow and it was over one billion in 2020. Slum dwellers are most prevalent in three regions, which are home to about 85% of the slum residents in the world—Central and Southern Asia (359 million), Eastern and South- Eastern Asia (306 million), and sub-Saharan Africa (230 million).

111. Data for 2020 from 1,510 cities around the world indicates that, on average only about 37% of the urban areas are served by public transport, measured as a walking distance of 500 m to low-capacity transport systems (such as buses or trams) and/or 1,000 m to high-capacity systems (such as trains and ferries). With variations in population concentrations within the cities, this translates to only about 52% of the world population having convenient access to public transport.

112. In 2022, the global average municipal solid waste (MSW) collection rate in cities is at 82%, and the average MSW managed in controlled facilities in cities is 55%. The MSW collection rates in sub-Saharan Africa and Oceania are less than 60%. Uncollected waste is the source of plastic pollution, GHG emissions, and incubation for infections.

113. Data for 2020 from 1,072 cities point to a poor distribution of open public spaces in most regions. In these cities, only about 38% of the urban areas are located within 400 m of walking distance to an open public space, which translates to only about 45% of the global urban population having convenient access to these spaces.

114. As of March 2021, 156 countries have developed national urban policies, with almost half (74) already in the implementation stage. A further breakdown shows that 40% of the countries are in the early stages of developing their plans, while 12% are monitoring and evaluating how well these plans are functioning.

115. By the end of 2021, 98 countries have reported having local governments with disaster risk reduction strategies, an increase from 51 countries in 2015 [74].

Achieving the goals of the 2030 SDG Agenda can be maximized through the Health in All Policies (HiAP) approach. The implementation of this approach can in turn be facilitated by the application in cities around the world, including those in less developed areas, of tools such as Health Impact Assessment (HIA). The availability of data, the consideration of equity issues, the involvement and collaboration of all the main stakeholders (experts, citizens and decision-makers) are fundamental elements to implement our ambitious but fundamental objectives [75].

As you can see, there is still much to be done.

References

1. World health organization (2016) WHO: health as the pulse of the new urban agenda: United Nations conference on housing and sustainable urban development, Quito. World health organization. https://apps.who.int/iris/handle/10665/250367. Last accessed 26 Jun 2022
2. United Nations (2019) Department of economic and social affairs population division: world urbanization prospects 2018 Highlights. https://population.un.org/wup/Publications/Files/WUP2018-Highlights.pdf. Last accessed 26 Jun 2022
3. Cyril S, Oldroyd JC, Renzaho A (2013) Urbanisation, urbanicity, and health: a systematic review of the reliability and validity of urbanicity scales. BMC Publ Health 13:513. https://doi.org/10.1186/1471-2458-13-513.Lastaccessed26Jun2022
4. WHO (2021) Non communicable diseases. https://www.who.int/news-room/fact-sheets/detail/noncommunicable-diseases. Last accessed 26 Jun 2020
5. WHO (1948) Constitution of the world health organization (WHO). Geneva (world basic documents). https://apps.who.int/gb/bd/PDF/bd47/EN/constitution-en.pdf?ua=1. Last accessed 26 Jun 2022
6. Barton H, Grant M (2006) A health map for the local human habitat. J Royal Soc Promot Health 126(6):252–253 (2006). ISSN: 1466-4240
7. WHO: European healthy cities network. https://www.who.int/europe/groups/who-european-healthy-cities-network. Last accessed 26 Jun 2022
8. United Nations (2015) Transforming our world: The 2030 agenda for sustainable development. https://sdgs.un.org/2030agenda. Last accessed 26 Jun 2022
9. Battisti A, Marceca M (2020) Urban health multidisciplinary actions promoting health in an urban environment. In: Battisti A, Marceca M, Iorio S (eds) Urban health. participatory action-research models contrasting socioeconomic inequalities in the urban context. Springer, Cham pp 19–26
10. GBD 2019 Risk factors collaborators (2020) Global burden of 87 risk factors in 204 countries and territories, 1990–2019: a systematic analysis for the Global Burden of Disease Study 2019. Lancet 396(10258): 1223–1249. https://doi.org/10.1016/S0140-6736(20)30752-2. Last accessed 26 Jun 2022
11. Lelieveld J, Klingmüller K, Pozzer A, Pöschl U, Fnais M, Daiber A, Münzel T (2019) Cardiovascular disease burden from ambient air pollution in Europe reassessed using novel hazard ratio functions. Eur Heart J 40(20):1590–1596
12. Marmett B, Carvalho RB, Dorneles GP, Nunes RB, Rhoden CR (2020) Should I stay or should I go: can air pollution reduce the health benefits of physical exercise? Med Hypotheses 144:109993. https://doi.org/10.1016/j.mehy.2020.109993.Lastaccessed26Jun2022
13. European Environment Agency (2020) Environmental noise in Europe—2020. EEA Report No 22/2019. https://www.eea.europa.eu/publications/environmental-noise-in-europe. Last accessed 26 Jun 2022. ISSN 1977–8449.
14. Münzel T, Sørensen M, Lelieveld J, Hahad O, Al-Kindi S, Nieuwenhuijsen M, Giles-Corti B, Daiber A, Rajagopalan S (2021) Heart healthy cities: genetics loads the gun but the environment pulls the trigger. Eur Heart J 42(25):2422–2438. https://doi.org/10.1093/eurheartj/ehab235,Lastaccessed26Jun2022
15. WHO (2010) UN-HABITAT: Hidden cities: unmasking and overcoming health inequities in urban settings (2010). https://www.who.int/publications/i/item/9789241548038. Last accessed 26 Jun 2022. ISBN 978-92-4-154803-8
16. Caminade C, McIntyre KM, Jones AE (2019) Impact of recent and future climate change on vector-borne diseases. Ann N Y Acad Sci 1436(1):157–173. https://doi.org/10.1111/nyas.13950.Lastaccessed26Jun26
17. European Environment Agency https://www.eea.europa.eu/. Last accessed 26 Jun 2022
18. United Nations: New urban agenda (2017). https://habitat3.org/the-new-urban-agenda/. Last accessed 2022/06/26. ISBN: 978-92-1-132731-1
19. UN-HABITAT: National reports on the progress in the implementation of the new urban Agenda (2021). https://www.urbanagendaplatform.org/member-states. Last accessed 26 Jun 2022

20. UN-HABITAT: National reports on the progress in the implementation of the new urban agenda (2016). https://www.urbanagendaplatform.org/member-states. Last accessed 26 Jun 2022
21. International Energy Agency (IEA), Nuclear Energy Agency (NEA), OECD: projected costs of generating electricity 2020 Edition (2020). https://www.iea.org/reports/projected-costs-of-generating-electricity-2020. Last accessed 26 Jun 2022
22. European Energy Research Alliance—EERA: white paper on the clean energy transition, European energy research alliance, Brussels (2021). https://www.eera-set.eu/. Last accessed 26 Jun 2022
23. European Environment Agency (2021) Urban sustainability: how can cities become sustainable? https://www.eea.europa.eu/themes/sustainability-transitions/urban-environment. Last accessed 26 Jun 2022
24. U.S. Department of Commerce (2019) U.S. census bureau: commuting by public transportation in the United States: 2019. https://www.census.gov/content/dam/Census/library/publications/2021/acs/acs-48.pdf. Last accessed 26 Jun 2022
25. Louiza H, Zéroual A, Djamel H (2015) Impact of the transport on the Urban Heat Island. Int J Traffic Transp Eng 5(3):252–263
26. Vujovic S, Haddad B, Karaky H, Sebaibi N, Boutouil M (2021) Urban heat island: causes, consequences, and mitigation measures with emphasis on reflective and permeable pavements. Civil Eng 2(2):459–484. https://doi.org/10.3390/civileng2020026.Lastaccessed26Jun2022
27. Warren TY, Barry V, Hooker SP, Sui X, Church TS, Blair SN (2010) Sedentary behaviors increase risk of cardiovascular disease mortality in men. Med Sci Sports Exerc 42(5):879–885. https://doi.org/10.1249/MSS.0b013e3181c3aa7e.Lastaccessed26Jun2022
28. Hoehner CM, Barlow CE, Allen P, Schootman M (2012) Commuting distance, cardiorespiratory fitness, and metabolic risk. Am J Prev Med 42(6):571–578. https://doi.org/10.1016/j.amepre.2012.02.020.Lastaccessed26Jun2022
29. Milner A, Badland H, Kavanagh A, La Montagne AD (2017) Time spent commuting to work and mental health: evidence from 13 waves of an Australian cohort study. Am J Epidemiol 186(6):659–667. https://doi.org/10.1093/aje/kww243.Lastaccessed26Jun2022
30. Humphreys DK, Goodman A, Ogilvie D (2013) Associations between active commuting and physical and mental wellbeing. Prev Med 57(2):135–139
31. Mueller N, Rojas-Rueda D, Cole-Hunter T, De Nazelle A, Dons E, Gerike R, Götschi T, Int Panis L, Kahlmeier S, Nieuwenhuijsen M (2015) Health impact assessment of active transportation: a systematic review. Prev Med 76:103–114
32. Giles-Corti B, Vernez-Moudon A, Reis R, Turrell G, Dannenberg AL, Badland H, Foster S, Lowe M, Sallis JF, Stevenson M, Owen N (2016) City planning and population health: a global challenge. The lancet 388(10062):2912–2924
33. Rueda S (2019) Superblocks for the design of new cities and renovation of existing ones: Barcelona's case. In integrating human health into urban and transport planning. Springer, Cham, pp.135–153
34. WHO (2004) Global strategy on diet, physical activity and health—2004. https://www.who.int/publications/i/item/9241592222. Last accessed 26 Jun 2022
35. WHO (2008) A healthy city is an active city. https://www.euro.who.int/en/health-topics/environment-and-health/urban-health/publications/2008/healthy-city-is-an-active-city-a-a-physical-activity-planning-guide. Last accessed 26 Jun 2022
36. WHO (2018) More active people for a healthier world. Global action plan on physical activity 2018–2030. https://apps.who.int/iris/handle/10665/272722?locale-attribute=de&. Last accessed 26 Jun 2022
37. Liikkuva koulu (Schools on the move) (2010) Finnish schools on the move. Increasing physical activity and decreasing sedentary time among school-aged children. https://schoolsonthemove.fi/. Last accessed 26 Jun 2022
38. Physical and health education Canada (PHE Canada): Passport for life Canada (2013). https://passportforlife.ca/. Last accessed 26 Jun 2022
39. Healthy Ireland. https://www.gov.ie/en/campaigns/8928d-healthy-ireland/. Last accessed 26 Jun 2022

40. Irish Government. https://www.gov.ie/en/publication/85fc0-getting-active/. Last accessed 26 Jun 2022
41. Department of health and children, health service executive: the national guidelines on physical activity for Ireland (2009). https://activeschoolflag.ie/wp-content/uploads/2020/08/GuidelinesPhysicalActivity.pdf. Last accessed 26 Jun 2022
42. Stathopoulou G, Powers M, Berry A, Smits J, Otto M (2006) Exercise interventions for mental health: a quantitative and qualitative review. Clin Psychol Sci Pract 13(2):179–193
43. Alexandratos K, Barnett F, Thomas Y (2012) The impact of exercise on the mental health and quality of life of people with severe mental illness: a critical review. Br J Occup Ther 75(2):48–60
44. Maynou L, Hernández-Pizarro HM, Errea Rodríguez M (2021) The association of physical (in) activity with mental health. differences between elder and younger populations: a systematic literature review. Int J Environ Res Publ Health 18(9):4771. https://doi.org/10.3390/ijerph18094771. PMID: 33947122; PMCID: PMC8124550
45. Allen L, Williams J, Townsend N, Mikkelsen B, Roberts N, Foster C et al (2017) Socioeconomic status and non-communicable disease behavioural risk factors in low-income and lower middle-income countries: a systematic review. Lancet Glob Health 5:e277-289. https://doi.org/10.1016/S2214-109X(17)30058-X
46. Dallmeyer S, Wicker P, Breuer C (2020) The relationship between physical activity and out-of-pocket health care costs of the elderly in Europe. Eur J Publ Health 30(4):628–632. https://doi.org/10.1093/eurpub/ckaa045 PMID: 32155251
47. Biddle SJH, Asare M (2011) Physical activity and mental health in children and adolescents: a review of reviews. Br J Sports Med 45:886–895
48. Kemel PN, Porter JE, Coombs N (2021) Improving youth physical, mental and social health through physical activity: a systematic literature review. Health Promot J Austr. https://doi.org/10.1002/hpja.553. Epub ahead of print. PMID: 34735738
49. Comune di Viano: I percorsi del cuore. Prevenzione e riabilitazione. https://www.comune.viano.re.it/vivi-viano/mappa-e-itinerari-naturalistici/i-percorsi-del-cuore/. Last accessed 26 Jun 2022
50. Blundo-Canto G, Cruz-Garcia GS, Talsma EF et al (2020) Changes in food access by mestizo communities associated with deforestation and agrobiodiversity loss in Ucayali. Peruvian Amazon Food Sec 12:637–658. https://doi.org/10.1007/s12571-020-01022-1,lastaccessed 2022/06/26
51. Hall CM, Rasmussen LV, Powell B, Dyngeland C, Jung S, Olesen RS (2022) Deforestation reduces fruit and vegetable consumption in rural Tanzania. Proc Natl Acad Sci 119(10):e2112063119
52. Lopes-Ferreira M, Maleski ALA, Balan-Lima L et al (2022) Impact of pesticides on human health in the last six years in Brazil. Int J Environ Res Publ Health 19(6):3198. https://doi.org/10.3390/ijerph19063198
53. Popkin BM, Ng SW (2022) The nutrition transition to a stage of high obesity and noncommunicable disease prevalence dominated by ultra-processed foods is not inevitable. Obes Rev 23(1):e13366. https://doi.org/10.1111/obr.13366
54. Monteiro C, Moubarac J, Levy R, Canella D, Louzada M, Cannon G (2018) Household availability of ultra-processed foods and obesity in nineteen European countries. Publ Health Nutr 21(1):18–26. https://doi.org/10.1017/S1368980017001379
55. Monteiro CA, Cannon G, Moubarac JC et al (2017) The UN decade of nutrition, the NOVA food classification and the trouble with ultra-processing. Publ Health Nutr 21:5–17
56. Chen X, Zhang Z, Yang H, Qiu P, Wang H, Wang F, Zhao Q, Fang J, Nie J (2020) Consumption of ultra-processed foods and health outcomes: a systematic review of epidemiological studies. Nutr J 19(1):86. https://doi.org/10.1186/s12937-020-00604-1. PMID: 32819372; PMCID: PMC7441617
57. Kliemann N, Al Nahas A, Vamos EP, Touvier M, Kesse-Guyot E, Gunter MJ, Millett C, Huybrechts I (2022) Ultra-processed foods and cancer risk: from global food systems to individual exposures and mechanisms. Br J Cancer. https://doi.org/10.1038/s41416-022-01749-y. Epub ahead of print. PMID: 35236935

58. Harvard department of nutrition. https://www.hsph.harvard.edu/faculty-research/. Last accessed 26 Jun 2022
59. UN system standing committee on nutrition. The UN decade of action on nutrition 2016–2025. https://www.unscn.org/en/topics/un-decade-of-action-on-nutrition. Last accessed 26 Jun 2022
60. Schroeder SA (2007) We can do better. Improving the health of the American people. N Engl J Med 357:1221–8. https://doi.org/10.1056/NEJMsa073350. PMID: 17881753
61. Vlahov D, Freudenberg N, Proietti F, Ompad D, Quinn A, Nandi V, Galea S (2007) Urban as a determinant of health. J Urban Health 84(3 Suppl):i16-26. https://doi.org/10.1007/s11524-007-9169-3.PMID:17356903;PMCID:PMC1891649
62. WHO (2022) Healthy cities vision. https://www.euro.who.int/en/health-topics/environment-and-health/urban-health/who-european-healthy-cities-network/healthy-cities-vision. Last accessed 26 Jun 2022
63. D'Alessandro D (2020) Urban public health, a multidisciplinary approach. In: Battisti A, Marceca M, Iorio S (eds) Urban health. Springer, Cham. https://doi.org/10.1007/978-3-030-49446-9_1
64. Lindström B, Eriksson M (2006) Contextualizing salutogenesis and Antonovsky in public health development. Health Promot Int 21(3):238–244. http://www.jstor.org/stable/45152879. Last accessed 26 Jun 2022
65. Katz AS, Cheff RM, O'Campo P (2015) Bringing stakeholders together for urban health equity: hallmarks of a compromised process. Int J Equity Health 14:138. https://doi.org/10.1186/s12939-015-0252-1,lastaccessed2022/06/26
66. Battisti A, Marceca M, Iorio S (2020) Urban health. participatory action-research models contrasting socioeconomic inequalities in the urban context. Springer, Cham
67. Aresi G, Marta E (2014) Predittori della civic participation: il senso di comunità e le sue dimensioni. In: Atti del 10° convegno nazionale della società Italiana di psicologia di comunità (S.I.P.Co.) "Costruire comunità ospitali e disponibili, nuove sfide per la psicologia di comunità". Cesena, giugno 2014 pp 19–21
68. Boniforti D, Ripamonti E, Rho B (2014) Abitare e convivere: sostenere comunità nei caseggiati popolari. In: Atti del 10° convegno nazionale della società Italiana di psicologia di comunità (S.I.P.Co.) "Costruire comunità ospitali e disponibili, nuove sfide per la psicologia di comunità". Cesena, giugno 2014, pp 19–21
69. Reyes S (2014) Verso una città di vicinati di strada il caso dei luoghi di sosta pedonale a Bologna. In: Atti del 10° convegno nazionale della società Italiana di psicologia di comunità (S.I.P.Co.) "Costruire comunità ospitali e disponibili, nuove sfide per la psicologia di comunità". Cesena, giugno 2014, pp 19–21
70. Findlay G, Tobi P (2017) Well communities perspectives in public. Health 137(1):17–20. https://doi.org/10.1177/1757913916680329
71. Dors Piemonte: CARE Catalogo di Azioni ben descritte Rivolte all'Equità. Jämställda platser I Malmö (Gender equal places) (2015). https://www.dors.it/tooldis/CARE/pratiche_completa.php?id=35. Last accessed 26 Jun 2022
72. WHO (2018) Regional Office for Europe: copenhagen consensus of mayors. Healthier and happier cities for all. A transformative approach for safe, inclusive, sustainable and resilient societies (2018). https://www.euro.who.int/__data/assets/pdf_file/0003/361434/consensus-eng.pdf. Last accessed 26 Jun 2022
73. D'Alessandro D, Arletti S, Azara A, Buffoli M, Capasso L, Cappuccitti A, Casuccio A et al (2017) Attendees of the 50th course urban health. Strategies for disease prevention and health promotion in urban areas: the erice 50 charter. Ann Ig 29(6):481–493. https://doi.org/10.7416/ai.2017.2179. PMID: 29048447
74. United Nations (2022) Department of economic and social affairs: sustainable development. Sustainable development goals: implementation progress. SDG progress report– advanced unedited version. https://sdgs.un.org/goals#implementation. Last accessed 26 Jun 2022
75. Ramirez-Rubio O, Daher C, Fanjul G et al (2019) Urban health: an example of a "health in all policies" approach in the context of SDGs implementation. Global Health 15:87. https://doi.org/10.1186/s12992-019-0529-z

Security, Health and Social Exclusion in Urban Contexts. A Sociological Perspective

Giuseppe Ricotta

Abstract This paper explores the theme of socio-spatial exclusion through two concepts from contemporary critical sociology: that of territorial stigmatization and that of abyssal social exclusion. These concepts are used to interpret a specific urban context characterized by marked socio-spatial inequalities: the city of Rio de Janeiro, Brazil. The dynamics of socio-spatial segregation are analyzed with particular reference to the issues of urban security and access to social and health services. The case of Rio de Janeiro, which has a paradigmatic value because of the deep urban division between *asfalto* and *favelas*, has here the function of stimulating the analysis of certain dynamics also found in other urban contexts globally. We then go on to discuss the relevance of activation and knowledge processes located in "bottom-up" civic and democratic participation practices to counteract the dynamics of social exclusion and foster equitable access to urban healthcare and security.

Keywords Urban security · Health services · Social exclusion · Colonial sociability · Rio de Janeiro · Favelas

1 Introduction

Critical reflections on modernity have long posed the need to reconsider triumphalist categories and views towards the Western modernization process [1–4]. These critical reflections have concerned the very development of the modern city and its contradictions in terms of equity and social inclusion [5]. Nevertheless, a vision of the "modern city" continues to exist on which the degree of development of metropolises and metropolitan sociability itself is measured globally; a vision that has found new life in the wake of the crisis of governance of nation-states and the emergence of a "new urban era". We refer to the renewed prominence of cities, specifically "global" cities [6], which took off over the last thirty years of the last century as a result of the changes affecting global capitalism. We can refer, in this regard, to the competition

G. Ricotta (✉)
Sapienza University of Rome, Rome, Italy
e-mail: Giuseppe.ricotta@uniroma1.it

A. Battisti et al. (eds.), *Equity in Health and Health Promotion in Urban Areas*, Green Energy and Technology, https://doi.org/10.1007/978-3-031-16182-7_3

engaged by cities to host so-called mega-events [7], a competition that is played out on the terrain of technological modernity of transport and information infrastructure, smartness, and at the same time security and "urban quality of life", all of which are decisive elements in asserting a specific city brand before the international audience of investors, tourists, and spectators.

At the same time, and consistent with neoliberal dynamics of production and transformation of urban spaces, risk factors are emerging in cities that intercept multiple social issues, including urban security and access to healthcare. In this paper we focus precisely on the risk factors of urbanization processes in the late modern era, with particular reference to the phenomenon of dualization [8], or urban divide [9].

The phenomenon of urban dualization, and the socio-spatial inequalities associated with it, are analyzed in light of two concepts from critical sociology: that of territorial stigmatization [10] and that of abyssal social exclusion [11].

These concepts are used for the interpretation of a specific urban context characterized by severe socio-spatial inequalities: the city of Rio de Janeiro, Brazil. The dynamics of socio-spatial segregation are analyzed with particular reference to urban security issues as much as to access to social and health services. The case of Rio de Janeiro, which has a paradigmatic value because of the deep urban division between *asfalto* and *favelas*, has here the function of stimulating the analysis of some dynamics also found in other urban contexts globally.

Finally, we discuss the relevance of the activation and knowledge processes located in "bottom-up" civic and democratic participation practices to counteract the dynamics of social exclusion and foster equal access to healthcare and urban security. Access to healthcare and community health models are particularly strategic issues in all those urban contexts that suffer most in terms of inequalities and social exclusion.

2 Social Exclusion and Urban Trends

The concept of social exclusion is relatively recent in the debate within the social sciences. Its analytical definition is complex, both because it is a multidimensional concept that is difficult to operationalize for empirical analysis [12], and because there is a dispute—or rather, a real competition—between alternative theoretical paradigms in the literature about the etiological factors of the phenomenon [13]. Our focus here is on the socio-economic, cultural and spatial factors that cause exclusionary dynamics toward individuals and human groups in urban settings. Specifically, we are interested in understanding how inequalities interact with socio-spatial segregation in urban and suburban contexts.

Social exclusion can be analyzed as much from the economic dimensions of relative material deprivation (caused by unemployment, low income, low educational qualifications, disability, etc.) as in relation to its socio-cultural aspects (isolation, absence of social ties). Especially in its socio-cultural reading, with reference to the

Durkheimian sociological tradition, social exclusion has been interpreted as a key player in social pathologies: a society characterized by widespread and/or increasing social exclusion undermines not only the socio-economic well-being of individuals suffering exclusion, but social cohesion itself. Indeed, among the negative consequences associated with the condition of exclusion is the increase in insecurity both for the individuals and social groups that existentially experience this condition and for society as a whole.

Robert Castel [14] has analytically isolated two dimensions of security: a social dimension, related to accidents that can deteriorate the human material condition (unemployment or low income, disease, precariousness and unhealthiness of living, etc.), and a civil dimension, related to threats to psycho-physical safety, the protection of one's property, and the protection of personal freedom and inviolability. The so-called *Trente Glorieuses* after World War II ensured in Western Europe a strong capacity for social inclusion through collective protections, among which the organization of universal health services was a decisive one. In this sense, following Castel, the contemporary re-emergence of insecurity finds its most important cause precisely in the crisis of the welfare state that began in the 1970s. The factors behind this crisis have been identified mainly in the transformations that have affected the economy (globalization, outsourcing and offshoring, financialization). Thus, the weakening of classical welfare coverage was associated with the rise of unemployment and job insecurity.

To the typical risks of Western modernity (or classical risks as Castel defines them), which re-emerge due to the weakening of national and local welfare systems, are added the "new" global risks, determined by the consequences of the development model underlying the modernization process. Within the sociological debate on the transition from the first to the second (or late) modernity, the so-called risk society [15, 16], it has been highlighted how the late-modern condition is characterized precisely by reflexivity towards the risks inscribed in the Western development model: among others, health, demographic, energy and environmental risks.

Social reflexivity about risks in the second modernity thus underlies the emergence of the theme of sustainability in its three interconnected components: environmental, economic and social. The very pandemic of COVID-19 can be read within this interpretive key—in which the "new global risks" act as amplifiers and accelerators of inequalities determined by the "classic risks of the modernization process", an event capable of radicalizing trends already taking place at the level of global society, Western democracies included: growth of inequality, crisis of central and local governments, crisis of public regulation and essential public services (health, education, training and labor). Risks typical of modern society and new global risks, rather than passing the baton, mix and add up [17].

Returning to the object of analysis of the city, which is what we are interested in here, the aforementioned crisis of social protections has had a set of consequences that have fostered the re-emergence of social insecurity, and in some ways have made urban dynamics comparable—albeit with their structural social–historical and political differences—globally. Starting from these considerations, sociologist Zygmunt Bauman [5] stated, with an expressive and evocative image, that "contemporary cities are dumping grounds for the mis-formed and de-formed products of fluid modern society". Products that derive as much from the old risks of early modernity as from the new risks of second modernity. To list just a few, think of environmental pollution and land erosion, radicalization of inequalities and processes of socio-spatial segregation, precarious housing and violence.

Contemporary cities can consequently be analyzed, within a sociological perspective, as spaces of activation of reflexive and conflictual processes revolving around the undesirable and sometimes unforeseen effects of urbanization processes and related urban dynamics. Processes and dynamics conditioned by neo-liberal policies [18] and the tensions of the current post-democratic phase [19].

It is especially in large cities that, along with population growth, the volumes of intensive housing settlements and informal urban conglomerates are increasing, and where the main social, economic and environmental problems mentioned above are concentrated. We speak, by the way, of a dual city or urban divide to refer to the occurrence of an intra-metropolitan duality between neighborhoods or areas where wealth is produced and which have high levels of quality of life and neighborhoods or areas characterized by relative poverty and spatial segregation. The former are urban territories that, due to their characteristics (e.g. centrality, infrastructure, etc.), are capable of intercepting global market opportunities; the latter, are territories that are less attractive for investment, trade and tourism and consequently increasingly socially peripheral [8].

3 Territorial Stigmatization and Colonial Sociability

To analyze the dynamics of socio-spatial exclusion we resort to two concepts from contemporary sociological theory. The first refers to severe forms of social exclusion that provoke and are in turn fueled by social processes of stigmatization aimed at specific urban territories and the populations that inhabit them. The second, which takes its cue from the postcolonial and decolonial debates, refers to a type of exclusion, termed abyssal, based on colonial sociability.

The first of the concepts analyzed, that of territorial stigmatization, takes its cue from Wacquant's work in the Black American ghettos and French urban periphery [10]. According to Wacquant: "The comparative sociology of the structure, dynamics, and experience of urban relegation in the United States and the main countries of the European Union during the past three decades reveals, not a convergence on the pattern of the US ghetto as the dominant media and political discourse would have it, but the emergence of a new regime of marginality on both sides of the Atlantic" [20]. This new regime of marginality generates forms of poverty that are neither residual nor cyclical or transitory, but are interpreted by Wacquant as structural, inscribed in the future of contemporary societies. This is because of the crisis of welfare and the fragmentation of waged labor relations, and the functional disconnection of marginalized neighborhoods from national and global economies—an element already highlighted as the cause of the process of dualization in contemporary cities.

Wacquant's thesis on territorial stigmatization ties together Pierre Bourdieu's theory of symbolic power with Erving Goffman's thesis on stigma and the management of "spoiled identity". Stigmatization processes, referring to urban spaces, act negatively on residents of deprived neighborhoods, favoring when possible exit strategies, on surrounding residents and business operators, on public street-level bureaucrats, on journalists, scholars, and politicians, on business operators, and on public policies.

Delica and Hansen [21] analyzed 119 peer reviewed articles devoted to the topic of territorial stigmatization. The analysis shows that it is a versatile concept that has become central to the study of territorial exclusion and urban inequality. However, its causes and conditions are still understudied. As such, through their timely review of the literature, the two authors argue—consistent with Wacquant's thesis—that the production of territorial stigma is an integral part of contemporary forms of neoliberal urban governance. Territorial stigmatization can be interpreted as a strategy for legitimizing current radical political measures of demolition, gentrification and re-privatization of stigmatized territories.

One of the possible outcomes of territorial stigmatization processes is the criminalization of specific urban spaces, as a result of labeling processes that arise from how political-economic forces structure urban space, determining the distribution of the population, particularly the poorest, in different neighborhoods [22].

What we are interested in here is to understand the way through which these processes of territorial stigmatization produce negative effects in terms of urban security and access to health services, with particular reference to severe forms of socio-spatial exclusion, forms that cause an expulsion of specific sectors of the population outside the symbolic framework of the social contract of modern citizenship. It serves this purpose to introduce the second of the concepts: abyssal social exclusion.

The concept of abyssal social exclusion is proposed by Boaventura de Sousa Santos, a sociologist whose thought is situated within a debate that embraces, on the one hand, post-colonial, decolonial studies, sociologies of globalization and critical theory, and, on the other, the analysis of alter globalization movements (or social justice movements). Santos places at the center of his reflection the "abyssal line" that separates two types of sociability: a "metropolitan" type and a "colonial" type [11, 23–25]. By sociability we refer here to the prevailing forms assumed by social relations in a given historical and geographical context, forms that determine social inclusion and exclusion. The modern Western project has been built on the metropolitan type of sociability, based on the metaphor of the social contract and the tension between regulatory mechanisms, necessary to guarantee order in the social system, and emancipatory pressures for the inclusion in the groove of civil, social and political rights of ever larger segments of the population. A process, the latter, which was historically substantiated in the twentieth century in Western Europe, in the transition from "restricted liberal modernity" to "organized modernity" based on a system of collective regulations [26]. Shifting the view from Western Europe to the world-system [27], however, since the sixteenth century another type of sociability has structured itself alongside the metropolitan one: colonial sociability. The latter is regulated by the tension between violence—understood as physical, material, cultural destruction—and appropriation—understood as incorporation, co-optation, assimilation.

In colonial-type social relations, social exclusion is abyssal in that the excluded cannot realistically claim their rights, as they are not considered fully human. Eurocentric theory, created on the basis of metropolitan sociability, ignores colonial sociability or, rather, reproduces it as non-being. Eurocentric rationality, in this sense, becomes abyssal thinking, failing to recognize as contemporary what happens in contexts characterized by colonial sociability. If this abyssal line originates with colonialism, it does not terminate with the end of historical colonialism, but persists in the post-colonial phase, transforming and entering powerfully within European societies themselves at a time when contemporary global economic logics have obscured the promises of progress, freedom and equality inscribed in the Eurocentric vision of modernity.

Rethinking social emancipation, according to Santos, requires post-abyssal thinking: questioning citizenship rights also from the perspective of noncitizens, human rights also from the perspective of those who are considered sub-human or non-human: those who live on the other side of the abyssal line, in fact, resist humiliation, discrimination and extreme social exclusion and are in search of solutions because they want to survive in the present.

Post-abyssal thinking is based on a "cosmopolitan reason" that aims to expand the present and contract the future through three sociological procedures: the sociology of absences, the sociology of emergencies, and translation. The sociology of absences allows for the expansion of the present by turning its interest to what Eurocentric thinking produces as not present and therefore invisible, not existing. The task of sociology is then to critically analyze the hierarchies produced by Eurocentric thought and thus transform absences into presences; the expansion of the present is, in fact, possible as we expand what can be considered contemporary. Hence the importance of noting the diversity and multiplicity of social practices, manifesting the experiences that oppose the destructive elements of globalization.

The sociology of emergencies, for its part, aims to contract the future by subjecting to critique its linear conception, the idea of limitless progress and an infinite future that does not need to be thought about. Such is the case with the modernizing ideology that absolutizes capitalist development. Instead, it is necessary to contract this future in order to think about it, a future that depends on care and caregiving. Santos invites sociology to focus on the alternatives contained in the horizon of concrete possibilities: the emergence of new anti-hegemonic experiences is based on a symbolic expansion of knowledge, practices and agents. Expectations legitimized through the sociology of emergencies are contextual and local and are able to open up concrete and radical new paths of social emancipation.

Translation work makes it possible to create mutual intelligibility among emancipatory experiences scattered around the world. Translation, in this sense, is at once intellectual, political and emotional work for the purpose of mutual understanding between possible and available experiences.

In contexts where abyssal forms of social exclusion operate, these often find a place in specific urban spaces, subject to processes of territorial stigmatization. In this sense, the approach proposed here consists of: on the one hand, analyzing how the forms of abyssal social exclusion and stigmatization suffered by specific territories and the populations that inhabit them affect urban security and the access to social and health services; on the other hand, analyzing how community empowerment represents an essential element for pathways of care and emancipation.

4 Urban Security, Health and the Struggle for Emancipation

In this section we put to work the concepts just expounded of "territorial stigmatization" and "abyssal social exclusion", using the city of Rio de Janeiro as a setting. The objective is not as much to delve into the specifics of the city of Rio in light of the themes discussed, but to test the heuristic value of the concepts introduced in an urban context that presents some particularly interesting elements in relation to urban dynamics globally.

According to data provided by the Instituto Brasileiro de Geografia e Estatística (IBGE) Rio de Janeiro had an estimated population in 2021 of 6,775,561 (it was 6,320,446 according to data from the last census, in 2010). The city has been home to a long season of mega-events (2007–2016). In particular, the mega-events hosted by Rio de Janeiro have been the XV Pan American Games (2007), the FIFA Confederations Cup (2013), the XXVIII World Youth Day (2013), the FIFA World Cup organized by Brazil in 2014, and the XXXI Olympic Games (2016).

This has meant the initiation of a series of urban transformation processes according to a project of a modern global city, understood here in the sense of: rational, well-organized and functional. This is in order to achieve an attractive city brand for trade and tourism [28].

There is a dual imaginary about Rio. On the one hand, it is renowned for being a dynamic metropolis full of unique natural and cultural attractions. On the other hand, Rio is known as: (a) a dangerous city, due to the high number of homicides and the territorial contiguity between *favelas* and *asfalto* (the urbanized city areas inhabited by the middle and upper classes); (b) as an unequal/unjust city, due to deep socioeconomic inequalities, which also have a major impact on access to health care. A *cidade partida*, a broken city, according to the title of a famous book published in 1994 by journalist and writer Zuenir Ventura [29].

These inequalities have a very marked socio-spatial connotation based on the division of the city between *asfalto* and *favelas*. The latter term refers to realities that are very diverse, both in terms of the number of dwellings and resident population, and the level of less or more urbanization and availability of services. According to 2010 census data, 763 favelas (*aglomerados subnormais*) were counted in the city of Rio de Janeiro for a resident population of 1,393,314, about 22% of the total population. The favelas developed widely throughout the city during the twentieth century, mainly through the initiative of poor, migrant workers, in many cases former slaves, because of the need to reside close to the areas where they were employed serving the middle and upper classes [30]. Favelas spring up numerous also near the city's business, political, and commercial center and the famous beaches and fine residential neighborhoods of the adjacent southern zone (*Zona Sul*), a renowned destination for national and international tourism. The city's nobler areas and their inhabitants, therefore, are also spatially close to the favelas.

Since their formation, favelas have been perceived as unsanitary places and refuge for criminals [31]. However, the issue of urban violence assumes relevance beginning in the 1980s, following the intensification of armed control over favelas territories by *tráfico* factions. A process fostered by the absence of institutions and the geographic location of the favelas (largely perched on the city's hills).

The *tráfico* factions became militarily organized in order to defend the drug markets, installed in the favelas, from possible attack by rival gangs, as well as from raids by the military police. Armed control of the territory has given the *tráfico* a parallel power of governance over the population residing in the favelas, where serious deficiencies in terms of road, energy and sewage infrastructure, absence of social-health services and public education remain—albeit in the diversity found according to contexts. Urban spaces where the civil and social dimensions of security intertwine and overlap.

The police have traditionally approached the fight against the drug markets in the favelas with an urban guerrilla approach, following a violent and repressive tradition against the poorer segments of the population that has its roots in the original function of security in colonial and imperial times: the defense of landowners' interests against potential "internal enemies" (poor, slaves, indigenous people) [32]. Role of internal enemy today inherited by the favela inhabitant—black, poor, and criminal [33]—a figure that stands in the way of the construction of a fully modern image of the city (and the nation).

The *modus operandi* of Rio's military police consists of raiding operations inside favelas in war gear in order to arrest specific suspects and then be able to return to their barracks located in the *asfalto*. Firefights between factions as well as between individual factions and police have, therefore, become part of the lives of favelas residents, with tragic consequences in terms of casualties and injuries due to stray bullets and the often arbitrary and violent methods of the police themselves. The deadly consequences of the firefights fall not only on the so-called *tráfico* soldiers—increasingly younger ones (or on the police officers themselves)—but dramatically involve ordinary residents who find themselves in the midst of the firefights. In the midst of the organization of mega-events, Amnesty International published a report denouncing that 15.6% of the murders in Rio in 2014 involved killings at the hands of military police [34].

On the eve of the decade of mega-events, so-called urban violence was placed on the Brazilian political agenda and public debate as a strategic issue to be addressed in order to reassure national and international audiences about the orderly and safe conduct of hosted activities. In 2008, the State of Rio de Janeiro launched a new police action for this purpose, the Pacification Police Units (UPP), composed of soldiers belonging to the military police. A project that, at least on paper, was presented by institutions as overcoming the model of armed raids inside favelas. This was through, on the one hand, the proposal of a permanent military occupation of the favelas; on the other, the promise of a model of community policing, more attentive to the human rights of the inhabitants. Not surprisingly, the initiative was welcomed by major international organizations, such as, for example, the United Nations [35] and the World Bank [36]. UPP settlement operations have been preceded by armed invasions with arrests and weapons seizures. The selection of favelas to which the UPPs were sent (38 in all) followed the interests related to the mega-events themselves: favelas located close to the most valuable tourist and commercial areas as well as near the districts affected by the mega-events and the main transit routes. The project to militarize the favelas was also to be accompanied by programs of a social nature. Specifically, the UPP Social project, created to facilitate military penetration of the favelas by policemen, was intended to promote urban, social and economic development of the "pacified" territories. Despite the ambitious premise, due to political and administrative misadventures and lack of public investment, the Social project ended in 2014 without achieving the hoped-for results. Since 2013, several critical issues have emerged for the UPP project: notably an increase in firefights between civilians and the military and an increase in complaints of abuse of residents of "pacified" favelas at the hands of soldiers [37].

The aspect that we are interested in emphasizing here is how, in a major investment opportunity such as the one related to mega-events, the favelas, due to the territorial stigmatization they suffer from and dynamics of colonial sociability still strongly operating against their residents, have seen as the main policy intended for them a military control operation with the aim of making the parts of the city deemed at risk as less visible as possible. A reference to the research I conducted at the Complexo da Maré [38] may be useful for this purpose. This is the most populous agglomeration of favelas in the city, with its 140,000 inhabitants. Surrounded by the main thoroughfares leading from the international airport to downtown Rio, the area is contested as a drug hub by all the main armed *tráfico* factions operating in the city. In 2012, the imminent deployment of UPP was announced in Complexo as well. However, close to the organization of the FIFA World Cup (June–July 2014), as the UPP Maré project had not yet started, the federal and state governments opted for an occupation of this vast territory through the use of the National Armed Forces (April 5, 2014–June 30, 2015). The research (September-December 2015) started immediately after the end of the occupation, at a time of great uncertainty regarding the security policies that would affect Maré on the eve of the last of the planned mega-events: the Olympic Games. The case study was conducted through interviews with personnel from *Organizações não governamentais* (NGOs) operating in the area, informal interviews, and observation through a series of visits to the Complexo.

The main criticism expressed by NGOs at the UPP project concerns the modernizing and civilizing intentions inscribed in the project itself, which can be summarized in the idea that the arrival of the UPP represents the entry of the rule of law into places, the favelas, hitherto abandoned in a state of nature. By reproducing a hierarchy between the civilized and the uncivilized, which in Rio translates into the hierarchy between the city (*asfalto*) and the non-city (*favelas*), the "civilizing logic" of the UPP project fails to recognize the favela as properly cities and the *favelados* (favela inhabitants) as fully citizens. During the season of mega-events, in this sense, the *favelado* continues to be socially reproduced as invisible and absent; this means, from the point of view of the "cosmopolitan reason" proposed by Santos, a process of undervaluing and wasting experiences of social struggle, such as those carried out by *favelados* and NGOs operating in the Complexo. Experiences that have meant over time the opening of numerous services in the fields of education, health, and culture. Experiences which, in the security projects aimed at the Complexo, are not taken into account in any way.

The idea that the state can enter the favela through military force is, therefore, the main misunderstanding on which Operation UPP is based. This vision of the favela is based on—and reproduces a—colonial sociability within which the state, called to assume a modernizing role, is legitimized to proceed using violent methods: from this vision derives, according to the interviewees, an attitude of the police force that is disrespectful of the lives of the residents. As if there were no civic community presence in the favelas.

The NGO activists' complaint focuses on a dual form of violence: indirect violence, which results in a devaluing representation of the *favelado*, and direct violence, relating to police abuse during military operations. To counter this dual form of violence, NGOs pursue community development goals for the local population (which they call *empoderamento*), mainly through combating stigma and social exclusion, enhancing local culture and commerce (highly developed in some of the Complexo favelas), promoting schooling and access to university studies, and promoting social and political rights and the right to security, health, and physical safety. These activities, according to the interviewees, are the indispensable condition, on the one hand, to free the territory from an isolation that favors its control by the factions, and, on the other hand, to make it less attractive for young *favelados* to join the factions.

The abyssal line Santos writes about is, therefore, found in the transition from the asfalto to the favelas, where the modes of public regulation change profoundly starting with the posture assumed by the police. The widespread representation of the *favelado* as an internal enemy populating unsanitary and uncivilized places—which characterizes the kind of stigma that has developed against these territories and those who inhabit them—has legitimized modes of law enforcement action that place themselves above the law, in a perpetual state of colonial sociability.

Turning now to the specific issue of access to healthcare and urban health, inequalities in health in Brazil are, like other factors of inequality and social exclusion, strongly intertwined with colonialism and slavery, and in this sense are affected by determinants that relate among other factors to race—understood as a socio-political construct [39]—social class, educational level, and urban spaces where populations in a condition of social disadvantage are concentrated. After the end of the military dictatorship, health was defined as a universal right in the new Brazilian Constitution of 1988. A year later, the largest government-run public health care system in the world, by number of users, the SUS—*Sistema Único de Saúde*, was born. Since then, despite difficulties stemming particularly from underfunding and pressure from the private health sector, the SUS has expanded access to health care and, especially during center-left presidencies (2003–2014), in synergy with other social interventions, contributed to improving the health status of the population and reducing social inequalities [40].

However, given the strong socio-spatial inequalities described, the SUS has not been sufficient to ensure equitable healthcare access to both *asfalto* and favelas. In a study published in 2000, for example, the socio-spatial connotation between health conditions and socioeconomic status in the city of Rio de Janeiro was analyzed [41]. The health indicators taken into account were "infant mortality rate"; "standardized mortality rate"; "life expectancy" and "homicide rate". The worst health situation was found in the sector of the city with the highest concentration of residents in favelas, where there is an extremely high homicide rate and a life expectancy seven years lower than in the rest of the city. The area that concentrates the highest well-being indices, composed of the geographical units located along the coast, showed the best health situation. Intermediate health conditions were found in the western zone, also characterized by poor living standards but with a low concentration of favelas.

It is from these structural inequalities in access to health and physical safety that experts and activists in grassroots movements are calling for local health and other social programs specifically targeting these communities. However, Brazil's more recent neo-liberal policies have challenged the SUS itself.

In such a situation, the COVID-19 pandemic has proven to be a multiplier of already existing inequalities. The rhetoric of "we are all in this together" vis-à-vis the virus immediately clashed with early evidence regarding the different contagiousness and mortality among human groups and subaltern communities. While, in fact, the idea of vulnerability in the face of the virus being unaffected by class distinctions (as much as, rather, by aspects such as age or prior illnesses) had characterized early public discourse on the ongoing pandemic, these rhetoric based on "equality" in the face of SARS-CoV-2 infection were soon joined by analyses that emphasized the worsening of pre-existing social inequalities as a result of the pandemic.

Bernardo, do Rosario, and Conte-Junior [42] analyzed data on total confirmed cases and deaths due to COVID-19 with reference to the top ten neighborhoods of Rio de Janeiro based on a social development index (all placed in the *asfalto*) and the top ten most populous favelas in the city. The index was constructed based on: (1) adequate water supply, sewage and garbage collection network, (2) number of bathrooms per resident per household, (3) illiteracy rate, (4) per capita income per household. Mortality rates were significantly higher in the poorest areas of Rio de Janeiro, reaching an average of 9.08% in the most populous favelas and an average of 4.87% in the 10 richest neighborhoods. Underlying these disparities, the authors identify poverty (and consequent malnutrition), unequal access to health facilities with intensive care units, and population density (ranging from 17 thousand inhabitants per km^2 in the favela of Acari, to 4148 in the Lagoa neighborhood).

Through a sociology of absence approach—following Santos—we have focused on how populations affected by abyssal social exclusion, who inhabit urban spaces subjected to processes of stigmatization, can suffer the negative effects: (1) of police actions that—instead of defending the safety of residents—become, due to their methods, an element of criticality for urban security; (2) of a structural lack of access to health services that, combined with precarious urban-health conditions, constituted an accelerator for contagion and deaths during the pandemic.

The common backdrop is the devaluation of the citizenship rights of favelas residents, in terms of physical safety, whether put at risk by gun violence or due to structural difficulties in being able to prevent contagion and the lack of adequate treatment against COVID-19.

The sociology of emergencies is interested in the forms of resistance and care produced in contexts characterized by colonial sociability. In this sense, returning to Complexo da Maré, experiences of social struggle, such as those carried out by *favelados* and NGOs operating in the Complexo, have over time meant the opening of numerous services in the field of health, as well as education and culture. With respect to the specific issue of urban security, the NGOs' commitment has been—during the period of the mega-events—to put forward a counter-hegemonic vision of the issue, in order to place the rights to the physical safety of favelas residents at the center, in lieu of the needs to reassure national and international audiences about the orderly and safe conduct of hosted activities that motivated the activation of the UPPs.

Similarly, with respect to forms of care and resistance with regard to the COVID-19 pandemic, in this same book Sonia Fleury delves into how activists from social movements and urban collectives in Brazil's favelas and suburbs worked together with the residents themselves to provide the collective services and means of consumption necessary for the well-being of the populations of these territories, in the absence of public policies dedicated to them. Just as we have seen for the activity of Maré NGOs in defending the safety of residents and their *empoderamento*, the process of articulation and mobilization in the pandemic context can also be interpreted as producing shifts in the meanings historically attributed to the inhabitants of these localities [43]. A process of de-stigmatization capable of showing a multifaceted set of experiences that claim and express the different potentials of life that exist in these territories.

5 Conclusion

The aim of the chapter was to analyze—from a sociological perspective—the dynamics of social exclusion in urban contexts with particular reference to issues of security and access to health services. Issues related to social and civic insecurities—following Castel's approach—were read together, focusing on their interconnections within urban spaces. Contemporary urban dynamics were read in light of the debate on second modernity and risk society, with particular reference to dualization tendencies that fuel forms of socio-spatial segregation. We have also analyzed how, from a world-system perspective, new risks that call into question the sustainability of the development model of Eurocentric modernity tend to graft onto and enhance the already existing forms of inequality and social exclusion related to the classical risks of modernity. Referring back to some critical sociology approaches, we have taken up two concepts we believe can analyze social exclusion in urban contexts with particular reference to urban security and access to health services. These were specifically the concepts of "territorial stigmatization," first developed by Wacquant, and "abyssal social exclusion," proposed by Santos. From these concepts, we analyzed the specificities in terms of inequalities and social exclusion in the city of Rio de Janeiro.

The in-depth study on the city of Rio de Janeiro—also in light of research I myself conducted—served as a case study for the analysis of processes of territorial stigmatization and abyssal exclusion and the activation of forms of civic participation, resistance and care. In particular, an in-depth study of some of the dynamics related to Rio's favelas, with particular reference to urban security policies in times of mega-events and thus to the effects of the more recent COVID-19 pandemic crisis, allowed us to focus on how populations affected by abyssal social exclusion who inhabit urban spaces subjected to processes of stigmatization, can suffer highly negative effects in terms of physical safety and access to health services, as much due to the absence of public intervention as to a way of operating of public powers—in the specific case of law enforcement—that follows colonial sociability logics.

Stigmatization and—consequently—devaluation of the human, civil and political rights of specific sectors of the population result in their expulsion from the symbolic social contract of modernity, which guarantees citizenship rights within a framework of metropolitan sociability.

At the same time, we pointed out how, in these contexts of strong suffering and exclusion, capacities of analysis, forms of action, protest and claim of citizenship are activated, which enact processes of de-stigmatization capable of showing a multifaceted set of experiences which reclaim and express the different potentials of life and sociability that exist in these territories. Civic participation allows the situated wisdom of those who have to deal with severe forms of exclusion on a daily basis to emerge. In this sense, academics and institutions have a decisive task that requires listening skills, understanding and co-design.

References

1. Appadurai A (2013) The future as cultural fact. Verso, London-New York
2. Harvey D (2003) The new imperialism. Oxford University Press, Oxford
3. Santos B de S (2018) The end of the cognitive empire. The coming of age of epistemologies of the South. Duke University Press. Durham-London
4. Wagner P (2016) Progress. A reconstruction. Polity Press, Cambridge
5. Bauman Z (2003) City of fears. City of hopes. Goldsmith's college, London

6. Sassen S (2001) The global city. Tokyo. Princeton University Press, Princeton, New York, London
7. Roche M (2000) Mega-events and modernity. Olympics and expos in the growth of global culture. Routledge, London
8. Borja J, Castells M (1997) Local and global. The management of cities in the information age. Routledge, London
9. United Nations (2007) Enhancing urban safety and security, United nations human settlement programme. UN-Habitat, Nairobi
10. Wacquant L (1993) Urban outcasts: stigma and division in the Black American ghetto and the French urban periphery. Int J Urban Reg Res 17(3):366–383
11. Santos B de S (2002) Para uma sociologia das ausências e uma sociologia das emergências. Revista Crítica de Ciências Sociais 54:197–215
12. Bak CK (2018) Definitions and measurement of social exclusion. A Conceptual and methodological review. Adv Appl Soc 8:422–443
13. Bowring F (2000) Social exclusion: limitations of the debate. Crit Soc Policy 20(3):307–330
14. Castel R (2003) L'Insécurité Sociale: qu'est-ce qu'être Protégé? Éd du Seuil, Paris
15. Giddens A (1990) The consequences of modernity. Stanford University Press, Stanford
16. Beck U (1992) Risk society. Towards a new modernity. Sage, London
17. Ricotta G (2022) Gli impatti diseguali della pandemia di Covid-19. Società del rischio e sociabilità coloniale. In: Millefiorini A, Moini G (eds) Covid, azione pubblica e crisi della contemporaneità Primato o declino della politica?. Sapienza Università Editrice, Roma, pp 29–42
18. Jessop B (2002) Liberalism, neoliberalism, and Urban Governance. A State-Theor Perspect Antipode 34:452–472
19. Crouch C (2004) Post-democracy. Polity Press, Cambridge
20. Wacquant L (2008) Territorial stigmatization in the age of advanced marginality. In: Houtsonen J, Antikainen A (eds) Symbolic power in cultural contexts: uncovering social reality. Sense Publishers, Rotterdam, pp 43–52
21. Delica KN, Hansen CS (2016) Pillars in the works of Loïc Wacquant: against a fragmented reception. Thesis Eleven 137(1):39–54
22. Hancock L (2008) The criminalisation of places. Crim Justice Matters 74(1):22–23
23. Santos B de S (2016) Epistemologies of the South: justice against epistemicide. Routledge, London, New York
24. Santos B de S (2017) The resilience of abyssal exclusion in our societies. Toward a post-abyssal law. Tilburg Law Rev 22:237–58
25. Santos B de S (2018) The end of the cognitive empire: the coming of age of epistemologies of the South. Duke University Press, Durham-London
26. Wagner P (1993) A sociology of modernity. Liberty and Discipline. Routledge, London
27. Wallerstein I (1979) The capitalist world economy. Cambridge University Press, Cambridge
28. Miagusko E (2012) Antes da copa, depois do pan. O Rio de Janeiro na era dos megaeventos esportivos. Civitas—Revista de Ciências Sociais 2(12):395–408
29. Ventura Z (1994) Cidade Partida. Companhia das letras, são paulo
30. Vaz LF (1994) Dos cortiços às favelas e aos edifícios de apartamentos. A modernização da mora-dia no Rio de Janeiro. Análise Social 3(XXIX):581–597
31. Zaluar A, Alvito M (eds) (2006) Um Século de Favela. FGV Editora, Rio de Janeiro
32. Zaluar A (2007) Democratização inacabada: fracasso da segurança pública. Estudos Avançados 61(21):31–49
33. Machado da Silva LA (2008) Vida sob cerco. Violência e rotina nas favelas do Rio de Janeiro. Nova Fronteira, Rio de Janeiro
34. Amnesty International (2015) You killed my son. Homicides by military police in the city of Rio de Janeiro, Anistia Int Brasil, Rio de Janeiro (2015).
35. United Nations (2015) UN-habitat global activities report 2015. Increasing sinergy for greater national ownership. United Nations human settlement programme. UN-Habitat, Nairobi

36. The World Bank (2012) Bringing the state back into the favelas of Rio de Janeiro. Understanding changes in community life after the UPP Pacification Process, Washington
37. Ricotta G (2017) En el territorio del enemigo. Las unidades de policía de pacificación (UPP) en una favela de Río de Janeiro, Brasil. Antípoda. Revista de Antropología y Arqueología 29:63–79
38. Ricotta G (2019) Ripensare l'emancipazione sociale. Sociologia delle assenze e delle emergenze. Quaderni di Teoria Sociale 1:179–198
39. Desmond M, Emirbayer M (2009) What is racial domination? Du Bois Rev 6(2):335–355
40. Azevedo e Silva G, Giovanella L, Rochel de Camargo Jr K (2020) Brazil's national health care system at risk for losing its universal character. Am J Publ Health 110(6):811–812
41. Szwarcwald CL, Bastos FI, Barcellos C, de Fátima Pina M, Pires Esteves MA (2000) Health conditions and residential concentration of poverty. A study in Rio de Janeiro, Brazil. J Epidemiol Commun Health 54:530–536
42. Bernardo Y, do Rosario D, Conte-Junior C (2021) COVID-19 pandemic in rio de Janeiro, Brazil. Soc Inequality Rep Med 57:596
43. Fleury S, Menezes P, Magalhães A (2021) Deslocando enquadramentos. Coletivos de favelas em ação na pandemia. Revista Brasileira de Sociologia 9(23):256–279

From the Phenomenological Redefinition of Body to Inequalities in Health

Silvia Iorio and Valentina Gazzaniga

Abstract In the international scientific arena, there is a clear understanding of the impact that the social gradient can have on the wellbeing of the population, as well as the consequent higher frequency of mortality and morbidity in the most vulnerable and discriminated population groups based on their social and economic position. By embracing the ecological perspective of health, this paper will attempt to connect the phenomenological paradigm of redefining the concept of the body with that of urban suffering, understood as an interpretative category of the encounter between the suffering of individuals and the social fabric in which they live. By drawing on various fields of studies and a multi-systemic approach, the authors attempt to show how the phenomena of gentrification can be seen as a form of structural violence that reinforces inequalities.

Keywords Health care equality · Embodiment · Structural violence · Urban suffering

For more than twenty years, the notions of the body, health, and disease have been the subject of a fundamental redefining process, freeing these notions of assumptions regarding "natural" realities, while highlighting cultural, social and historical modalities that subtend their makeup. The concept of corporeity is defined by a fundamental ambiguity: on one hand we have the experience of the body itself, while on the other there is the objectification of the biological body and how it is represented.

The distinction between experience and representation of the body, typical of many philosophical reflections, does not find adherence in the experiential reality. In real life, in fact, we find ourselves having a body to represent and, at the same time, being bodies through which we know the world. This dichotomy is a "facade" that arises within the Cartesian philosophical-scientific system and that dualism mind/body that has permeated Western science; a paradigm in which the human subject is conceived only as a thinking being, while the body is only a physical instrument, completely

S. Iorio (✉) · V. Gazzaniga
Department of Medical-Surgical Sciences and Biotechnologies, Unit of the History of Medicine and Bioethics, Sapienza—University of Rome, Rome, Italy
e-mail: silvia.iorio@uniroma1.it

A. Battisti et al. (eds.), *Equity in Health and Health Promotion in Urban Areas*, Green Energy and Technology, https://doi.org/10.1007/978-3-031-16182-7_4

detached from thought. The distinction between *res extensa,* a physical substance that can be measured and divided, and *res cogitans*, a thinking substance and as such neither measurable nor divisible, is the basis of this dualism, which sees body and mind as independent entities that cannot be conditioned by one another.

Beginning with Descartes, Western philosophical thinking regarding mankind has generally developed on a theoretical level and not on the basis of actual historical and social experience. Western science has welcomed the Cartesian dualism while denying those contradictions that oppose the philosophical theory rather than daily practice ([1]: 56).

Since the thirties, the theme of the body has become the subject of studies in the field of humanities through the development of the concept of "Techniques of the Body" by Marcel Mauss, who defines this concept as follows: "The ways in which men, from society to society, men know how to use their bodies" ([2]: 385). The body is mankind's first tool, through which we interact within the fields of culture, society and history. Starting at this moment, in which the body exceeds its mere biomedical definition, studies then turn towards how social processes and cultural forms act on the body and therefore on the biological aspects of the human being. In this sense, technique is a form of learning that reflects the specific con- text in which it arose, becoming natural to the point of appearing as a practice belonging to biology rather than socio-cultural orders.

If the body technique varies based on the contexts in which it develops, it is therefore possible to investigate the nature of what Mauss defines as *habitus.* With this concept, the author indicates all daily practices—such as sleeping, eating, talking, gesticulating etc.—that, while apparently "natural", are actually culturally learned in ways that may not be based on verbal communication. In many cases, this can be "silent" learning ([1]: 31), absorbed by the body through observation and imitation in ways that do not require an explanation. In this sense, the positioning of the body in the world—posture—are body techniques and the product of the cultural modelling that takes place as part of the relational experience, camouflaged processes that are triggered when we interact.

The notion of *habitus* led to a recognition of the body as the result of an extensive social and cultural process, and contemporary thinking, through the elaboration of the concept of *embodiment*, has made fundamental progress towards the deconstruction of the scientific paradigm founded on the Cartesian dichotomy. This concept, which has become the central point, defines "the ways in which humans experience the body in the world and produce its representation" and refers to "the historical process of construction of corporeity and bodily ways in the production of history" ([1]: 37–40). This concept considers the experience and representation of the body as inseparable: it is the body that experiences the world and, at the same time, produces representations that arise from this understanding in the broadest sense of the cultural production of itself and the natural and social reality. The subject and the object of representation and experience are therefore inseparable—embodiment is, in this sense, the human condition, which appears mystified, due to the effect of naturalisation that the body itself inevitably produces because it arises from the imagination of reality, therefore tending to be naturalised.

The concept of embodiment assumes the role of a methodological principle: Thomas Csordas, in an article published in1990, proposes the concept of embodiment assumed as a new theoretical perspective useful in order to investigate the socio-cultural forms and the ways in which the Cartesian mind–body dichotomy expresses itself. From the reinterpretation of the concept of embodiment elaborated by Maurice Merleau Ponty [3] and Pierre Bourdieu [4], and through the analysis of particular ritual practices of Christian charismatic movements, Csordas develops what he calls "phenomenology", within which the body assumes the value of "subject":

The approach I will develop from the perspective of psychological anthropology leans strongly in the direction of phenomenology. This approach to embodiment begins from the methodological postulate that the body is not an object to be studied in relation to culture, but is to be considered as the subject of culture, or in other words as the existential ground of culture [5].

Therefore, the body is the starting point for the analysis of the culture and the self. By analysing perception and practice (*habitus*), there is the collapse of the distinction between subject and object—it then becomes possible to investigate the experiences and representations as constituting a continuous corporeality process. In this sense, historical, social and cultural processes are body products—namely cultural and natural—and the result is the embodiment of the external actions and forces, as well as the objectification of our bodily experiences; "The body therefore becomes a product of history, and history can be viewed as a bodily process" [1]. The individual's ability to act—and consequently exercise power over others—passes through the body, through which power relationships are expressed.

Csordas' analysis served as the basis for more recent studies on the concept of embodiment in medical anthropology, through which we began to look at the concepts of body, health and disease as a form of knowledge embodiment, based on the perception of historical, social, cultural and political realities. Scientific work, which took on the basic principles of this phenomenological tradition, has had the merit of assaying biomedical classifications related to health and disease, revealing these as various cultural products, configured within corresponding frameworks of the mind/body dualism. For the French philosopher, the origin of everything is the body: a system in relationship with the world and that perceives the world. Perception does not lie in the external stimuli that the body would passively register; rather, it is in the body and is indeterminate until it encounters an object. This is based on the idea that before the sentient body, there is no object, and nothing can be grasped objectively regardless of an operation of objectification-perceptual abstraction that is already culturally organized. A body in the world is abstracted and represented, gives meaning to the indeterminacy of the world by projecting its consciousness towards cultural interpretation of the surrounding reality. The body can only perform these operations in accordance with cultural values and manners, through which it aims its perception into the uncertainty—in itself meaningless—that surrounds it. The body as a subject of culture is agent at the same time acted upon, due to the fact that it is the object of cultural systems that guide perception. Bourdieu, determined to overcome the analysis of social systems, leads the reader towards a discussion that start with a concept of *habitus*, for which Csordas offered the following definition:

A system of perduring dispositions which is the unconscious, collectively inculcated principal for the generation and structuring of practices and representations ([5]: 11).

A socially shaped body, in every sense, internalizes and embodies *habitus*. However, in addition to being culturally structured, the body in turn becomes a part of cultural structure—bodies that cultures produce are the same bodies that live in the world producing culture, practicing it and recreating it in a subjective manner. Introjecting means turning knowhow and skills into something that is your own, up to assimilation—capacities that become productive. The process of embodiment of the experience is related to processes from the body and of the body, the processing of social life and cultural production. From the body as the subject, we see it as the active producer of knowledge, and the body in fact as a product of social, cultural and historical dynamics, regarding hegemonic practices rooted in everyone's life and in the biographies of each and every one of us, receding from the sphere of awareness, moving towards unquestioned common sense. The arbitrariness of social life from culture becomes nature, shaping corporeality and turning into hegemony.

In this regard, the work of Nancy [6] and Margaret Lock is truly important. In an essay from 1987, the authors make a careful critique of the Cartesian dichotomy as "cultural model" to which they held that the same medical anthropology has long been subordinate. The task of medical anthropology is therefore that of revealing the historical and cultural nature of mind/body separation, which has managed to rise to a universal category by virtue of its "natural" definition. The body is in fact simultaneously natural and cultural, meaning that it is part of a specific historical context; there- fore we can define it as a "thinking body". Based on this phenomenological interpretative perspective, we can reach the relationship between what the two scholars indicate as the "three bodies": the individual body, the social body and the political body. The individual body is that which the person experiences, meaning "in the phenomenological sense of the experience of the conscious body (body-self)" ([6]: 154) as a set of its constituent parts (mind, matter, psyche, self). This was categorized in Western epistemology through the opposition of the individual and society, according to a concept of the self that is highly individualized, theorized as universal, but which, however, is not accepted by many groups.

The Eurocentric conception of a unitary self, based on individuality, according to a Western philosophical tradition of where Descartes is considered one of the leaders, is not universal. The individual body must therefore be considered in relation to the social body, which refers to the means by which man thinks and represents nature, society and culture, and the political body, which refers to the powers and social forces that guard bodies, both individual and collective, in all areas related to reproduction, sexuality, work, health and disease. Mediation between the three dimensions of the body is through emotions, which represent a bridge between the individual, society and the political body, as they imply at the same time feeling and cognitive guidelines, a public morality, as well as ideology. The model of the three bodies therefore helps expose the artificiality of Cartesian dualism, on which Western science and clinical medicine are founded, allowing for the pursuit of a sort of radically materialistic thinking tied to a mechanistic view of the body and its functions.

The paradigm—to which medical knowledge refers—is built, in fact, on the foundation of biology. Diseases reside in the physical body and they are biological and universal entities that transcend the social and cultural context. This "model" is defined by Byron Good:

the "medical model" typically employed in clinical practice and research assumes that diseases are universal biological or psychophysiological entities, resulting from somatic lesions or dysfunctions. These produce "signs" or physiological abnormalities that can be measured by clinical and laboratory procedures, as well as "symptoms" or expressions of the experience of distress, communicated as an ordered set of complaints. The primary tasks of clinical medicine are thus diagnosis—that is, the interpretation of the patient's symptoms by relating them to their functional and structural sources in the body and to underlying disease entities—and rational treatment aimed at intervention in the disease mechanisms. ([7]: 14).

Biomedicine does not take under its jurisdiction that which is not an objective pathological condition, however there is a contradiction in this practical work when this field bases much of its diagnosis on the narratives and experiences of the patient, their symptoms. Medical science has in this way made a distinction among the signs, objective evidence of an illness amenable to direct or indirect observation, and symptoms or subjective evidence of a disease as perceived by the patient. The symptom is the narrative of an experience of suffering, rich in symbolism and socio-cultural references, because it was built by the patient starting from the embodiment of one's life experience. In light of the concept of embodiment, the distinctive sign/symptom is the revival of the Cartesian dichotomy in the objective/subjective opposition.

The notion of embodiment makes it possible to analyze the relationships between human suffering and social relationships and power: the body moves in a network of power relations that define healthy or ill, according undeniable authorities of medical science. The concepts of health and disease, far from being considered objective factual data, take on a different meaning when viewed from the point of view of an embodied experience.

Based on these assumptions, it is necessary to question the concept of disease. M. Augé, in one of the most famous and profitable studies on contemporary medical anthropology, defines disease as "elemental form of the event" [8]. With this term he refers to all those biological individual events whose interpretation, imposed by the cultural model, is immediately social. With this in mind, birth, death and disease are elementary events because they are individual and collective at the same time. Disease is subject to the paradox of being both "the most individual and the most social events":

The paradox is made up of the fact that disease is at the same time the most individual and the most social of events. Each of us experiences it on his or her own body and may die. Feeling it ominously grow within themselves, an individual can feel a sense of detachment from others in everything that constituted their previous social life. Yet, everything in it is at the same time social, not only because a number of institutions take charge of the various stages of its evolution, but also because the thought patterns that allow you to identify it, to give it a name and to cure it, are eminently social: thinking about your illness means already making reference to others. ([8]: 34).

Disease makes the link between individual perception and social symbolism explicit; this relationship needs to be explored in the intersection of its components, taking into account those that Augé says are the common foundations of the disease developed in all societies: (1) they speak of the individual (its definition, its components, its destiny, its accidents); (2) they speak of the society (the social causes of the disease, the threat they pose to the values and social situations structurally in terms of heritage, affiliation, affinity …); (3) are based in part on observed facts: symptoms and circumstances of the illness" ([8]: 37–38).

Disease, as a social aspect, is thought of as a representation, or as a production that refers not only to thoughts and words but also to behaviour of a particular group. The quest for meaning that this creates in the subject or person requires that he or she were to give an explanation built using different reference systems, which vary depending on the context in which the event of illness occurs. To build the chain of causation in which to classify the disease, the person then draws on the social meanings connected with it, showing its links with institutions that go well beyond those that are connected to medicine.

Analysis of disease as an elementary event must take some factors into account that influence interpretation: the existence of a social order already thought out and defined, symbolized and set up prior to the event; the arbitrary nature of the event and the autonomy of the series of events in relation to the institutions that seek to understand and master them; as well as symbolic patterns on which these interpretations are based.

Health and disease are not so simple physiological states, but rather conceptual figures that respond to instances of definitions that are culturally and socially determined, and which vary according to the geographical and historical context in which they develop. The same diseased condition is not objectively given, rather it is a status resulting from the explicit recognition by the community of a condition to which they give meanings commonly recognized by the community, and that the person lives with discomfort and malaise. The different diseases identified by medical science are not automatically perceived as such by those affected by the disease or the group to which it belongs. Ethnographic research has shown how the concepts of health and illness are not objective data that are mutually exclusive. On the contrary, there are categories whose boundaries fade ac- cording to historical time and geographical context, thus encroaching upon each biomedical definition. Health and disease processes are historical, cultural and socio-political concepts that try to enter the real experience of the living body in an abstract representation, which responds to moments that are culturally defined and socially determined. They cannot be separated from the collective fields and the historical forces that actively intervene in their construction.

In an attempt to restore the complexity of such concepts, the term "disease" has been questioned, in a thought process aimed at renaming the phenomenon through the deconstruction of biomedical designations. The anthropology of the English language, especially the US, has adopted three terms to define three distinct dimensions of the disease: illness, disease, and sickness. The term *illness* can be translated in Italian with "malessere" and refers to the subjective experience of disease, the state of suffering as perceived by the subject; *disease* translates in Italian with the word "*infermità*" and identifies the biomedical definition of disease, the pathological condition objectified as an alteration of the body according to signs and symptoms. On the other hand, *sickness* is translated as the "state of disease" that is socially recognized: "the social role of the patient formalized at the time of diagnosis" ([3], pp. 45).

Through this breakdown, we are then able to highlight the semantic complexity of the concept of disease, while also revealing the contradictions inherent in a definition that is solely biomedical. There may be a disease without illness or, conversely, an illness without disease—these dimensions may be different, but even overlapping.

From this tripartite division, this approach has created a thriving production—great importance must be given to current studies that focus specifically on the opposition of *illness/disease.* In this context, a major role has been that of scholars from Harvard University who have carried out a dialogical and interpretative study on the various narrative forms, which focuses on the subjective perception of the experience of illness. This approach, known as *meaning-centered*, was introduced by Arthur Kleinman in the seventies, and Byron Good was known among its best-known exponents. At the centre of their work, there is the *illness*, which is expressed through these narratives, designed as "cultural tools that aim to reconstruct the irregular experiences of illness in an order of meaning" ([1]: 86). The goal is to distance the disease from the definition given in biomedicine in order to highlight the cultural dimension inherent to it. Narratives are one of the tools available to the subject in order to meet the need for sense that the onset of disease creates—illness carries out a modification of the *habitus* and activates the need to represent the disease in a way that can be communicated—in order to define the experience in a meaningful order. This approach, while denaturalizing disease and highlighting the cultural dimension, also turned out in many ways to be a debasement. Narratives do not bring into play only the individual dimension of the illness, but there is a connected web of other dimensions, such as those related to social, economic and political relations, as well as the historical processes.

The breakdown of terminology has been the subject of strong criticism by the French anthropologist [9], who considers this terminology subordinate to the notion of biomedical disease as a debasement—disease has a variety of aspects that are impossible to categorize in only three dimensions; doing so will also create the risk of not detecting the interaction between the three orders, those found in between, and many others. Important criticism of the approach that focused on *illness* are found in the work of [9, 10], who challenge the lack of consideration given to the processes of historical construction of biomedical categories of disease, the benefit of the exclusive attention individual experience of the illness, in an approach that is essentially clinical. They therefore propose greater attention to processes of disease formation and the socio-political and historical causes on which categories of biomedical disease are built. On the other hand, importance must also be given to the sickness as a process of socialization of illness as well as disease. In this way, the medical anthropology of disease and sickness is developed, through which the limited space of the doctor-patient relationship opens up to a more complex reality of relationships and each therapeutic act is to be considered as a power confrontation that is played out in the complex socio-political field of power relations ([1]: 89).

Following the review of the tripartite division of the concept of dis- ease, two main theoretical currents were defined. On the one hand, the *meaning-centred* approach, whose members, once again [7, 11], propose an observation of disease as a cultural construction of meaning, through the adoption of a hermeneutic perspective. This thesis is based on the concept of *explanatory models*, which Kleinman calls "belief patterns that contain explanations of some or each of these five questions: etiology, early symptoms, pathophysiology, course of the disease (severity and type of role of the sick person), and therapy" ([12]: 13). This concept refers to a set of terms used by those involved in the therapeutic process patients, doctors, family members—to reconstruct the causes and meaning of an episode of illness and develop useful knowledge for the therapeutic action. We are dealing with models of knowhow and understanding that are set up in models of explanations, able to reconstruct the meaning and causes of the disease and that belong to both the patient and the doctor. The explanatory model of the patient and their family is founded on informal knowledge about the disease, in relation to strong emotions that guide those choices regarding the therapeutic route to take. The biomedical explanatory model, however, is based on the disease and combines knowledge acquired during training with those resulting from the therapeutic practice. The clinical reality of the care relationship is established through negotiation of explanatory models that are individual, family, professional or "traditional", all involved in relationship among the therapist-patient-family, making the transaction a therapeutic phenomenon of hermeneutic nature. According to the Harvard School, conflicts in medical communication would be the leading cause of non-compliance and therefore of therapeutic inefficacy. Biomedicine should deal with curing ailments and not reprocessing experiences, therefore avoiding the need for patients to give meaning to their experience.

The "explanatory model" is to be found in a "semantic networks illness", a concept introduced in 1977 by B. J. Good during ethnographic research on epilepsy in Iran. This term indicates:

A "syndrome" of specific experiences, a set of words, situations and feelings that typically "contribute" to the members of a society, those symptoms and emotions through which the sufferer gives meaning to their disease. This syndrome is not only a reflection of symptoms linked in natural reality, but a set of experiences associated through networks of meaning and social interactions within a society. ([7]: 33).

Good believes that only a semantic network can investigate the meaning of the categories of the disease—research should therefore focus on the words, emotions and all aspects of social interaction used to express forms of experience related to the illness. Networks of meaning that connect the experience of illness to the cultural values of a specific social context appear structured around a symbolic element; "heartache" in Iran is the central symbol around which narratives are constructed about several incidents to illness in women, such as childbirth, pregnancy, abortion, contamination, menstruation, oral contraception, and sterility. The concept of a semantic network takes into account the emotional and experiential elements that give meaning to a particular episode of illness and condenses the set of personal, social and cultural meanings that aggregate around suffering.

The second school of thought, developed from the critical review of the concepts of disease, illness, and sickness, adopts a perspective of analysis that aims to track, within the categories and the cultural meanings of the disease, frameworks and structures of domain and power. The vast array of political, social, and economic powers that come into play in a given context, become the subject of research, therefore outlining the shift from a "culturalist" approach to illness, focused on doctor-patient relationship, to a social-political approach towards the understanding of disease and sickness. G. Pizza summarizes this approach as follows:

Every therapeutic act is always a confrontation of powers, which is played in a more complex field of socio-political power relations. The doctor-patient relationship is always stuck in a field of relationships that is wider and broader. Just think, for example, of how that relationship is in fact crossed by external logic to the dyadic relationship, reflecting the dialectic hegemonic socio-political space—in relation to health policies and institutional activities of the State and in relation to families and others social subjects, depending on the situations and contexts. ([13]: 89).

This theoretical approach, in direct opposition to that of Harvard, has created a thriving literary production; for reasons of relevance to the issues treated by the author of this study, I will simply mention the work that, even within the same theoretical current, has taken on the concept of "social suffering" as a specific subject of research. This is a concept that aims to investigate the relationship between the historical and social processes and experiences of discomfort, revealing how disease represents one of the ways in which social suffering arises.

Social suffering […] includes a common set of human problems whose origin and whose consequences sink their roots into the devastating fractures that social forces can exert on human experience. Social suffering is the result of what the political, economic and institutional powers do to people, and, reciprocally, how these forms of power may themselves influence responses to social problems. Included in the category of social suffering, there are conditions that generally refer to different fields, conditions that simultaneously involve issues of health, welfare, but also legal, moral and religious aspects. [14], quoted in Forty 2006: XXI).

This perspective focuses on the relationship between the subject and the social order, and the ways in which some forms of power may be involved in producing discomfort.

1 Types of the Embodiment of Inequality, Social Injustice and Environmental Distress

Urban suffering is a social fact, which deserves to be investigated as a result of the actions of the political, economic and institutional power. In this sense, the task of those who analyse social suffering is to understand the pathogenic role of this authority, which is equivalent to the assumption of a political commitment to promote social equity and, where necessary, to denounce human rights violations. It is not limited, in fact, to the analysis of cultural representations, and appears to be highly critical of those forms of relativism that tend to conceal social inequality.

One of the most significant contributions on these issues is that of Paul Farmer, advocate of a theoretical view that suggests we consider as an area of study the embodiment of historical, social and political processes in individual biographies, through an in-depth historically and geographically vast analysis ([15]: 283). Considering the case of AIDS and tuberculosis in Haiti, he highlights how social forces of various kinds can produce what he calls "structural violence". This expression refers to Farmer "iatrogenic effects produced by a social order characterized by deep inequalities"; a particular type of violence that is exerted in an indirect way, since it does not require a person to be performed, but rather it is produced within the same social order and by the inequalities that are produced within it.

"The term is particularly appropriate since this suffering is "structured" by forces and processes created through history (often economically driven) that conspire through routine, ritual or, as more often happens, the harshness of life limiting the ability to take action." (ibid: 280). This is "structured and structuring", because not only is it inherent in the social makeup, but it also limits the capacity for action of those who occupy more marginal positions within contexts marked by deep social inequalities. In Haiti, AIDS and tuberculosis, and with them, racial, political violence and gender inequality, are considered various ways in which social suffering materializes in people's lives, as individual embodiment of wider social, historical and political processes. Farmer raises the question as follows: "Through what social forces, ranging from poverty to racism, are to be embodied as individual experience?"; we need to understand how to hold together the individual experience of suffering with social forces and processes of large-scale in which cultural forms and social forces are involved. For the analysis of "structural violence", Farmer suggests considering three fundamental "axes of suffering":

Social factors including gender, ethnicity ("race"), and socioeconomic status may each play a role in rendering individuals and groups vulnerable to extreme human suffering. But in most settings these factors by themselves have limited explanatory power. Rather, simultaneous consideration of various social "axes" is imperative in efforts to discern a political economy of brutality. ([15]: 284).

"The axis of gender" helps us understand why two people with the same status may fall victim to violence different; being a woman, in fact, often means suffering a subordinate relationship that hits directly in the intimacy of domestic life. In Haiti, the majority of women who die of AIDS, in fact, lived in a state of deep poverty.

"The axis of the race" or ethnicity offers the opportunity to reveal how the definition of the differences in racial and ethnic manages to conceal the problem of economic and social inequality. The concept of "race" and that of "ethnicity" are often used to deprive the fundamental rights specific social groups—their use as explanatory criteria of suffering hides social inequalities "biologizing" or "ethnicizing" them, covering the fact that they are consequences of an unequal distribution of resources.

The axis that sees the combination of structural violence and "cultural difference", in conclusion, must be considered in order to critique the viewpoint that has confused, through a narrow relativist approach, social inequality with cultural differences. Approaches based on a concept of culture as an "essence" that men seem to have, has today led to a "culturalization" of suffering. Issues related to the management of power and institutional structures were frequently raised as an issue of alleged cultural changes in local contexts, to the detriment of the analysis of the structural elements affecting real balance of power. These axes of oppression must be considered as a simultaneous act, since there are factors that, if considered individually, may be decisive.

Only the concomitant action of social forces with varying nature is able to frame and give structure to the daily risk of exposure to certain diseases. In most situations, gender in itself is not enough to create a risk for this type of aggression to the dignity of the person. Poor women, in fact, are the most defenceless against these attacks. This applies not only to domestic violence and rape, but also to AIDS and its distribution in the population (ibid: 286).

These are issues that call into question the statistical and epidemiological parameters that currently govern health policies and humanitarian interventions, in areas where the suffering is related to a condition of structural violence, inherently positioned in the global economic and policies from which they are derived.

The complex traits of suffering can only be grasped through the personal stories and biographies. That which is shared by the victims, past and present, are neither, in fact, attributes of a personal or psychological character, nor can the common experience of suffering be generally attributed to culture, language or race. What the victims share is rather the experience of occupying the lowest point on the social ladder in inegalitarian society (ibid: 31). Therefore, ethnographic work must come from biographies, which are located within the historical and social systems in which they develop. Farmer shows that the same mechanisms that create inequalities to restrict the ability of individual action in life choices, so they are crucial for understanding what he calls "pathologies of power" [16]. Ethnography in disease experience is aimed at showing how the relationship between history, power and processes of embodiment are inscribed directly into the body, which becomes not only a place of organ dysfunction, but a reflection of a social order characterized and defined by deep-rooted inequalities.

Within this theoretical perspective, there are many works that welcome the concept of Foucauldian bio-politics [13, 17, 18]. Dissertations of the French philosopher around this concept have, in fact, been widely reported, and were accepted within the scientific debate by virtue of their ability to question the relationship between power and biological life. According to Foucault, since the eighteenth century, we have been witnessing a radical transformation of the relationship of power with life and death. Up to the age of the Enlightenment, in fact, the sovereign power was the holder of the right to take life or let live, a right not absolute but relative to the defence and survival of the sovereign state. Sovereign power is exercised, therefore, as withdrawal, such as the right to take life. The eighteenth century, however, led to a major transformation: political power takes on the task of "managing life"; it transforms human life and enters the field of explicit calculations, for whom death is no longer the instrument with the most important domain, but rather the limit to continuously remove.

One might say that the ancient right to take life or let live was replaced by a power to foster life or disallow it to the point of death. This is perhaps what explains that disqualification of death, which marks the recent wane of the rituals that accompanied it. That death is so carefully evaded is linked less to a new anxiety that makes death unbearable for our societies than to the fact that the procedures of power have not ceased to turn away from death. In the passage from this world to the other, death was the manner in which a terrestrial sovereignty was relieved by another, singularly more powerful sovereignty; the pageantry that surrounded it was in the category of political ceremony. Now it is over life, throughout its unfolding, that power establishes its dominion; death is power's limit, the moment that escapes it; death becomes the most secret aspect of existence, the most "private" [19].

What Foucault calls bio-power does not eliminate sovereignty, but rather penetrates and carries out life management through specific techniques. Between the seventeenth and nineteenth centuries, biopower is developed in two main forms: the first has the body as its objective, the reinforcement of attitudes, the growth of its value in relation to the needs of the structures in which it stands. It is a discipline that Foucault calls "political anatomy of the human body" ([19]: 123). The second is the "Bio-politics of the population" and takes place in a series of regulatory controls related to demographic phenomena, birth and mortality, levels of health or lifespan; a term which refers to the way in which we have tried to rationalize the problems posed to governmental practice by specific phenomena of its population. These two forms of power over life in the eighteenth century still appear separate, but are an articulation in the nineteenth century, when for the first time the biological reality begins to be reflected in this policy, and the fact of life is no longer the inaccessible base that emerges only sporadically in the events of the death and fatality. It passes, at least in part, into the field of knowledge control and intervention of power ([19]: 126).

In relation to this process of articulation, Foucault highlights the important role of the state, defined as a form of power that is also a power of collectivizing and individualizing. In the modern state, the body and bio-politics of the population tend to be articulated in particular ways. This can be achieved because it is able to integrate into a new political form and that of a power technique: that which is pastoral. Already present in Eastern societies, and introduced to Europe by Christianity, this power has certain characteristics. It rules over a multitude of people and not a territory; it guides the individual during the course of his or her life to ensure his safety; unlike the royal power the person must be able to sacrifice for their flocks; it is a form of power that can be exercised only by knowing the feelings of men, urging them to reveal their deepest secrets. Pastoral power is not limited to compel the individual to perform certain tasks, but seeks to determine the relationship they have with themselves. The modern state must be considered a new form of pastoral power; it is an attempt to meld the political power exercised on the "legal entities" with the pastoral power exercised on living individuals. The art of governing therefore moves from the scope of the Christian pastoral power to that of civil society; it no longer guarantees the salvation in the hereafter but rather guarantees it in this world: health, hygiene, birth rates, longevity, well-being, and security are taken over by this new power. Bio-power has been one of the elements essential to the development of capitalism, which could not have been achieved without the inclusion of bodies in the apparatus of production and without an adaptation of the phenomena of population to these economic processes.

This new pastoral power is exercised by public institutions, the family, and complex structures, such as medicine. The first pole in which bio-power is made up of the disciplinary techniques, which allow for the detailed management of the population through direct intervention on individuals and aims to make them "docile". The other pole is that of bio-politics of the population, which indicates the ways in which they have tried, since the eighteenth century, to rationalize the problems posed by the population to governmental practice. The procedures for standardization to regulate subjects invade more and more the scope of the law. The norm applies, in fact, to the body of individuals with regard to the population, creating a "society of normalization". This expression means not a generalized disciplinary society, but rather a society in which norms of discipline and the norm of regulation both interact. An emblematic case is found in medicine, which since the nineteenth century has acted a great deal on bodies as well as on the population. In *Birth of the Clinic*, Foucault highlights the establishment of a process of "medicalization" of society, through which the doctor's view enters social space in order not only to cure diseases, but also to identify and provide specified health parameters. In this manner, the clinic assumes a role of legislation, laws, and norms.

Bio-power affects bodies and the population, also acting in areas outside of disease—this is even more evident if we look at sexuality.

With this background, we can understand the importance of sex as a subject of political struggle [...] On one hand, sex participates in the disciplines of the body [...] while on the other it participates in the regulation of all peoples through the global effects that it induces. It fits simultaneously on two registers; it gives rise to infinitesimal surveillance, constant control, as well as organization of the space of an extreme meticulousness, a medical or interminable psychological examination, and an entire micropower over the body; but also gives rise to massive measures, to statistical estimates, with interventions that target the entire body or social groups as a whole. ([20]: 129).

Sexuality allows bio-power to reach and affect life, providing access to the life of the body and that of the species. Sexuality is related to power strategies, and it is the set of the effects produced in bodies, certain behaviour and social relations from a specific device that is dependent on complex political technology ([20]: 113). Sexuality is so disciplined, pursued in our existence, and at the same time becomes the theme of political operations, economic interventions (such as incitement or brakes on procreation) and ideological campaigns of moralization or empowerment.

If Foucault, through the concept of bio-power, clarifies the relationship between politics and health, identifying a particular historical break that occurred in the West in the age of Enlightenment, Didier Fassin, while accepting to address the concept of bio-politics, develops a thesis that exceeds that specification and considers the geographical and temporal power in local forms in which it works.

In his famous work *L'Espace Politique de la Santé*, he provides us with a new definition of health, which takes on a double meaning:

Health therefore appears simultaneously as a concept and as a space defined by the relationship between the physical and the social body. [...] A notion where we find meanings developed both by common sense and by the learned knowledge. This is a space that connects an ensemble of agents that meet there as patients, professionals and administrators. ([19]: 35).

Health, insofar as a "notion", comes forth as a cultural creation, in which common sense and official knowledge interact—health as a political construction, on the other hand, describes a space in which the action unfolds in a multiplicity of social protagonists who vie for the meaning and definition of the aforesaid "notion". Conceiving health as a political space offers the opportunity to reveal those power relations inherent to the processes of health and disease, freeing them from a description that conceives them as natural and objective reality. Therefore, we can investigate the links between "official knowledge", represented by the powers of the state, and "common sense". It is at this point that a space opens up for interaction with the analysis of processes of embodiment, which aims to highlight the link between physical well-being and social, historical, and political forces.

Much like Farmer, the French anthropologist sees disease not as an objective reality inscribed in the body, but rather as a social reality from which power relations emerge. Social order is mirrored, consequently, in the body, which can become an expression of the unequal distribution of resources of care and, consequently, the different possibilities of surviving the disease or not. The analysis of the relationship between physical well-being and state policies shows that health may be included as the possibility of access to tangible and intangible resources that ensure high levels of life satisfaction; the disease can be, on the contrary, the impossibility of access to these resources, and therefore a form of embodiment of inequality. According to this perspective, health is set up as a social and political problem, and the difficulty of access to resources and services that protect people become an expression of social injustice that characterize a given context. Social inequality produces disparities, and differences in status or wealth can be inscribed to bodies, turning social aspects into biological issues.

Within the political world of health and health care, a set of powers takes action. The powers are involved in the political management of bodies: "public health", understood as collective health management governed by the state, to raise the issue of the possibility of access to resources that guarantee wellness. It is therefore a place of interaction of a set of powers that play a central role in the definition of the concept of health and ensuring, or not, access to resources that ensure the well-being.

The state plays, in this respect, a key role. The state is responsible for the collective management of disease.

The role of the state and therefore central: as the monopoly of legitimate violence and founder of social protection systems, in terms of the embodiment of inequality; as the supreme example of legitimization of actors and arbitration of conflicts regarding the power to heal; as defender of the public good and guarantor of public order, with regard to governing lives [13].

Violence informs the aforesaid state policies and through them these bodies are inscribed. An exemplary case is found in French policies on immigrants without residence permits; regulatory policies adopted by European states for access to territories of illegal aliens has been delayed by issues regarding the right of asylum as well as the right for care—following amendments to legislation, all possibilities of obtaining a residence permit have been limited, while health and disease have become progressively more useful for obtaining legal status. If citizenship is the basis in order to claim certain rights, illegal immigrants cannot be considered *holders of such rights*; only in cases where there is a clear threat to the biological existence of immigrants will the immigrant be granted the right to enter or remain in France without papers. "The legitimacy of the suffering body, offered in the name of a common humanity is opposed to the illegitimacy of the racialized body, promulgated in the name of an insurmountable difference. […] The body has become the site of inscription for politics of immigration, defining what we can call, using Foucauldian terminology, a bio-politics of otherness" ([18]: 306). The Bio-politics of "Otherness" must be understood as the extreme reduction of social to biological systems. The suffering body has imposed its legitimacy whereby there were no other bases that would guarantee legal status; this became the place of last political legitimacy: only as that "bare life" [1] do illegal aliens receive recognition. Violence lies not only in the countries from which they are forced to flee, but also in the hospitality and immigration policies and practices of the host countries.

2 Conclusions

Social exclusion, marginalisation, absolute and relative poverty, unemployment and discrimination make up different and often intersecting axes of the psychosocial vulnerability of numerous minorities. Clearly, the notion of 'suffering' goes far beyond that of illness, due to the fqct that there are many individuals and groups who can be defined as suffering without being '*sick*'. Moreover, there are many other conditions of vulnerability that are expressed through forms of individual and collective suffering without the possibility to define them as diseases. Physical illness, mental illness, psychological suffering, social suffering and their expression through the body are actually nodes of a complex network whose simplification can be risky. An unforgivable mistake could lead to reading the dynamics of urban suffering by focusing our attention solely on the pathological, "integrational" spread of values and behaviour. Such an approach would conceal the influence of history, culture and political-economic and social structures on individual biographies, narratives, and bodies. On the contrary, the subjective and intersubjective experience of suffering must be observed through the cognitive transactions that take place within the local morality, as well as in the interaction between cultural elements, social structures and psychophysiological processes. Perceived subjective wellbeing, defined as the overall assessment of one's physical, mental and social-emotional conditions, is able to influence the body, individual health, the quality of social relationships, work productivity and adherence to pro-social behaviour and attitudes. This means that the individual perception of subjective wellbeing does not exclusively affect the individual level of individuals. However, this perception can become a problem for the entire community, if the feeling of malaise becomes particularly widespread, triggers\ing a spiral in which the widespread perceived malaise ends up feeding systematic and equally pervasive self-destructive and antisocial attitudes and behaviour in life. This is one of the reasons why in the last ten or twenty years, many governments and international organizations have begun to compare the subjective wellbeing perceived in the various nations in order to identify the social and economic policies that allow the sustainable social development of a nation. Consistent with the biopsychosocial model, research indicates that this perceived wellbeing can be influenced by numerous factors, including innate genetic variables as well as the various situational and circumstantial determinants that can originate with the individual's interaction within their socio-cultural, political-economic and environmental context.

References

1. Pizza G (2005) Antropologia Medica. Saperi, pratiche e politiche del corpo. Roma, Carocci
2. Mauss M (1965) Techniques of the body. In: Mauss M (ed) Outline of a general theory and other essays. Torino, Einaudi
3. Pandolfi M (1986) Dall'antropologia medica all'antropologia della malattia. Antropol Med 1:45
4. Bourdieu P (2003) Per una teoria della pratica. Con tre studi di etnologia cabila. Milano, Raffaello
5. Csordas TJ (1990) Embodiment as a paradigm for anthropology. Ethos J Soc Psychol Anthropol 18(1):5–47
6. Sheper-Hughes N, Bourgeois P (2004) Violence in war and peace. Blackwell publishing, An anthology. Malden
7. Good BJ (2006) Narrare la malattia. Lo sguardo antropologico sul rapporto medico paziente. Torino, Piccola Biblioteca Einaudi
8. Augé M Herlich C (1986) Le sens du mal. Anthropologie, histoire, sociologie de la maladie. Paris, Des archives contemporaines
9. Zempleni A (1985) La maladie et ses causes. L'ethnographie, Paris
10. Frankenberg R (1980) Medical anthropology and development: a theoretical perspective. Soc Sci Med (24) 14B:197–207
11. Kleinman A (1975) Explanatory models in health care relationships. Washington, D.C., NCIH
12. Kleinman A (1988) The Illness Narratives. Suffering, Healing, and the Human Conditio. New York Basic Books,
13. Fassin D (1996) L'éspace politique de la santé. Presses Universitaires de France, Paris

14. Kleinman A, Das V (1997) Lock, M. Berkeley, University of California Press, Social Suffering. London
15. Farmer P (2004) An anthropology of structural violence. Curr Anthropol 45(3):305–325
16. Farmer P (2003) Pathologies of power: health, human rights, and the new war on the poor. Berkeley, University of California Press, London
17. Agamben G (1995) Homo sacer. Einaudi, Il potere sovrano e la nuda vita. Torino
18. Fassin D (2004) Entre la politicas de lo vivente y las politicas de la vida. Hacia una antropología de la salud. Rev Colomb de Antropol 40:283–318
18. Foucault M (1999) Gli anormali. Corso al Collège de France (1974–1975). Milano, Feltrinelli
20. Foucault M (1998) Nascita della clinica. Un'archeologia dello sguardo medico. Torino, Einaudi

Well-Being in Urban Agglomerations

Pathways for Therapy and Urban Health in the Field of Mental Suffering. Illness Narratives from a Residential Complex for Public Housing Assistance in Rome, Italy

Silvia Iorio, Alessandra Battisti, Valentina Gazzaniga, Maurizio Marceca, Giuseppe Ricotta, Lorenzo Paglione, Alberto Calenzo, Livia Calcagni, and Marco Tofani

Abstract The aim of this paper is to analyse and interpret, using a qualitative approach, the relationships between mental health and social vulnerability, by studying a limited population group of in the city of Rome, Italy. Specifically, we analysed two aspects. On the one hand, we looked at the representation, perception and therapeutic management of mental distress based on meanings and symbols that are associated with these issues by the local population. On the other hand, we also extended our analysis of this discomfort to the action of political-economic forces that lead to a sort of *incorporation* of inequality and social injustice. Through the analysis of illness narratives, there is the possibility to demonstrate how socio-economic and spatial segregation are intertwined with health and social inequalities. From these results, the authors highlight the need to adopt a multidisciplinary approach to equity in health with regard to 'urban health'. The goal is that of overcoming inequalities in health and social-health care through the analysis of psycho-social-environmental

---

S. Iorio (✉) · V. Gazzaniga
Department of Medical-Surgical Sciences and Biotechnologies, Unit of the History of Medicine and Bioethics, Sapienza-University of Rome, Rome, Italy
e-mail: silvia.iorio@uniroma1.it

A. Battisti · A. Calenzo · L. Calcagni
Department of Planning, Design, and Technology of Architecture, Sapienza-University of Rome, Rome, Italy

M. Marceca · M. Tofani
Department of Public Health and Infectious Diseases, Sapienza-University of Rome, Rome, Italy

G. Ricotta
Department of Social Sciences and Economics, Sapienza-University of Rome, Rome, Italy

L. Paglione
Department of Civil, Constructional and Environmental Engineering, Sapienza-University of Rome, Rome, Italy

M. Tofani
Department of Human Neurosciences, Sapienza-University of Rome, Rome, Italy

A. Battisti et al. (eds.), *Equity in Health and Health Promotion in Urban Areas*, Green Energy and Technology, https://doi.org/10.1007/978-3-031-16182-7_5

processes and the impact that these processes are able to have on objective and perceived health.

Keywords Marginality · Mental health · Illness narratives · Health care seeking behaviour

1 Introduction

In recent years, there has been an increasing interest in the study of the relationship between the area of residence and health. Internationally, relationships among environment, social vulnerability and health have been observed in several metropolises. However, there is currently a lack of standardised tools that allow for a proper reading of the phenomenon of local inequalities in health and daily life. Since 2016, our team at the Sapienza University of Rome on Urban Health and Equity in Health—in collaboration with ASL Roma1, Municipio XIII, INMP (National Institute of Health, Migration and Poverty); and the DEP (Department of Epidemiology of the Regional Health Service of Lazio)—has worked to put together an infrastructure of prototypical analysis that can facilitate further studies aimed at adequately grasping the complexity of the relationships between inequality in health, socio-environmental and economic discomfort, as well as individual and collective health. Faced with the interest in achieving meaningful, fair and lasting solutions for contrasting and reducing health inequalities, the current lack of analytical reconstructions of the system suggests the need for new multidisciplinary approaches, oriented towards the quality of life within an 'ecological' model of health [1].

The goal of this research work is that of gathering a greater understanding of the phenomenon of mental health of the population living within the "temporary accommodation" (housing assistance) complex called "ex Bastogi" in Rome, Italy. Interest in this type of housing stems from the peculiarities and unique characteristics of the area under investigation–after being delineated over the last twenty years as an impregnable fortress, these apartments appear to be now geographically isolated and culturally distinct from the rest of the city. Referring to other studies that analyse its specific characteristics, the complexity of the discomfort found in Bastogi is outlined as a spiral of marginalisation due to several correlated factors: urban degradation, illegal occupation and squatting, unemployment, relational and economic poverty, social exclusion of fragile subjects (minors and elderly in a state of abandonment, irregular migrants, former prisoners), intra and intra-family violence, prostitution, crime and others. In addition, there is also a noteworthy part of the population suffering from some of the most tragic social diseases, including drug addiction and HIV. Moreover, the inadequacy of housing, the illegal occupation of common spaces, the deteriorating conditions of the buildings, the precariousness of the housing situation, due to the vain expectations for the allocation of permanent houses by the Municipality, have all strongly influenced the daily life of the inhabitants, negatively affecting the efforts of integration with the rest of the citizens and nullifying the hopes for an effective recovery of their condition of discomfort [2]. From the framework outlined to date, there is a clear relationship between the condition of degradation and marginality experienced by the inhabitants of Bastogi and any obstacles to access and accessibility of social and health services, generated in part by bureaucratic and organisational barriers, but above all structural issues, with significant risks to individual and collective health. Specifically, our analysis focuses on two aspects: on the one hand, the representation, perception and therapeutic management of mental distress based on meanings and symbols that the local population connects to mental unease and healthcare; on the other hand, the analysis of this discomfort to the action of political-economic forces that make it a form of incorporation of inequality and social injustice. In this regard, a structuralist perspective highlights how "risky behaviour" of the local population does not depend solely on individual choices, but also on the social, cultural and material conditions in which this type of behaviour is embedded [3]. Consequently, the processes of treatment cannot be limited within the space of the doctor-patient relationship. Importantly, efforts must be also directed towards the removal of the social structures that cause disease and illness. This theoretical paradigm therefore makes it possible to recognize, within the social-health field, the etiological agents and their effects, combining structural processes with personal perceptions and experiences of pain, trauma, stress, and discrimination. The complexity of certain phenomena, however, necessitates new models of integrated social services and health care based a "proximity", with a close and synergistic collaboration between the different actors of social services and health care in the public sector and even in the private social sector. This needs to be done without forgetting the importance of mental health, through the focus of scientific and operational interest on the relationships between the individual and the environment, where mental suffering itself indicates the lines of fracture and marginalization of the relationship between institutions and the population.

2 Methodology

The methodology used is based on qualitative analysis, typical of corresponding and pertinent anthropological science (1) in an ethnographic study within the housing and residence over a period of about two years, (2) to an experimental culture that combines the perspectives of biomedical, psychological and social disciplines through the formulation of interviews with local and regional social and health institutions (for a total of fifteen interviews), (3) the legitimacy of the data produced by the practice ensured participant observation, (4) carrying out thirty in-depth interviews and semi-structured interviews.

Primo Levi developed the concept of "grey area" (or "grey zone") to describe the ethical desolation imposed by the Nazis interned in concentration camps—in this zone, survival imperatives prevail over personal dignity, forcing prisoners to inflict upon one another unbearable cruelty. Far from wanting to draw a parallel between the Nazi extermination and social exclusion strategies implemented in a modern metropolis, it seems nevertheless extremely useful to think about the agglomeration in question as a "grey zone" of contemporary society, where unbearable conditions are structurally imposed and naturalized. It is certainly not a closed placed, or rather of a total institution in Goffmanian sense, yet it is essential to read the collected data and important factors such as drug addiction, unemployment, lawlessness and more, with a mindset that shows the borders of a scenario where vulnerable social groups find themselves.

This forcibly materialistic attempt [4, 5] to approach the area, as opposed to the approach of personality culture [6], allows for the framing of gentrification phenomena in the real estate market, the industrial crisis, labour restructuring, flexibility of the outsourcing, and the precariousness of educational institution and social and health institutions as forms of structural, political and symbolic violence, in turn outwardly expresses in daily violence that reinforces inequalities. The concept of "everyday violence" used by the anthropologist Scheper-Hughes (1996) places attention on the social production of indifference to the brutality expressed in interpersonal interactions and in daily routines. The residents of Bastogi, much like those who live in other contexts of exclusion:

Far more numerous are the victims of economic change or institutionalized discrimination by a perverse political and economic system. They do not passively accept their fate as fourth-class citizens. They struggle, with determination, to earn money, gain respect, and lead lives that make sense. Tragically, however, it is precisely this struggle against—but within—the social system that aggravates the suffering of their community and destroys hundreds of thousands of individual lives ([4]: 9).

Among all the problems that individuals face, those that involve the sphere of mental health put in place the manifestations of uncertainty or more precisely of lability, question in a critical sense the values on which social and personal life recalls. Ernesto [7] had highlighted the cruciality of the condition of lability, as an agent of construction of meaning at the origin of the social drama.

This anguish is not really about anything, but [rather] about the relative non-being that is the non-existence of the presence in the historical becoming, the non-existence as a centre of decision and choice according to distinct operational powers: it is the experience of a definitive catastrophe. The forms of the vital or existential risk of presence are manifold: the collapse of the distinction between self and world; the outflow of presence in the world or feeling "acted", "possessed", "invaded" by the world; the experiences of incompleteness and strangeness and the loss of the sense of reality; the specular imitation of [what is] happening and [the person's] will blocked by catatonic amazement; the shattering of essential unity in the plurality of simultaneous or subsequent psychological existences; the cyclical alternation of depression and mania; the uncontrolled discharge of destructive impulses; and further, becoming more specific, according to the indications that psychopathology provides in a heuristic manner. These psychic conditions of crisis, where they remain without redemption or with inadequate redemption, are incompatible with any form of cultural life, and precisely in this lies their extreme riskiness, their catastrophic character that anguish denounces and emphasises [7]: 58).

In this sense, for the inhabitants of Bastogi, talking about mental health means allowing for the expression of social tensions that run through this environment. Through the language of psychological malaise, worries about poverty, housing insecurity, domestic violence, loneliness, and job discrimination all emerge. Those interviewed bring their own conception of their illness to the plot, as a dynamic product of the relationship between a subject and the socio-cultural environment. Depression, schizophrenia and other disorders narrated by displaced and marginalized inhabitants of the residence become metaphors codified through which they express the precarious and unacceptable existential condition—metaphors through which they make clear the link between the socio-political order and that of the personal discomfort.

The information gathered in the transcripts of the numerous interviews constitutes a *corpus* of stories of psychic suffering, crisis and other experiences, highlighting the cause or effect of personal or family hardships over time. During this research work, thirty-two interviews were gathered from people who were diagnosed by the local Mental Health Center and Health Service Clinic. Of these, twenty-two were women and ten were men, all regular or irregular residents inside the residence. The stories told in their interviews underlined different textures through which mental suffering was evident. Two models under which the experiences of the disease can be defined as: (1) The most common form of story tells of how the physical and mental suffering started from a great emotional trauma due to precarious housing or job loss. In these narratives the trauma associated with the initiation of the disease acquires a powerful effect in forming the central meaning and nature of the story; (2) the second form of story regards relationships in general, defined by conflicting factors and inequality.

3 Discussion: Therapeutic Pathways and Incorporation of Inequalities

The data that emerged from this study showed a great discrepancy between local representations of mental distress and the institutions and those who classify disease and illness. These considerations lead us to look at the problem of normality and abnormality in the conceptual framework of a local cultural model. In a community context in which violence, deprivation and dependency are delineated as "normalized" factors, it is clear that the perception of discomfort reaches degrees that are quite distant from that which is representative of the general classification parameters for tolerability. In this regard, Didier [8] proposes an analysis that allows for the consideration of the individual dimension of the disease as well as the political and social setting. Therefore, health is to be defined as a field full of struggles, with the aim of obtaining legitimacy, which, in turn, constantly redefine this field. Health is thus analyzed at the same time in terms of concept and space, as culturally and politically determined. An even more interesting concept in this regard is offered again by Fassin—the idea to approach the issue of public health through the analysis of these dynamics, continuous adjustments, route changes, contradictions, negotiations in which actors are involved or to which they give rise, in turn putting different resources and capital into play, in relation to historical and social changes. An important role in this field is that of the studies and work of Paul Farmer [9]. As we have already highlighted, he has developed an analytical perspective that allow us to grasp the subtle links between the individual experience of suffering and networks of economic and political relations, emphasizing the individual incorporation mechanism of collective dynamics. Starting from an analysis that is geographically large and historically deep, Farmer tries to develop a perspective that can explain suffering by including the individual biography in the wider matrix of culture, history and political economy, going beyond what is ethnographically visible. The analysis of the individual aspect of suffering makes it possible to grasp the influence that visible social and political forces only have on the individual at a macro-level, which act silently in the daily lives of the most vulnerable social groups.

The analysis of etiological reconstructions is certainly useful for a first level of investigation, in order to highlight the specificities of the different cognitive and value-based approaches. Starting from the study of single etiological interpretations, the analysis carried out in the residence was extended to the study of important social issues that were sometimes overlooked, such as economic insecurity and existential consequences, domestic violence and the perception of the crisis of a local culture. This crisis is also evident in the increasingly apparent disconnection, created between the level of interpretation of illness and the structuring and planning of a course of treatment. Therefore, taking into account the use of therapeutic resources available in a given territory, without being limited only to health services, the behaviour of the population of the area was analysed in order to determine how its inhabitants make use of multiple therapeutic strategies put into place when distress is recognized by the individual as well as their family group.

The therapeutic pathway, defined by Anglo-Saxons as "health care seeking behaviour", is understood here as a process that consists in the diagnosis-treatment course of action in response to a pathological case, as well as the set-up of networks, roles and behavioural procedures that are defined in specific circumstances [10]. We must also consider that the course of treatment, at a structural level, is a constantly ongoing process in which individuals can make different choices, alternating explanatory models and different therapeutic approaches. The people studied and interviewed move in the field of therapy in a pragmatic fashion, often not taking into account criteria such as consistency and incompatibility, yet rather returning to their own choices, experimenting with strategies and alternative solutions on their own bodies. In fact, there are a number of people whose therapeutic behaviour is characterized by the strategy of "intermittence of care", based on moments in which the person continues the dialogue with Health Services, alternating with times in which they suddenly detach and distance themselves from public health care.

Marcia

She is 60 years old. She works, obviously paid under the table, at the home of an elderly lady who also lives in the residence. "I've lived here for many years, it's gotta be more than twenty years! I've always got by with these chores at home of those who are better off than me. Of course, since I got sick, it has been a bit more difficult." A friend advised her to contact the Mental Health Center of the local clinic [ASL in Italy] about 5 years ago. "No one had ever helped me out, then came this man, and as we talked about my situation he recommended the CSM [Mental Health Centre]. So I went a few times to talk to the psychiatrist and social worker. Sure, at first I wondered if I was really that crazy by having to go to visit that place, but then I asked around and I realized it was quite normal to go over there." Marzia had her first episode of great suffering at eighteen. She describes it as a "breakdown" and attributed the causes to her concerns at that time. "You know, I lived with my family in public housing nearby and I had a little girl with me … I was living alone, because the child's Father had the bright idea of getting engaged to another girl after I got pregnant. So I was not exactly happy. In my house we lived between the screams and despair, not knowing what to eat and where to get money to get by … and so, at that time, I was sick for the first time, I spent months on end just crying! ". She arrived here at the housing facilities after being raised in public housing, so passing from an already critical housing situation to an even more precarious one. The second incident took place six years ago, at the time when her current partner was indicted for drug dealing. "I'm always sick, I have headaches. You know how long I've tried to figure out why the hell I had this pain? I thought I had a brain tumour, I thought of so many horrible things and I got a number of tests prescribed. I am exempted [she doesn't pay copayment or fees for health care] so I've always done check-ups but nothing ever came out." Marzia reports that the doctor never gave much notice to the descriptions of her illness. The prescription of clinical tests was generally the result of her persistent requests. "No one has ever helped me. Here we are all in bad shape, and what can I say to a doctor? At best, they tell you to go see a social worker, but if you think you have a disease that's not where you are looking for help. You ask all around to find people who have the same problem and go down so many roads." Once she arrived at the CSM [Mental Health Centre] and after receiving a diagnosis of depression, Marzia followed, for a few months, the plan and drug treatments that were chosen, however she later moved gradually away from the health care setting. "What can I say … the CSM prescribed me drugs, advised me to find more stable and rewarding work, but after a while I moved away. I have always had odd jobs, that's fine work as well. Then, with the drugs, I was also better, but the idea of depression, for me, was not enough to explain my illness." During these five years, starting from the first interview, she has periodically called the CSM in order to try to resume the interrupted path, but after a few meetings Marzia always go back to her request for prescriptions of further clinical tests.

Investigation and studies of the therapeutic approaches and pathways focus on what people do when they feel sick—while behaviour, rituals, words and therapeutic options of the sick are closely related to their interpretation of disease, elaborated within a social context and setting. These ideas include the interpretation of symptoms and recognition of the disease as such, its name, the etiology and prospects regarding possible remedies. It is a body of representations and orientations of which the individual and their group have as part of their culture, which, as we have seen, the body order and social order are correlated [11]. As Sylvie Fainzang wrote:

I start from the hypothesis that the search for a medical cure cannot be regarded as the only determining factor in the choice of therapy. This choice is also connected with the interpretation of the illness end with the social tensions which that interpretation expresses. On this basis, I study the behaviour of sick people in the context of their personal histories end cultural identity, and in the light of the wider life of the commune. This will lead to a reconstruction of the situation of elements belonging to different levels of social life and thought systems, and will provide an explanation for paradoxes like the apparent recourse on the part of a patient to what he regards as less effective medical treatment [12]: 42).

The study of the therapeutic approaches and planning should therefore allow for an understanding of the behaviour of those suffering, within the context of his or her individual experience, characterized historically and then inserted in a wider social dimension and setting.

The case of Marzia shows a rough road and setting, where the role of the primary care physician is a rather marginal figure, while the informal support received from acquaintances was decisive. Knowing how people reach, and who has sent them, the Mental Health Centre is undoubtedly useful because it highlights the visibility of the Centre for the community and the network of social and health services. Moreover, this aspect highlights the importance seeking help on your own, or the presence of people, formal and informal mediators, as well as the network of friends or acquaintances relatives. It is clearly known that a treatment strategy, regardless of its institutional legitimacy, consists in addressing all of the medical system resources through the use of practices, logic and symbols within the context of the suffering person. For Marzia, the her arrival at the Mental Health Service Clinic was part of a long, complex process which translated into an intermittent relationship that today involves moments of approach and detachment.

Starting from the evidence gathered from the area's residents and statements from the local ASL CSM [Public health care clinic/Mental Health Centre and Clinic] staff, we found that 60% of those who sought the mental health assistance went through Rome's City Social Services, while a smaller percentage went there on their own, helped by local support networks, while only a fraction thanks to their primary care physician. In the latter case, the dominant tendency on the part of the users interviewed is to interpret being sent the Mental Health Centre as neglect and disregard on the part of the referring physician or GP. As it often happens when pain becomes chronic, doubt is cast on the authenticity of the experience and the patient, who by not encountering a solution to suffering, tends to feel disregarded or abandoned. *"No one has ever helped me. Here we are all in bad shape, and what can I say to a doctor? At best, they tell you to go see a social worker, but if you think you have a disease that's not where you are looking for help. You ask all around to find people who have the same problem and go down so many roads".* Chronic pain involves the inevitability of failure. Communication between different explanatory models finds consistency where the sufferer interprets the words of the doctor in order to better understand the disease from which he or she suffers, and the therapist listens to the words of the patient in order to identify the disease. However, if the patient comes from a context such as the residence in which "*we are all in bad shape*", the patient will feel labelled as subject at risk, a loather, depressed and hopeless, in such a way as to read a referral to local social services as a form of de-legitimization of the pain felt. As it often happens in the field of mental health in many other narratives collected in this area, the causes of the malaise are sought mainly through the exploration of the body, because the suffering must have a location, and description of a psychological malaise cannot explain the intensity of the suffering endured. Physical symptoms are those that are felt first, and those who are of greater concern: "*the idea of depression, for me, was not enough to explain my illness*". Nevertheless, in the sample observed the use of primary care seems to represent only a marginal factor, while self-referral is used more frequently and are structured on three levels. In the first level, reference is made to the request for help addressed to residents of the area who have worked or are working in any health care setting. It's not important what role they play, as long as they belong to an environment recognized as therapeutic—they could be people who handle cleaning of hospitals or people working in the field of care for the elderly or other related fields. This category of persons is often elected by the sufferer as a source in order to address a course of treatment. A second level of support in the field of self-referral (going there on one's own) is seen in people who have had a therapeutic relationship with the service, which serve as mediators between the patient and the Centre and are considered by respondents in the interview as those who offer advice on the based on personal experience. These figures, tested within the territorial mental health in some Italian regions and identified as social facilitators, encapsulate the meaning of initiation to a path of suffering and membership in a therapeutic institution. The third level identified in the field regards community involvement in the process of care and addressing those who are suffering. This level, which is a rather limited phenomenon and generally does not involve people who are subject to social withdrawal, is a mobilization turned against those who disturb or show serious health problems that clearly involve the body. In the residence, in order for Community support to be activated, it is necessary that meets specific standards of borders that do not allow intrusion or interference in the private sphere. Issues regarding couples, for example, despite being outsourced, and experienced in the public sector, do not arouse any intervention from services in the area. This is the case of a great deal of pain suffered by a woman we'll call Costanza, who was been abused by her partner for about one year. Neither she nor her companion was pushed to ask for help, even though both showed obvious signs of physical pain, and episodes of violence and self-harm had occurred in housing's common areas.

No one ever stepped in to help; yet the house's walls are very thin and you hear the screams. A. Not even friends ever come to help him when he went crazy and said he wanted to kill me and kill himself; one of them lives right here in front of us. I was the one who went to look for a lady who lives here and who had the same problems. With her I started a long ordeal that then, after a year, took me to Social Services, the CSM [Mental Health Centre,] and filed a formal complaint. But nobody helped him. Well, he wasn't even aware that he was sick, because in those moments he believed that everything he did was right. He had his reasons at the time. His friends, who today I meet on the stairs, look at me disgusted because I went to the cops, and now

I want to get out of here. No one understands that I have also done this to protect my children! They are all small and the house we live in is tiny ... it was not right that they experienced those situations. In any case, I will not ever get out of this situation, and nor will my partner. We are now scarred for life!

Costanza is now alone inside the residence and is often verbally attacked by residents, because along with her friend, she involved local institutions to resolve a private matter [13]. This story, which will be detailed further in the text through the testimony of her husband Alessandro, allows us to approach the understanding of the role played by the various institutions within the setting of local treatment.

As touched on in the previous paragraph, the percentage of referrals and access in the field of mental health is very often due to Social Services. In the case described above, discrimination directed at Costanza regards use of the police and not that of Social Services. This factor introduces an important aspect on the degree of tolerance that the Town Hall Service has succeeded in stimulating within the cultural context of the residence. Specifically speaking, Social Service for minors, since 2000, has developed an approach they call "relational systemic approach", which includes the concept of "family as a resource" within those interventions aimed at the residential population.

Once we had started working in 2000, we began a project that today has shown good results in the population of the residence (buildings). From the prejudice that labelled social workers as "those who take children away", we worked through complex levels of intervention. For example, we start from the financial contribution granted to people who come to us for help, and slowly, after a max of two years, the granting this assistance-tool is cut off. The family begins to take a more complex level of concern regarding, for example, their relationship with their children. So, we work with professionals who enter the domestic space of the family, and we increase their degree of understanding regarding internal dynamics. From this level, we move to dialogue with other services, such as local health clinic, and working on individual malaise, couples or the issue of parenting. This is how the population arrives at the Mental Health Centre. Municipal Social Service Professionals.

The professionals of the Mental Health Centre confirm the close link between the local people and the department for minors at Social Services in the path of access to health facilities. This situation, however, appears to be totally absent as far as adults without children are concerned. In this case, the communication between services is almost non-existent. As with Marzia, to prevail is the doctor look at the single that induces professionals to underestimate the social, cultural and economic aspects of illness and treatment. Biomedicine is indeed effective in treating various acute diseases, however it is not appropriate to deal with the structural and social problems that ravage those living on the margins of society. As shown in a study of the *Mental Health Department*, Laziosanità—ASP and the Department *Social and Community Psychiatry, Queen Mary University of London*, focused on the analysis of health and social care for people with mental health problems, within marginalized groups in the area of several European cities, many services openly stated their inadequacy in dealing with therapeutic interventions for socially-marginalized groups. In several interviews with mental health professionals, we see the impossibility, and difficulty, in reaching certain segments of the population due to the fact that the complexity of the needs of marginalized people extends not only to the poor socio-economic conditions, inadequate housing and social isolation, but also lack of readily available information on health and social services.

Support of this scenario is also found in some of the data regarding the area in question, taken from epidemiological system of the Department of Mental Health of the local health clinic (ASL).

By way of example, from 1997 to 2015, users living in the complex who have turned to the local mental health services appear to be 3.8% of the total population, of which the highest percentage is female (65%). Since the diagnostic totals of the S.I.S.P. (ICD IX C. M.) used by the Mental Illness Department (DSM—local ASL) we find a high prevalence of neuroses (60%) and following, in descending order, affective psychoses, oligophrenia, addictions, schizophrenia-paranoid states, and organic psychoses.

Patients from the residence who were taken on for care or treatment from the different territorial services reach only about 10%.

Regarding the information above, specifically on the lack of social and health interventions that should see the integration of the different services, we should remember that every modern state should be equipped with a system of social protection defined by the four elements of competition: education, social security, assistance, and health. The mental, physical, and social health of people depends on individual variously-integrated responses and calibrated in relation to specific needs to be met. Not unexpectedly, large hospitals and tertiary-care clinics are of little use for those families who, much like the residence of the investigations, live in a single, unhealthy room and do not have enough money to eat. In essence, a good social security system must be based on the balanced development of all four of the elements listed above. A health care institution will hardly be able to function effectively in a context where the other aspects are reduced and insufficient. Indeed, the health care system will be forced to act on improper needs—such as long hospitalizations aimed at people without home care—using more and more resources and, worse still, using health care facilities for need not related to actual health care. Therefore, in short, a health system cannot be planned and managed if not within the social protection system of which it is part. If there is not a sufficient degree of security, care and education, no system can work, due to the fact that it would be forced to resort to more resources, making use of health care services for needs that have nothing to do with health.

Our working conditions, when we face the care of a patient from the residence, are really very complicated. Sometimes we do not assign a diagnosis to avoid the risk that the subject could be psychiatrically diagnosed, while we are well aware that the problems are socio-economic in nature. Or we are in charge of diagnoses in order to obtain economic benefits because the patient needs to get out of a situation. Or again, we find ourselves putting people in health facilities when the person absolutely needs assistance from social services. Professionals of the Mental Health Centre of the local ASL unit.

The legislative system in recent years has led to the strengthening of those cultures and administrative practices, operations and policies aimed at the active promotion of "local" aspects, seen as the institutional political space for the development of social cohesion. This is the way they were defined, between the various institutions of the "territorial pacts [agreements] for Mental Health" aimed at setting-up policies and programs for local development aimed at social cohesion, environmental promotion, prevention-promotion and protection of mental health.

On a more general level, we can say that the current approach is aimed at solving problems related to prevention. However, this prevention, albeit considered on a whole, should be divided, even within a psychiatric hospital, in primary, secondary and tertiary care. Specifically, primary prevention is oriented to eliminate those factors that are judged likely to cause or contribute to the onset of mental disorders and that develop in the context of so-called primary institutions: family, school, and work. When you consider that the answers available for prevention programs are usually rather limited, it is clear that there is a difference between the positive intent and operational reality involving a complex situation like that of the Bastogi. This is not to say that simply with primary prevention we can eliminate the causes that underlie a disease. Such a view is pure utopia, especially when you consider that the nature of risk factors for mental health are attributable to structural forces, due to the fact that it relates to the political and economic organization of society.

Secondary prevention is seen as the set of measures and interventions aimed at reducing the prevalence of psychiatric cases, along with the average duration of mental disorders, through early diagnosis, effective treatment and the identification of those at risk. The reduction of prevalence, epidemiological measure in which covers all cases of reported disease (new cases and those already in treatment) in a given population, can in fact be obtained through the clear distinction of two types of interventions: one aimed decreasing the onset of new cases by means of a modification of the factors that determine or facilitate their beginning, while the other works to shorten the course of the disorders by means of a treatment that is as effective as possible. The first type of intervention falls in the field of primary prevention, while the second will have greater success, based on how early is put into place and the number of people to whom it is applied. The possibility to make an early diagnosis requires the identification of early symptoms from both the sufferer and those around him (family, friends, etc.)—and, above all, by the primary care physician. Early referral requires vast workings of health education and public awareness in terms of the recognition of the symptoms, as well as the elimination of the stigma attached to mental disorders. At this stage of secondary prevention, the primary care physician plays a central role, however, as reported in the first part of this paragraph, the primary care physician is almost never present in the therapeutic itineraries of end users and patients from the Bastogi residence.

The last tool supporting secondary prevention is found in the contact with the population at psychopathological risk. In practice, this means the identification of groups and individuals who, for reasons related to age, specific social conditions and problems related to the dominant culture, are more at risk than others, due to the fact that they are more exposed to the devastating effect of social issues. Based on this last aspect, we find tertiary prevention—aimed at reducing the degree of suffering, disability and social disability due to chronic mental disorders, while also promoting the recognition, development and use of the functional capacity of the individual. Indeed, it is considered as a set of interventions and medical-welfare projects that works with the entire communities, or catering to chronic psychiatric patients as a general category.

Within the territorial context of the Bastogi residence, we can see the almost total absence of the different programs and contents in the "territorial pacts for mental health" and in the three levels of prevention described above. In this regard, we find an explanation in the two objectives contained in the sole memorandum of understanding (14 June 2012) that exists between the Social Services of the City Hall and the locals CSMs [Mental Health Centres]. The goals of the following protocol are: to Avoid duplicate interventions; to favour the identification of priorities, services, and resources to be used. Far from representing an institutional integration model that encourages the building of policies and programs for local development, reference to these two objectives only involves the management and organizational context of the resources of these Services.

The integration of services is completely lacking. Theoretically they are all ready, but in practice it does not do anything. When the town hall [city government] has no resources, it turns to us in search of a diagnosis that can start benefits, job placement assistance, and so on. In turn, we are accused of sending to the Town Hall psychiatric cases that should involve our resources, and not those of the municipalities. This accusation, however, does not take into account the fact that health services can pay structures and health interventions but not social work. Therefore, if we have a patient, who is using social services, we can only send him or her to a health facility. Local ASL Mental Health Centre Professionals.

The dialogue between these services, played mainly on issues unrelated to those concerning the states of health and disease in the individual, appears to highlight the power relations that arise from the conflictual coexistence of different institutions in constant trouble or disrepair due to periodic spending cuts carried out by the State.

As shown in Giorgia's story, the conflicts between the territorial services can greatly affect the course of treatment for individuals suffering from mental illness.

Giorgia

She is 60 years old. She has left behind a long period of time working as a prostitute. Today she is physically and psychologically debilitated. Due to obesity and related joint pain, she is not able to move independently, and therefore she has the same problem for work. She is alone and has no children. She has lived in the residence for several years. Her therapy began ten years ago when it turned to the social workers of the City Hall. She received subsidized economic support for about a year and then took part in work placement that ended after a short time because of her physical condition. Giorgia is unable to manage her condition and has hardly ever referred to her primary care physician in order to be able to fight the severe pain. "Once I went to a doctor who told me that I probably had thyroid problems and diabetes. I was supposed to do some tests, analysis, but I do not want to go around, to wait in line and everything else. So I do not even know what makes me sick." Social Services, after the attempts described above, decided to contact the local Mental Health Centre. "For years I've gone to the CSM [Mental Health Centre], and sometimes I go back. Those people from the City Hall have advised me to go to them, because there was the possibility that I would get a check for disability, but it didn't happen. They gave me a diagnosis of depression and then started the request for disability, but they have failed to obtain it. I know very well that I'm handicapped. I cannot move, I'm always bad, I feel pain all over, but I was not given this blessed certificate ... I'm asking myself why they could not accompany me to do the certification? By myself I can't, everything is difficult and tiring. I'm sure if someone had come with me to do all these things I had to do, at this point I would have what is mine. Instead they invited me to do the trips, to do this and that and pass me around from side to side. Social Services have stopped following me and now the CSM does not help me anymore. Sometimes they call me and I go with great difficulty, but then nothing." Giorgia is described by the professionals of the CSM as a non-cooperative patient, interested only obtaining the subsidy. This outlines an incomplete course of treatment where none of the services has taken account of the pain that torments and blocks the life of this woman.

4 Conclusions

In the narratives presented, we can find all the existential depth of the experience of uprooting caused by economic marginality, as well as all the repercussions of the vital sadness and the innumerable physical pain caused by daily activities and routes. Importantly, we also see all the biographical fractures that affect the perception of roles, gender, life cycle, material and symbolic violence.

Urban suffering is an interpretative category of the encounter between the suffering of the people and the social factory they inhabit. Therefore, this proves to be an extremely effective paradigm in order to shed light on the deficit of social capital and relational quality produced by those welfare policies that trap weak social agents in the meshes of temporary housing assistance and assisted living. Such a perspective would make it possible to frame the phenomena of the gentrification of the real estate market, the industrial crisis, the restructuring of work, the flexibility to tertiarization, the precariousness of the educational institution as forms of structural violence that are expressed in a daily violence that reinforces inequalities [14].

In the Bastogi residential area, the identity of belonging to the local community is determined by recognising oneself as a group made up of people living in conditions of strong economic hardship, high dependence on institutions and poor integration into the world of legal work. There is a sense of belonging that does not exclude the frustration and suffering experienced in recognising oneself as belonging to a specific social marginality. In the street culture of the Bastogi residence, which permeates the behavioural codes of many young people and local adults, one can easily encounter opposing identities representing a proud rejection of social marginality and a defensive denial of one's own vulnerability. Here a closed horizon prevails around a suffering corporeality that progressively relegates itself to a situation of isolation. From here, the individual finds no other way out than that of painful emotions. Job disappointments dot the collected narratives, and their attempts to leave illegal work or stay within the conventional labour market tend to find painful resistance, leading eventually to self-destructive behaviour. This resistant culture does not define a coherent and conscious universe of opposition, but rather a spontaneous archipelago of practices that in the long run have grown into opposing lifestyles and behavioural patterns. In a tragically ironic manner, illegality pushes these individuals into a lifestyle characterized by violence, abuse and inner fury. Consequently, in an intrinsically contradictory essence, street culture rests on the self-destruction of its members, or on their complete withdrawal from any social reality, including those that are internal, within the context of their homes and neighbourhood.

References

1. Battisti A, Marceca M, Iorio S (2020) Springer International Publishing: Cham, Switzerland, pp 27–42
2. Iorio S, Battisti A, Salvatori LM, Tofani M, Angelozzi A, Caminada S, Paglione L, Rinaldi A, Barnocchi A, Calenzo A et al. (2020) Equity in health. Community-based action research in a compound of the metropolitan area of Rome an experience of urban health. In: Battisti A, Marceca M, Iorio S (eds) Urban health: participatory action-research models contrasting socioeconomic inequalities in the urban context. Springer International Publishing, Cham, Switzerland, pp 27–42
3. Iorio S (2016) health equity? social exclusion and psychological suffering within a housing assistance program in Rome, Italy; Edizioni, Nuova Cultura, Rome
4. Bourgois P (2010) Recognizing invisible violence: a thirty-year ethnographic retrospective. In: Rylko-Bauer B, Whiteford L, Farmer P Global Health in Times of Violence, Santa Fe, NM, School for Advanced Research Press
5. Wilson WJ (1987) The truly disadvataged: the inner city, the under class, and the public policy. University of Chicago Press, Chicago
6. Lewis O (1966) La vida: a puerto rican family in the culture of poverty-New York. Random House, New York
7. De Martino E (1959) Sud e Magia. Feltrinelli, Milano
8. Fassin D (1996) L'éspace politique de la santé. Presses Universitaires de France, Paris
9. Farmer P (2003) Pathologies of power health. University of California Press, Berkeley, Human Rights and the New War on the Poor
10. Kleinman A (1988) The Illness narratives: suffering, healing and the human condition, Basic–Books, New York
11. Augé M, Herzlich C (1986) Il senso del male. Antropologia, storia e sociologia della malattia, Il Saggiatore, Milano
12. Fainzang S (2000) Of Malady and Misery. An Africanist perspective on European Illness, Amsterdam, Het Spinhuis
13. Battisti A, Calcagni L, Calenzo A, Angelozzi A, Errigo M, Marceca M, Iorio S (2021) Urban health: assessment of indoor environment spillovers on health in a distressed urban area of Rome. Sustainability
14. Iorio S, Salvatori LM, Barnocchi A, Battisti A, Rinaldi A, Marceca M, Ricotta G, Brandimarte AM, Baglio G, Gazzaniga V et al. (2019) Social inequalities in the metropolitan area of Rome. A multidisciplinary analysis of the urban segregation of the "formerly-Bastogi" compound. Ann Ig 31:211–229

Does Urbanization Correlate with Health Service Assistance? an Observational Study in Rome, Italy

Enrico Calandrini, Lorenzo Paglione, Anna Maria Bargagli, Nera Agabiti, Alessandra Battisti, Livia Maria Salvatori, Maurizio Marceca, Maria Alessandra Brandimarte, Enrico Di Rosa, Silvia Iorio, Marina Davoli, and Laura Cacciani

Abstract The urban context of the city of Rome is the result of an urban but also socio-economic stratification. From the frenetic development of the central areas at the end of the nineteenth century, up to the building speculation of the first half of the twentieth century and throughout the sixties, Rome today is characterized by highly urbanized areas, and dispersed nuclei of cities in an area of over 1200 km^2. Municipalities XIII and XIV constitute in this a real representative cross section of the Roman context. The dense fabric of the more central historical periphery becomes gradually more rarefied, re-aggregating around the GRA motorway ring, and then dispersing again into the countryside to the north. Within this fabric there are areas of Public Residential Housing (PRH), built between the 40 and 70 s, which still today constitute, in the perception of the population, real "urban islands". These are characterized by a lower socioeconomic level than the surrounding deprived areas, and a significant increased risk level regarding the access rates to the emergency room and hospitalization. All this in the context of an evident centre-periphery gradient of

E. Calandrini (✉) · A. M. Bargagli · N. Agabiti · M. Davoli · L. Cacciani
Department of Epidemiology, Lazio Regional Health Service, ASL RM1, Rome, Italy
e-mail: e.calandrini@deplazio.it

L. Paglione
Department of Civil, Constructional and Environmental Engineering, Sapienza-University of Rome, Rome, Italy

L. Paglione · M. A. Brandimarte · E. Di Rosa
Department of Prevention, ASL Roma 1, Rome, Italy

A. Battisti
Department of Planning, Design, and Technology of Architecture, Sapienza-University of Rome, Rome, Italy

L. M. Salvatori
Health District III, ASL Roma 1, Rome, Italy

M. Marceca
Department of Public Health and Infectious Diseases, Sapienza University of Rome, Rome, Italy

S. Iorio
Department of Medical-Surgical Sciences and Biotechnologies, Unit of the History of Medicine and Bioethics, Sapienza-University of Rome, Rome, Italy

A. Battisti et al. (eds.), *Equity in Health and Health Promotion in Urban Areas*, Green Energy and Technology, https://doi.org/10.1007/978-3-031-16182-7_6

these indicators, which can be correlated not only with socio-economic indicators, but with the development of these portions of the city itself. The complexity of the historical and urban stratification of Rome makes this methodology capable of reading in depth the socio-economic dynamics with an impact on health, and of effectively planning health, territorial and hospital services.

Keywords Urban health · Health inequalities · Urban spatial segregation

1 Introduction

The urban context of the city of Roma Capitale has specific features that make it unique in its kind. Its urban development, quite recent despite the long history of the city, can in fact be traced back to 1870, the year in which the unification of Italy was completed thanks to its conquest by Italian troops. At that time Rome had just over 200,000 inhabitants, and it was little more than a small town surrounded by a vast agricultural territory, partly malarial. The first regulatory plans, up to the beginning of the twentieth century, set a radial development of the city, but it is above all due to the great impulse to building speculation but above all to the urban sprawl given by the regulatory plans of the fascist period that Rome begins to assume the today's form. Today, in fact, the city occupies an area characterized by a very low population density, which involves major problems related to the availability of services and transport in areas that are still dispersed and fragmented in the Roman countryside. Furthermore, unlike many other global metropolitan areas, Rome does not have a real conurbation, but rather a "valley" of territory, dedicated in various forms to primary economy (extractive, to the east, agriculture, and livestock to the north and south–east, the sea to the west). The inhabited centers that make up the "Metropolitan City" are located at a considerable distance from the center of Rome, and, with the exception of the south-east border of Rome, along the Appia and Tuscolana routes, two important consular roads [1], the actual inhabited center of Rome "has no borders" [2] as it gradually disperses in a sort of "urban explosion" [3], where the inhabited area interpenetrates with the Roman countryside.

The triggering of this process is traced back to the Fascist era, when, continuing with the alleged "modernization" of the medieval-Renaissance urban fabric of the center of Rome (process already planned by the first post-unitary General Regulatory Plans [3, 4]) thousands of buildings are demolished, with the consequent displacement of hundreds of families from the central areas to the so-called "*Borgate Ufficiali*" (intended for Official Villages or Hamlet) [5]. These newly built neighborhoods are arranged in a crown in the Roman countryside, often kilometers from the first buildings of the compact urban fabric, with a dual purpose: to remove the "classes dangereuses" [3] from the urban center (the official villages are also located in the immediate vicinity of the fortresses of the "Fortified Belt" (from *Campo Trincerato*) of Rome [3], and act as urbanization nuclei, with a real strategy of land speculation, thanks to the increase in the value of the land located between the center and the villages, which have been equipped, at the expense of the community, of the services necessary for the urbanization of the hamlets (water, roads, electricity) [3].

New neighborhoods of a higher socio-economic level than the Borgate will be born around the "*Borgate Ufficiali*", which will always be perceived as "hostile" areas within the urban fabric that was consolidating, with the real estate boom of the 1960s [3, 6]. This real stigma still has important consequences today, both on the integration of the population of the hamlets first, and of the public housing areas of the 70 s and then [5], both in socio-economic terms, and in terms of health [7].

1.1 Administrative Divisions

The Municipality of Roma Capitale (from now on, Rome) covers an area of 1286 km^2. From an administrative and toponymic point of view, considering the long urban stratification that insists on Rome, the Municipality since 2013 has been divided into 15 Municipalities, autonomous bodies but dependent from an economic point of view on municipal central transfers [8]. Municipalities I and II cover the historic center, the first, and a first thrust towards the north of the historic periphery, the second a half-moon of territory within the first road and railway ring road of Rome. From the III to the XV the Municipalities are arranged like the wedges of a cake, including a vertex placed towards the center, and a base towards the countryside, except for the V and the VI (which however together constitute a further segment, divided into as it is among the most populous in the entire Municipality). A further toponymic subdivision is that of urban areas (*Zone Urbanistiche* in Italian, Urbanistic Zones or UZs in the text), 155 areas of different sizes and populations, but homogeneous from a historical-urban development point of view, uniquely identifiable within each Municipality. Finally, at a lower level, we find the Census Sections, or the basic units of the census survey, identifiable with an isolated block, also uniquely identifiable within the UZ.

The combination of these subdivisions therefore allows us to read the city from multiple points of view: historical-architectural, urban, socioeconomic, and finally health [9, 10].

1.2 Historical and Urban Planning Overview of the Contexts Analyzed

The context in question is the area of Municipalities XIII and XIV of the Municipality of Rome Capital. Like most of the Municipalities of Rome, these are in fact real segments of the territory, with an apex towards the center, represented by the I Municipio, and a base that borders on the Roman countryside [11]. From a strictly geographical point of view, therefore, we have represented in the two Municipalities under examination various aspects of the urban fabric of the city, from the most central compact fabric, which characterizes the first part of the so-called "historical periphery", that is the strip that immediately surrounds the Aurelian Walls, up to the so-called "city-countryside" [3], or those flanges of urban fabric deeply dispersed in the countryside surrounding the city of Rome to the north. As can be seen in Table 1, there is a real center-periphery gradient as regards the main socio-economic position indicators, with a greater concentration of deprivation in the UZs immediately behind the GRA, the motorway ring over 50 km long. which surrounds most of the built fabric of the city. This phenomenon, already extensively documented [3, 12], could be mainly due to a "filter effect" [13], due to the price of the properties, already correlated to health outcomes in the Municipality of Rome [9]. In fact, starting from its construction, the GRA has constituted an immense flywheel of urban development, connecting areas and "hamlets", even if they have arisen illegally, favoring their development and horizontal integration, but not vertical integration, with the most central districts.

In detail, the area consists of a total of 14 Urban Areas, covering approximately 40 km^2, equally divided between the two Municipalities. The population density is not distributed uniformly, and, in 2018 [14] the UZs with the highest population density/km^2 are those of the compact historical periphery (Aurelio Nord, Aurelio Sud, Medaglie d'Oro), born and developed between the 40 and 70 s of the twentieth century, and Primavalle, with the urbanization nucleus constituted by the Historic Village at its center. Outside these UZs the urban fabric thins out, gradually leaving space for the building typology of the "building", planned or self-built [15], parallel to the compact city, often by the same workers who built the curtained buildings of the planned historical suburb [16]. This very extensive phenomenon, well documented in the socio-urban literature on Rome [2, 3, 15] has given life to a suburb that gradually breaks up into the countryside, agglomerating and dispersing according to the opportunities offered by small urbanization nuclei dispersed before, and then along the GRA route. These are neighborhoods almost completely devoid of public transport [17], services [18], but also places of aggregation, such as squares, libraries, or cinemas [19], where meeting places are reduced to large shopping centers that have sprung up along the entire GRA [20], and in fact, as previously mentioned, without vertical lines of connection with the rest of the Roman urban fabric.

Within this heterogeneous fabric from a socioeconomic but also urban-architectural point of view, the units of Public Residential Housing (ERP, from *Edilizia Residenziale Pubblica, PRH in the text*) are inserted. In the area under analysis, those planned and built thanks to public initiative, or the result of self-organization were considered. These are:

- Primavalle, the historic village built starting in the 40 s to house the deportees from the demolition of the historic center. The initial project was drastically transformed into a base to the needs of the moment, and only six buildings respect the original layout of Guidi (the only, according to some authors, to have a minimum of dignity and livability). The building typology is that of the house in line, with buildings from three to four floors, and apartments rather small, accessible above all through

Table 1 Socioeconomic and Urbanistic characteristics of UZs and PRH areas

	Area (he)	Average population (2017–2019)	Density (av. population/km^2)	Low level of education	% Buildings in a poor state of conservation	Unemployment rate	Rent or other titles	Crowding index
Urbanistic Zones								
18a Aurelio Sud	286.6	24,608	8585.2	16.2	4.2	4.8	32.3	2.2
18b Val Cannuta	711.1	33,297	4682.6	21.4	10.2	5.7	26.3	2.7
18c Fogaccia	476.4	29,719	6238.1	25.0	6.0	8.4	37.5	3.1
18d Aurelio Nord	133.1	18,132	13,619.6	17.9	5.2	6.2	30.7	2.2
18e Casalotti di Boccea	311.8	17,511	5616.7	26.3	26.2	7.7	29.8	3.1
18f Boccea	4774.2	7595	159.1	23.0	14.3	6.6	28.4	2.7
19a Medaglie d'Oro	476.2	39,259	8244.5	12.6	1.7	4.5	25.6	2.0
19b Primavalle	562.5	56,539	10,051.1	25.5	14.9	6.8	34.0	2.8
19c Ottavia	560.0	15,444	2757.8	23.6	29.3	9.1	35.6	2.8
19d Santa Maria della Pietà	847.3	24,698	2915.0	24.0	14.7	7.7	36.7	2.9
19e Trionfale	359.7	16,955	4714.3	20.9	7.0	6.9	27.0	2.7
19f Pineto	165.3	1894	1145.8	15.1	0.0	3.8	17.9	2.1
19g Castelluccia	5657.3	28,689	507.1	23.3	7.1	7.0	29.1	2.7
19h Santa Maria di Galeria	4724.5	3690	78.1	30.0	12.7	7.9	25.4	2.5
Public residential housing areas								
Bastogi	5.1	1118	21,921.6	32.4	100.0	18.9	97.6	4.4

(continued)

Table 1 (continued)

	Area (he)	Average population (2017–2019)	Density (av. population/km^2)	Low level of education	% Buildings in a poor state of conservation	Unemployment rate	Rent or other titles	Crowding index
Primavalle	32.8	5920	18,048.8	35.7	58.9	12.6	92.5	3.2
Quartaccio	9.2	2656	28,901.0	25.5	56.4	10.9	70.5	3.2
Torrevecchia	15.2	2436	16,026.3	37.7	14.7	14.2	97.9	3.3

galleries [21]. Since its construction, during the 1940s, the neighborhood has revealed itself to be a real ghetto for the inhabitants, mostly coming from the gutted areas of the historic center.

- Quartaccio and Torrevecchia [22, 23], two large PRH complexes resulting from the housing assistance policies of the 1960s. Built in the late 1970s, based on contested and problematic projects, these appear as structures made up of large volumes of concrete, with an architecture characterized by elements that can be traced back in all the PRH interventions implemented in Italy in those years.
- Former-Bastogi (or simply Bastogi), built as a service motel for an airline, abandoned and finally occupied in the mid-1980s by the housing struggle committees. The complex consists of six buildings of 4 floors each, with the ground floors originally used as services which, except for some spaces used for common use (a kindergarten, associations, a gym), have also been divided and occupied. The whole complex, which covers an area of about 5 hectares, is surrounded by a retaining wall that delimits the perimeter. Around there are very few services and a lot of green in a state of neglect. All these characteristics combine in the Bastogi as an island, from a physical point of view but also "cultural", especially as regards the perception that the surrounding context has.

2 Objective, Materials and Methods

2.1 *Objective*

The aim of this work is to describe demographic, socioeconomic, and urbanistic characteristics of neighborhoods that include ERP areas and evaluate whether there are differences in hospital care and Emergency Department (ED) in populations living in PRH areas in the Municipality of Rome compared to those living in the surrounding urban areas, within neighborhoods.

2.2 *Materials and Methods*

This observational study was conducted considering areas identified based on a preliminary knowledge of the territory, as descripted previously. As for the identification of the PRH areas, these have been bounded using Google Earth Pro software. The same software, through the GIS functions, has allowed the identification of the correspondent census tracts. The shapefile, available on the ISTAT institutional website, containing the codes of the 2011 Census Sections [24], the territorial survey units, was superimposed on the perimeter polygon. Once the codes were identified, for each Section the information available on the public record layout of the 2011 Census was extracted, and the data were regrouped by Municipalities and UZs.

The participants in the study were the residents in the areas of interest as registered in the registry office of Rome. Regularly, the registry office provides the Department of Epidemiology with a complete extraction of the individuals registered at that moment. In addition to personal information, these databases contain the census section of residence of the individuals that was used to select the study population.

The hospitalization and access to ED rates were calculated from 2011 to 2019. First, for every year under study, all the hospital discharge records were extracted from the regional Hospital Information System (SIO). This database contains either demographic and clinical information about all the hospital discharges in the Lazio region since 1997. In addition, any discharge of residents occurred outside the Lazio region were also considered. From the total number of hospitalizations, only acute hospitalizations were selected, while the records of healthy newborns were excluded.

Next, as regards access to Emergency Department (ED), all the access records in the same period were extracted from the regional Emergency Department Information (SIES, from the Italian *Sistema Informativo per Emergenza Sanitaria*). This database contains clinical information on all the visits in the emergency departments of the Lazio region since 2000.

All the Information Systems cited above, and the registry office data can be deterministically linked together using an anonymized code uniquely assigned to everyone. This code made it possible to select hospital discharge and emergency department visits only for individuals residing in the areas under study.

Access to emergency room and hospitalization rates were stratified by sex and UZs and calculated using 10-year age classes with the oldest group being 70 or more years. Rates were also calculated in the same way for the PRHs, except for Bastogi that required further aggregation by age, with the oldest age group being 60 years or more. Rates were calculated for either the entire period and stratified for three-year periods 2011–2013, 2014–2016, and 2017–2019. Age-standardized rates were also calculated using the 2011 Italian population as a reference to allow comparison between the PRHs and the UZs.

3 Results

As stated before, XIII and XVI municipalities extend from the city centre to the suburbs incorporating heterogeneous urban and socio-economic contexts. Table 1 contains some socioeconomic and urbanistic indicators calculated by PRH and UZ. Considering the UZs, the population density ranges from high values in the more central areas to low values in the more peripheral. As regards the percentage of buildings in bad conditions, the XIII municipality shows an urban–rural pattern with a minimum of 4.2% in Aurelio Sud (18a) and a maximum of 26.2% in Casalotti di Boccea (18e), while in the XIV municipality it doesn't seem to be present such pattern with a minimum of 1.7% in Medaglie d'Oro (19a) and a maximum of 29.3% in Ottavia (19c), excluding Pineto (19f) which is mostly covered by the homonymous urban park. The unemployment rate in the XIII municipality ranges from 4.8% of the UZ of Aurelio Sud (18a) to a maximum of 8.3% of Fogaccia (18c) while, in the XIV municipality, from a minimum of 4.5% in Medaglie d'Oro (19a) to a maximum of 9.1% in Ottavia (19c). As regards the percentage of families living in non-owned houses, the XIII municipality shows higher values in the more central areas, more expensive on average. The XIV municipality, instead, shows similar percentages in UZs very distant from each other (Medaglie d'Oro, 19a and Santa Maria di Galeria, 19h) with a maximum in Santa Maria della Pietà (19d). Finally, the crowding index, which relates the population with the living space of the houses, shows low values in the more central UZs (Aurelio Sud 18a, Aurelio Nord 18d and Medaglie d'Oro 19a) and high values in UZs next to GRA, like Casalotti di Boccea (18e) and Santa Maria della Pietà (19d).

From a demographic perspective (Table 2), also, there are significative differences among the UZs that make up the two municipalities. Considering the central year of the study period (2015) the age distribution results more concentrated on the youngest ages as getting away from the city centre: in the XIII municipality the median age ranges from 41 years (IQR: 33) in the UZ of Boccea (18f) to 50 years (IQR: 36) in the UZ of Aurelio Nord (18d) while in the XIV municipality it ranges from 39 years (IQR: 31) in the UZ of Castelluccia (19 g) to 49 years (IQR: 38) in the UZ of Medaglie d'Oro (19a). As can be seen in the Fig. 1, which shows the standardized rates stratified by sex, there is also a considerable heterogeneity in the hospitalizations and ED visits that, in both cases, display an urban–rural gradient.

The PRH areas under study are located within 3 different UZs: Fogaccia (18c), Primavalle (19b) and Santa Maria della Pietà (19d). From a socio-economic point of view the PRHs represent a disadvantaged portion of the UZs to which they belong: higher share of individuals with low education except for Quartaccio, higher share of buildings in bad conditions, higher unemployment rates and higher crowding index. Also, the individuals residing in the PRHs represent a demographically different population with respect to the total population of its UZ. Table 2 shows the mean number of residents, the median age and the age interquartile range of the population in the PRHs and in the UZs to which they belong, stratified by sex and three-year periods. Looking at the temporal trends of the number of residents, it is interesting to note that while in all the UZs this number remains rather stable in the second period and increases in the last one, in the PRHs it shows a constant decrease.

Tables 3 and 4 show the crude and standardized rates of hospitalization and access to ED visits only for the PRHs under study and the UZs that contain them. As it can be seen from those tables, there is an excess of hospitalization and access to ED visits in the PRHs either in crude or in standardized measures.

This excess is made clearer by looking at the Table 5 that shows the rate ratio of standardized rates in each PRHs using the corresponding UZ as reference, with Torrevecchia having the lower and Bastogi the highest excess in hospitalizations and ED visits.

Table 2 Demographic characteristics of population living in PRH areas and in the corresponding UZs

Sex	Urbanistic zone/public residential housing	2011–2013		2014–2016		2017–2019	
		Average population	Median age (IQR)	Average population	Median age (IQR)	Average population	Median age (IQR)
Male	18c FOGACCIA	13,926	41 (33)	13,922	42 (34)	14,337	43 (34)
	Torrevecchia	1323	44 (39)	1240	46 (39)	1129	48 (41)
	Bastogi	597	34 (32)	595	35 (34)	547	34 (35)
	19b PRIMAVALLE	27,062	44 (34)	26,476	45 (34)	31,128	48 (36)
	Primavalle	3019	43 (35)	2920	44 (36)	2729	46 (36)
	19d SANTA M. DELLA PIETA'	10,534	39 (32)	11,155	40 (33)	12,096	40 (34)
	Quartaccio	1592	37 (31)	1441	39 (32)	1293	41 (34)
Female	18c FOGACCIA	14,909	43 (33)	14,993	45 (33)	15,382	46 (33)
	Torrevecchia	1477	50 (34)	1412	51 (35)	1307	53 (36)
	Bastogi	641	36 (31)	632	39 (32)	571	42 (32)
	19b PRIMAVALLE	31,495	47 (35)	31,128	48 (36)	30,475	49 (36)
	Primavalle	3452	48 (38)	3405	49 (38)	3191	50 (37)
	19d SANTA M. DELLA PIETA'	11,048	40 (31)	11,662	41 (31)	12,602	42 (31)
	Quartaccio	1716	41 (31)	1512	42 (31)	1363	45 (32)

4 Discussion

The results show an interesting pattern of the distribution of the variables under consideration. There is a strong center-periphery gradient, consistent with the urban development of Rome in terms of socio-economic composition. This gradient, within a large and complex urban context such as that of the Municipality of Rome, takes on peculiar forms. The distribution of the investigated outcomes, in fact, corresponds to a possible urban-architectural reading of the history of urban development in Rome, which follows a precise socio-economic pattern due in part to the phases of birth and growth of these contexts, described above.

The main indicators of social deprivation, i.e. low level of education, unemployment rate, share of residents in rent or other title, and crowding index, have the lowest values in the most central UZs, which are not only the richest but also, as described previously, more compact, and generally more urbanized than the peripheric ones, and an increasing gradient moving away from the more central areas, but with a tendency to concentrate in the UZs close to the GRA, i.e. 18e Casalotti di Boccea,

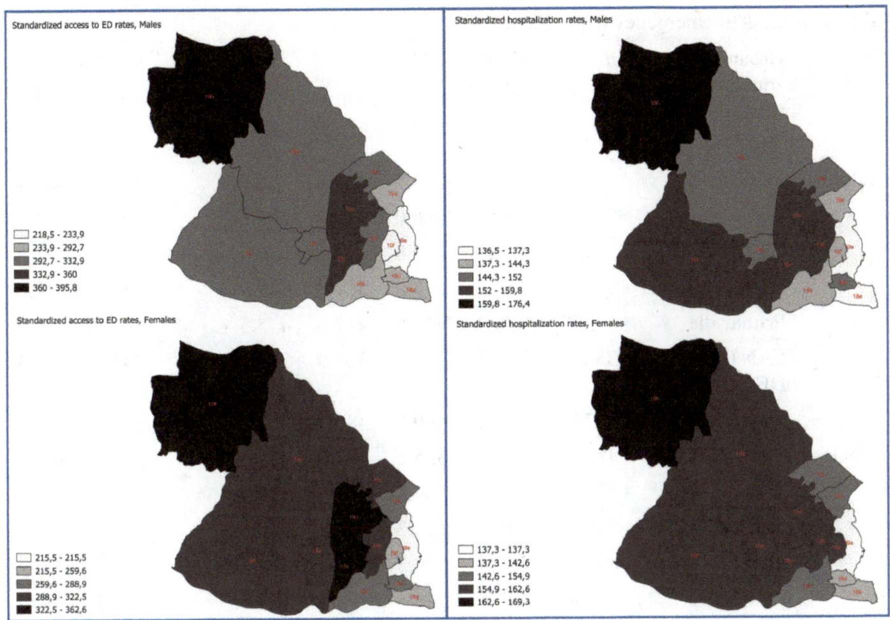

Fig. 1 UZs standardized ED access and hospitalization rates

Table 3 Hospitalizations

Sex	Urbanistic zone/public residential housing	*n*	Crude rates	CI 95%		Standardized rates	CI 95%	
				inf	sup		inf	sup
Males	FOGACCIA	18,528	146.4	146.4	146.4	157.9	155.6	160.3
	Torrevecchia	2110	190.5	190.0	191.1	180.5	172.8	188.5
	ex-Bastogi	976	187.2	186.1	188.2	246.1	226.7	267.1
	PRIMAVALLE	38,531	161.3	161.3	161.4	159.8	158.2	161.4
	Primavalle	4865	187.1	186.9	187.3	188.4	183.2	193.8
	SANTA M. DELLA PIETA'	14,177	139.9	139.8	139.9	159.7	156.9	162.5
	Quartaccio	2234	172.1	171.8	172.5	206.6	196.7	217.0
Females	FOGACCIA	21,906	161.3	161.2	161.3	162.6	160.5	164.8
	Torrevecchia	2600	206.5	206.0	207.1	190.1	182.6	197.9
	ex-Bastogi	1167	210.9	209.6	212.2	238.7	223.9	254.5
	PRIMAVALLE	47,318	169.4	169.4	169.4	158.8	157.3	160.2
	Primavalle	6036	200.3	200.0	200.5	188.1	183.2	193.1
	SANTA M. DELLA PIETA'	16,388	154.7	154.7	154.7	161.5	159.0	164.0
	Quartaccio	2566	186.3	185.9	186.7	200.2	192.2	208.5

Table 4 Access to emergency department

Sex	Urbanistic zone/public residential housing	*n*	Crude rates	CI 95%		Standardized rates	CI 95%	
				inf	sup		inf	sup
Males	FOGACCIA	44,879	354.6	354.5	354.8	360.0	356.6	363.4
	Torrevecchia	5644	509.7	506.0	513.4	509.6	496.2	523.3
	Ex-Bastogi	3295	631.8	619.8	644.1	720.7	689.5	753.3
	PRIMAVALLE	75,910	317.9	317.8	317.9	317.4	315.1	319.6
	Primavalle	12,377	476.0	474.6	477.4	475.5	467.2	484.0
	SANTA M. DELLA PIETA'	35,243	347.7	347.5	347.9	353.4	349.5	357.3
	Quartaccio	6274	483.4	480.5	486.3	515.8	501.1	531.0
Females	FOGACCIA	48,293	355.5	355.3	355.6	359.9	356.7	363.2
	Torrevecchia	5753	457.0	454.4	459.6	463.0	450.7	475.7
	Ex-Bastogi	3564	644.1	632.3	656.2	647.5	624.6	671.4
	PRIMAVALLE	89,487	320.4	320.3	320.5	318.7	316.6	320.9
	Primavalle	13,489	447.5	446.5	448.6	454.0	446.1	462.0
	SANTA M. DELLA PIETA'	36,599	345.5	345.3	345.7	346.4	342.8	350.0
	Quartaccio	6541	474.9	472.4	477.6	478.6	466.6	490.8

18c Fogaccia, 19d Santa Maria della Pietà. The outermost areas (18f Boccea, 19g Castelluccia and 19h Santa Maria di Galeria), although with overall slightly better indicators than 18e, 18c, 19d, as low education or unemployment rate, show rather absolute high deprivation indicators, in line with what has been described by other authors [2, 6, 19]. These results, however, are affected by the small population, scattered over a territory which, only for the portion outside the GRA of the two Municipalities in question, exceeds 150 km^2. This dynamic could be partly due to the urban history of each of these areas: the most central ones were born and developed on a unitary project, which framed them from the planning stage as towns (with large buildings, a compact fabric, well-functioning articulated on the territory). The areas of the extreme periphery, on the other hand, can be defined as a real "city-countryside" [18]. Those close to the GRA have a semi-spontaneous origin, with a tumultuous and fragmented development starting from small, very localized places of interest (small factories, commercial activities, historic villages,), while the one between the central compact fabric and these semi-disperse developed mainly with a medium–low socio-economic connotation during the phases of the Italian real estate boom [3].

This socioeconomic, and urbanistic, gradient certainly has repercussions [25] on the use of health services, with an evident gradient, as highlighted in Fig. 1, which can be roughly defined as "center-periphery", also in this case with the specification concerning the UZs close to the GRA, which present the worst indicators overall. As

Table 5 Hospitalization and ED access rate ratio between PRH areas and the corresponding UZs

Health service assistance indicators	Urbanistic zone/public residential housing	Males				Females			
		n	Rate ratio	CI 95%		*n*	Rate ratio	CI 95%	
				inf	sup			inf	sup
Hospitalizations	FOGACCIA	18,528	1.00	–	–	21,906	1.00	–	–
	Torrevecchia	2110	1.14	1.09	1.20	2600	1.17	1.12	1.22
	Bastogi	976	1.56	1.43	1.69	1167	1.47	1.37	1.57
	PRIMAVALLE	38,531	1.00	–	–	47,318	1.00	–	–
	Primavalle	4865	1.18	1.14	1.22	6036	1.18	1.15	1.22
	SANTA M. DELLA PIETA’	14,177	1.00	–	–	16,388	1.00	–	–
	Quartaccio	2234	1.29	1.23	1.36	2566	1.24	1.19	1.29
Access to Emergency department	FOGACCIA	44,879	1.00	–	–	48,293	1.00	–	–
	Torrevecchia	5644	1.42	1.38	1.46	5753	1.29	1.25	1.32
	Bastogi	3295	2.00	1.91	2.09	3564	1.80	1.73	1.87
	PRIMAVALLE	75,910	1.00	–	–	89,487	1.00	–	–
	Primavalle	12,377	1.50	1.47	1.53	13,489	1.42	1.40	1.45
	SANTA M. DELLA PIETA’	35,243	1.00	–	–	36,599	1.00	–	–
	Quartaccio	6274	1.46	1.42	1.51	6541	1.38	1.34	1.42

highlighted by the literature on social inequalities in health [26], these indicators not only are associated with exposure to risk factors, but also affect the health outcome following exposure. This is therefore reflected in greater social vulnerability both in terms of risk and in terms of people's ability to deal with the disease once it manifests itself. In this case it is therefore evident how a socio-economic gradient, in particular concerning "strong" determinants such as education and work [10, 27], in a global context of increased exposure, leads to worse consequences for health, with a necessary increased use of secondo level assistance services such as hospitals and emergency departments.

The PRH areas, on the other hand, always show far worse socioeconomic and urbanistic indicators than the UZs in which they insist. The population density in particular shows a clear difference between the PRH area and the corresponding UZ, even if the data obviously suffers from the non-built-up areas, which inevitably are greater when the data is evaluated on the neighborhood scale. A more specific indicator is certainly the crowding index, for which the PRH areas have values (calculated on the 2011 Census) higher than all the UZs examined. These results indicate a particular concentration of socioeconomically deprived population within the PRH areas, which, at least according to these results, are like ghettos within which a population with poor perspectives of real improvement of their material conditions.

Consistently with the socio-economic evaluation, the PRH areas identified show very high ED visits rates, even three times higher than those of the more central UZs of the XII and XIV Municipalities. In particular, the figure of Bastogi, despite having a rather young population (with an average age of around 40yo for females and 35yo for males in the time intervals considered), stands out for impressive results, especially as regards the accesses to ED of females. This result is partly explained by late access to services [28], partly due to stigma, partly due to geographical accessibility problems, which leads the population to directly access second-level services rather than following the process of territorial health services. This has repercussions in a consistent increase also in the hospitalization rate. The results highlighted in terms of rate ratios confirm what is highlighted by the rates: the PRH areas under analysis present constantly increased risks compared to the UZ in which they insist. Once again, while the nuclei of Quartaccio, Torrevecchia and Primavalle are substantially aligned, with risks increased between 10 and 30% as regards hospitalizations, and with risks increased between 30 and 50% as regards instead access to ED compared to the population residing in the surrounding areas in the same UZ, Bastogi stands out. The population residing in Bastogi has in fact a 50% higher risk of hospitalization compared to the Fogaccia UZ, and a double risk of access to the emergency room for males and increased by 80% for females.

The measures presented have limitations to answer the study question proposed. Although the use of hospital and emergency care are relevant indicators of the quality of health assistance offered to the population, both in terms of accessibility and appropriateness of care, they should be supported by other data and indicators to allow a comprehensive evaluation of the level of the quality of care, as they are affected by many other different dimensions, such as the prevalence of diseases, the number of providers in the territory, the organization of primary health care, the individual socioeconomic status. In addition, we did not include relevant confounders, such as the individual socioeconomic status, which affects health and in turn the access to care. However, the results match with those derived from the Census, which indicate the more deprived areas as those with the highest rates of hospitalization and emergency room use. At last, limitations inherent of the study design should be mentioned: the population was not followed-up as in a longitudinal study, rather averaged populations was used as denominators of the rates that can reduce the accuracy of the measures.

5 Conclusions

Complex and stratified urban contexts such as that of Rome require an integrated reading possibility, which considers the qualitative tools of urban planning, architecture and urban sociology, and the quantitative tools of current statistics [29]. Alongside these, as a possible further model for further study and conjunction, there may be social epidemiology which, through the reading of health information flows, can also allow forms of socio-health intervention based on the principle of equity [30]. This study, albeit with the limitations highlighted, is intended to be a contribution in this direction. Furthermore, this approach makes it possible to highlight the existence of social inequalities in health that exist even in very limited urban areas, such as PRH areas, even when these are integrated from an urban point of view within the surrounding urban fabric [31]. The existence of these inequalities demonstrates the need to build a model of assistance and care capable of reading the complexity of urban contexts.

References

1. Frondoni R, Mollo B, Capotorti G (2011) A landscape analysis of land cover change in the Municipality of Rome (Italy): Spatio-temporal characteristics and ecological implications of land cover transitions from 1954 to 2001. Landsc Urban Plan 100(1–2):117–128. https://doi.org/10.1016/j.landurbplan.2010.12.002
2. Tocci W (2020) Roma come se, Alla ricerca del futuro per la capitale, Donzelli editore, ISBN 978-88-5522-038-5
3. Insolera I (2011) Roma Moderna, da Napoleone I al XXI Secolo (1° ed. 1962), Edizione ampliata con la collaborazione di Paolo Berdini, Einaudi, Torino
4. Piano Regolatore Roma 1883 Approvato dal Consiglio Comunale il 26 giugno 1883, Legge 8 marzo 1883
5. Berlinguer G (1960) Della Seta P. Borgate di Roma, Editori Riuniti, Roma.
6. Berdini P (2018) Roma, polvere di stelle, la speranza fallita e le idee per uscire dal declino, Edizioni Alegre, Roma.
7. Paglione L, Cacciani L, Baglio G, Brandimarte MA et al (2020) Characterising a setting with a high level of informality, integrating national and specialised surveys, administrative and census data. In: Urban health: participatory action-research models contrasting socioeconomic inequalities in the urban context. Springer. https://doi.org/10.1007/978-3-030-49446-9_6

8. Official List and Names of Municipality and Urbanistic Zones of Rome [Roma Capitale. Denominazione Municipi e Zone Urbanistiche. Available on: https://www.comune.roma.it/web-resources/cms/documents/ElencoZ_Urbanistiche_rg_A.pdf, Last accessed 23 March 2022
9. Cesaroni G, Venturi G, Paglione L et al (2020) Mortality inequalities in Rome: the role of individual education and neighbourhood real estate market. Epidemiol Prev 44:(5–6 Suppl 1):31–37. https://doi.org/10.19191/EP20.5-6.S1.P031.071
10. Cacciani L, Bargagli AM, Cesaroni G et al. (2015) Education and mortality in the Rome longitudinal study. Dalby AR, ed. PLOS ONE 10(9):e0137576
11. Lelo K, Monni S, Tomassi F (2019) Le Mappe della Disuguaglianza, una geografia sociale metropolitana. Donzelli Editore, Roma
12. Smith N (1987) Gentrification and the rent gap. Ann Assoc Am Geogr 77(3):462–465. https://doi.org/10.1111/j.1467-8306.1987.tb00171.x
13. Bier T (2001) Moving up, filtering down: metropolitan housing dynamics and public policy. Brookings Institution, Center on Urban and Metropolitan Policy, Washington, DC
14. 2020 Statistical Yearbook of Rome [Annuario Statistico 2020–Roma Capitale. Available on https://www.comune.roma.it/web-resources/cms/documents/Annuario_statistico_2020_agg_giugno2021_1.pdf. Last accessed 29 March 2022
15. D'Eramo M (2017) The not so eternal city. New Left Rev 106:77–103
16. Erbani F (2013) Roma: Il tramonto della città pubblica, Gius. Laterza and Figli editore, Bari
17. #mapparoma10–Muoversi a Roma con il trasporto pubblico locale (2016). Available at:https://www.mapparoma.info/mappe/mapparoma10-muoversi-a-roma-con-trasporto-pubblico-locale/. Last accessed 19 Apr 2022
18. #mapparoma16–Sport, salute, sicurezza e centri anziani nei quartieri di Roma (2017). Available at: https://www.mapparoma.info/mappe/mapparoma16-sport-salute-sicurezza-e-centri-anziani-nei-quartieri-di-roma/. Last accessed 19 Apr 2022
19. Lelo K, Monni S, Tomassi F (2021) Le sette Rome, La capitale delle disuguaglianze raccontata in 29 mappe. Donzelli editore. ISBN: 9788855221597
20. Tomassi F (2013) Disuguaglianze, beni relazionali ed elezioni nelle periferie di Roma. Rivista di Politica Econ 1–3:403–450
21. Trabalzi F (1989) Primavalle: urban reservation in Rome. J Architec Educ 42(3):38–46
22. ArchiDiAP (2017): Quartiere di Torrevecchia, curato da Musacchio, Mancini, Tofanelli. Link al: http://www.archidiap.com/opera/quartiere-di-torrevecchia/. Last accessed 23 March 2022
23. ArchiDiAP (2017): Quartiere del Quartaccio, curato da Lenci, Pignanelli, Ianiri, Ginnetti, Di Santo. Link al: http://www.archidiap.com/opera/quartiere-delquartaccio/ Last accessed 23 March 2022
24. ISTAT, 15° Censimento della popolazione e delle abitazioni 201. Available on: https://www.istat.it/it/censimenti-permanenti/censimenti-precedenti/popolazione-e-abitazioni/popolazione-2011 Last accessed 24 March 2022
25. Fayet Y, Praud D, Fervers B et al (2020) Beyond the map: evidencing the spatial dimension of health inequalities. Int J Health Geogr 19:46. https://doi.org/10.1186/s12942-020-00242-0
26. Diderichsen F, Andersen I, Manuel C et al (2012). Health Inequality-determinants and policies. Scand J Public Health. 40(8_suppl):12–105
27. Paglione L, Angelici L, Davoli M et al. (2020) Mortality inequalities by occupational status and type of job in men and women: results from the Rome Longitudinal Study. BMJ Open, 10(6):e033776. https://doi.org/10.1136/bmjopen-2019-033776
28. Caminada S, Turatto F, Iorio S et al. (2021). Urban health and social marginality: perceived health status and interaction with healthcare professionals of a hard-to-reach community living in a suburban area of Rome (Italy). Int J Environ Res Public Health 18:8804. https://doi.org/10.3390/ijerph18168804
29. Corburn J, Cohen AK (2012) Why we need urban health equity indicators: integrating science, policy, and community. PLoS Med 9(8):e1001285. https://doi.org/10.1371/journal.pmed.1001285

30. LeBrón AMW, Torres IR, Valencia E et al (2019) The state of public health lead policies: implications for urban health inequities and recommendations for health equity. Int J Environ Res Public Health 16:1064. https://doi.org/10.3390/ijerph16061064
31. Weiss L, Ompad D, Galea S, Vlahov D (2007) Defining neighborhood boundaries for urban health research. Am J Prev Med 32(6 SUPPL.):S154–S159

A Walkable Urban Environment to Prevent Chronic Diseases and Improve Wellbeing, an Experience of Urban Health in the Local Health Unit Roma 1

Lorenzo Paglione, Giada Gigliola, Maria Carla Marrero Cabrera, Stefania Scalingi, Antonio Montesi, Jessica Bonfini Petraccone, Anita Fanti, Riccardo Aucone, Maria Alessandra Brandimarte, Enrico Di Rosa, Letizia Appolloni, Simona Guida, and Daniela D'Alessandro

Abstract Cities play a vital role in promoting health, as most of the world's population lives in urban areas. Urbanization and city planning are both factors that must be considered to improve the health of communities. Walkability is a measure of how friendly an area is to walk. The Walking Suitability Index of the Territory (T-WSI) measures the pedestrian viability of the streets of a environmental islands. It includes 12 indicators, distributed into four categories: practicability, safety, urbanity, pleasantness. The goal of this study is to establish a model of connection between universities, local authorities, and health institutions to improve the walkability of urban areas. Five Environmental Islands were identified in the Municipality of Roma Capitale. First step concerned multidisciplinary training, sharing the goal between professionals in both the health and non-health fields. The theoretical acquisition, for Public Health personnel, on the use of the "walkability" assessment tool T-WSI was concretized by applying the assessment in training inspections. The on-site measurements showed that the main critical issues in terms of unfavorable factors for walking are the obstacles on the sidewalks, concerning the safety of pedestrian crossings and protection from vehicular speed. Measurement was associated with a characterization based on census data, obtained from satellite imagery. It is important to develop tools that are easy to apply and that can be easily used, also by health personnel. This is necessary in the light of recent developments in the Italian regulatory framework, and international guidelines, toward a growing integration of professional skills with the common objective of Urban Health.

Keywords Urban health · Walkability · Prevention and health promotion

L. Paglione (✉) · L. Appolloni · D. D'Alessandro
Department of Civil, Constructional and Environmental Engineering, Sapienza-University of Rome, Rome, Italy
e-mail: lorenzo.paglione@uniroma1.it

L. Paglione · G. Gigliola · M. C. M. Cabrera · S. Scalingi · A. Montesi · J. B. Petraccone · A. Fanti · R. Aucone · M. A. Brandimarte · E. Di Rosa · S. Guida
Department of Prevention, ASL Roma 1, Rome, Italy

A. Battisti et al. (eds.), *Equity in Health and Health Promotion in Urban Areas*, Green Energy and Technology, https://doi.org/10.1007/978-3-031-16182-7_7

1 Introduction

The relationship between the built environment, urban development, and health is an ancient theme, but of strict topicality. In 2020, more than half of the world's population lives in urban environments [1], and, despite the SARS-CoV-2 pandemic showing how great the health challenges are for cities, urban growth continues, albeit at a slower pace [2]. While until the nineteenth century the main challenges concerned infectious diseases, today, net of the problems that emerged during the SARS-CoV-2 pandemic, more and more attention is being paid to the prevalence of chronic-degenerative diseases, in terms of social, economic, and human costs, also due to the growing impact of social inequalities in health [3]. This attention has been translated, by international organizations, into the definition of the Sustainable Development Goals (SDGs), in particular: Goal 3—Good Health and Well-being, and Goal 11—Sustainable Cities and Communities [4]. Cities play an important role in promoting health, with 70% of the world's population living in urban areas, and increasing urbanization requires adequate spatial planning. Improving health policy and designing a fair, shared, and harmonious urban system is an objective to be achieved.

Precisely in the context of these initiatives, the National Prevention Plan [5], the main public health programming tool in use in Italy, has paid strong attention to the theme of urban planning, and how skills in this area must be increasingly present in the professional baggage of public health professionals. In particular, the plan foresees a strong investment in PP1—Health Promoting Schools, PP2—Active Communities, PP5—Safety in Living Environments. These include a series of actions aimed at communities, political decision-makers, and institutional stakeholders to intervene on the urban environment improving ergonomics, usability with particular attention to the most fragile people, accessibility in safety, and in general terms, equity in access and use.

1.1 The Context of Rome

In this sense, the City of Rome Capital represents an important challenge, both in terms of urban planning and public health [6–8]. Rome is the capital (henceforth Rome) is a city of about 2.7 million inhabitants, therefore not particularly populous, especially compared to the great Asian megalopolises, but distributed over an area of over 1200 km^2, just under the extension of Greater London [9]. The result is therefore that of a deeply dispersed city, with a central nucleus, corresponding approximately to the perimeter of the Aurelian walls (III century DC), an expansion belt dating back to the period of transformation of the city into the capital of Italy (late '800, the '10 s of the twentieth century), a historic suburb developed between the two world wars, alternated with the compact fabric of urban development of the'60 and '70 s, and finally a crown of so-called "boroughs", planned or abusive, which have accompanied the entire development of Rome, from the Unification of Italy to today [6, 10, 11]. It is, therefore, an urban fabric, and social, heterogeneous but well recognizable, characterized by a mixed morphology, in which alternate compact cities, especially characterized by large curtain buildings, a semi-peripheral belt but still wealthy, cottages and especially buildings, and finally a fabric dispersed in the Roman countryside, sometimes distant dozens of kilometres from the city centre, characterized by cluttered agglomerations of buildings and single or multi-family villas.

There are therefore more cities in the urban context of Rome [12], each with its own urban, morphological, socio-cultural, and socio-economic specificities. However, a feature that unifies the whole city is its very strong dependence on private transport in terms of mobility. The rail network is very deficient, consisting of two complete subway lines, one line now open only for half of the planned route, three suburban regional railway lines, and a railway network with very few stations, despite its extension, even and above all because of the lack of a "network effect" considered the lack of connection between its parts and the almost total absence of real intermodal nodes, necessary for a real "network effect" [13], so much so that only 1% of the movements detected can be classified as "intermodal".

The urban form of the city itself, therefore, is developed to ensure the maximum availability of space for private cars, both in terms of road sections and parking, but the demand is so high that Rome is one of the most congested cities in the world and with the highest rate of cars per capita in Europe, or about 900 vehicles per 1000 inhabitants [14]. Despite this, most of the journeys could be replaced by public transport or sustainable mobility, as proposed by the PUMS (*Piano Urbano della Mobilità Sostenibile* - Urban Sustainable Mobility Plan) of the Municipality of Rome, which indicates, at the level of the plan scenario, the transfer of 10% from private mobility to public mobility and rapid mass transport [15].

Surely therefore it will be necessary to improve the infrastructural endowment of the city, and in this sense moves also from the European Recovery Plan, integrated with governmental resources, that allocates 5,393 € million, precisely for the strengthening of infrastructures, in particular railway and metropolitan of the Municipality of Rome, as they will be destined to the recovery of this gap consisting national and local funds also tied to great events. Alongside this "macro" work, however, it is necessary to develop a finer, more widespread work that acts on the consolidated urban context in terms of timely adjustments and neighbourhood interventions, capable of changing the perception of public space to promote its liveability, usability, and ultimately, improve the health of the population.

1.2 Walking as a Component in the Urban Mobility

Walking is therefore one of the main ways of moving within the urban environment. It is a modality that can be used exclusively, i.e., without using public or private means, but it is also and above all the main way to integrate the others [16]. As for all other forms of mobility, it requires compatible individual characteristics (obviously linked to the motor skills of the individual) [17], but also spatial characteristics that favour it, or at least do not hinder it [18]. If the individual characteristics depend on the single person, and there are very few possibilities of control over them beyond the possible biomedical interventions, the spatial characteristics, linked to urban design, can be measured, even stratifying them based on the motor skills of the individual., but above all they can be modified, acting on the project and the very shape of the urban space [19].

Decomposing the factors related to walkability into measurable elements of the urban space requires qualitative and quantitative analysis, capable on the one hand of identifying the main dimensions linked to it from the individual point of view of the pedestrian, in the various age groups, based on individual needs and collective, on the other hand to understand those structural elements that may or may not favour it.

The pedestrian component represents a significant share of Roman mobility with over 5% of the total journeys in the territory of Rome carried out on foot [14]. The evaluation is carried out based on a series of integrated actions for the promotion of pedestrian traffic in all areas, whether central or peripheral, of the urban territory.

The objective of this study is to present a model of the connection between health institutions, universities, and local administration for the measurement of walkability, the development of urban projects, and interventions to promote walkability. In this sense, the proposed work is a contribution to the discussion, from a scientific point of view, but also from a cultural point of view, with the proposal of an integrated approach for measuring the walkability of neighborhoods, integrating different characterization methodologies with the purpose of public health [20, 21].

2 Objective, Materials and Methods

In this article data coming from different sources are integrated, to obtain a complete picture of the territory. Census data have been collected for the following purposes:

- identify some "test areas" with different social and building characteristics, where apply the integrated analysis.
- collect information in each selected area about demographic, social and housing condition of the population.

At the same time, to understand the territorial appeal for the population, in terms of safety, pleasantness, urbanity and practicability, an already validated method to evaluate these streets characteristics has been used. Five test areas, each corresponding to a portion of a specific neighborhood, have been identified as settings in the Municipality of Roma Capitale (Fig. 1). These all fall within the territory of the ASL Roma 1, and are: San Saba, in the I district, Trieste-Salario and Villaggio Olimpico, in the II district, Sacco Pastore and Tufello, in the III district.

Fig. 1 Environmental Island identified in the context of the urban fabric of Rome

2.1 Census Data

The identification of the test areas included in the study took place based on a preliminary knowledge of the territory. These are in fact in the Municipalities I, II, and III of Roma Capitale, falling within the area of ASL Rome 1, as already said before. Once the areas were identified, the five test areas were then perimetered using Google Earth Pro software. The same software, through the GIS functions, has allowed the identification of the road sections under examination, and some preliminary measurements (length of the sections, slope, surface of the Environmental Island). The shapefile, available on the ISTAT institutional website, containing the codes of the 2011 Census Sections [22], the territorial survey units, was superimposed on the perimeter polygon. Once the codes were identified, for each Section the information available on the public record layout of the 2011 Census was extracted, and the data were regrouped by Environmental Island and Urban Zones.

2.2 T-WSI, Training and Measurement

A method used was already applied to assess the walkability of several districts of the city of Rome, based on direct observation. The instrument, called the Walking Suitability Index of the Territory [23], measures the pedestrian usability of the streets of a neighborhood.

The scoreboard includes 12 indicators, distributed into 4 categories: walkability, safety, urbanity, pleasantness [23]. This instrument has been previously tested, evaluated, and validated [24].

1. practicability: describes the real possibility of practicing the road, focusing on the difficulties caused by existing physical defects; this category includes the following three indicators: bottom (state of the pavement), obstacles (existence and frequency of encumbrance), and slope.
2. safety: the protection against accidents that the road equipment provides; this category includes: protection from speed (vehicle speed limitation provisions), lighting, and crossings.
3. urbanity: takes into account all aspects of hospitality, comfort, attractiveness, vitality that a road can develop, depending on the facilities available; this category includes: width (width sidewalk), equipments, and social and commercial activities and services (eg shops, churches, post offices or functional complexity of the exercises on the road and that make it alive).
4. pleasantness: concerns the sphere of well-being, considering that the subjective perception of environmental pleasantness can influence the choice of taking a walk; this category includes: traffic, building context (type of buildings present, how many low and separated, and how many high and compact) and green.

Each indicator is given a score: excellent (val. 1), voucher (val. 0.7), poor (val. 0.35) and very bad (val. 0). The tool allows you to measure the pedestrian accessibility in each street of an area, highlighting the possible critical issues that could hinder pedestrian accessibility. The assessment aims to highlight how much the overall situation leads to walking on the road, even for users with difficulties.

The first step concerned multidisciplinary training, to standardize technical skills during the survey. There was an opportunity for a meeting between figures from different disciplines and contexts, sharing the goal between professionals in both the health and non-health fields. With the participation of the Department of Construction and Environmental Civil Engineering for the operators of the Prevention Department, such as doctors, prevention technicians, and nurses, the training action was, from the outset, action oriented. The theoretical acquisition, for Public Health personnel, on the use of the "walkability" assessment tool, was concretized by applying the assessment in training inspections.

The training objective was, considering the multidisciplinary and skills, to innovate the knowledge of all the professionals involved in the project. The path has been structured in three distinct but preparatory phases to each other:

- first phase: classroom training activities;
- second phase: field training;
- third phase: inspection activities.

It has been a fundamental process because the role of the Health Service in the field of urban policies has become, over time, increasingly relevant, and there is a need to develop activities in the Prevention Departments such as preventive assessments and analyses on territorial health. It is necessary to involve all personnel who can contribute to urban and environmental regeneration and have a positive impact on health in the Community, as this could be a good basis for supporting public administrations in the decision-making process on local development policy to foster improvement.

3 Preliminary Results and Discussion

The Municipality of Rome has various levels of territorial subdivision, those of interest of the study are the administrative subdivision and the toponymic subdivision: the first concerns the Municipalities, the second the Urban Zones (UZs, from the italian "*Zone Urbanistiche*, ZU") [25].

Starting from 1972 in the city of Rome 20 districts were established and subsequently reorganized in 2013 into 15 Municipalities, at the same time in 1977 the municipalities were divided into 155 Urban Zones, characterized by an alphanumeric code, consisting of the number of the decentralization body (district/municipality), and a letter indicating the relative territorial portion, this to allow a better planning and management of the territory, also for static purposes.

The population density of the Roman territory in 2019 was equal to 2213.3 inhabitants per km^2. The most densely populated areas are Municipality V (9049.5 inhabitants per km^2) and Municipalities II and I located in the central area of the city (respectively 8525.4 and 8330.5 inhabitants per km^2). On the other hand, the less densely populated ones are Municipality XV (857.2 inhabitants per km^2) and Municipality IX (1001.3 inhabitants per km^2) [15]. In terms of density, three municipalities, the I, II and V, are characterized by a density that is four times the average of the entire city with the V municipality reaching 2255.69 ab./km^2.

With the PGTU (General Urban Traffic Plan) approved in 2015, Rome has decided to update its mobility planning tool in relation to the criticalities that have emerged and the transformations that have taken place in recent years. The intervention areas of the new PGTU include the "environmental islands" (EI, from the Italian "*Isola Ambientale*") which are defined as urban areas enclosed within each grid of the main road network, and the road network it serves is therefore made up only of local roads [26]. They are called "islands" as they are internal to the main road network and "environmental" as they are aimed at recovering the liveability of urban spaces.

3.1 *Census and Context Variables*

The table shows the concentration of the population in the UZs and EIs under study, the breakdown into age classes, and the relative percentage, comparing the EIs with the UZs in which they insist and with the average of the Municipality of Rome. The UZs and the related EIs considered appear to be different from each other. The

UZ 2E-Trieste is the one with the highest number of inhabitants: 49,259 while 2A-Villaggio Olimpico is the one with the smallest number of inhabitants 2677. For the EIs, we have values ranging from 8704 (the highest value for Sacco Pastore) to 1308 people residing in the Villaggio Olimpico.

The ZU 2E-Trieste has a larger area (371 ha), 4H-Sacco Pastore the smaller one (47 ha) while it is different for the EIs: it goes from the Villaggio Olimpico with 19.10 ha to the Tufello with 27.40 ha.

All the urban planning areas and the related EIs under study have a population density higher than the average of the Municipality of Rome, an expected result as areas of consolidated urban fabric have been included, also based on the dispersion problems present in Rome and previously discussed. In particular, the EIs are more densely populated than the average of their Urban Planning Zone, with Sacco Pastore that exceeds, as an EI, 42,000 residents per km^2.

For the age class 0–19, the UZ and the EI of the Villaggio Olimpico is the lowest (well below the average of the Municipality of Rome), while the highest value of population residing in this age group belongs to the UZ/EI 2E-Trieste/Trieste Salario. All the EIs and UZs considered have a resident population in the 0–19 age group below the average of the Municipality of Rome. This result is also in line with expectations, as there is an unequal distribution of the resident population by age groups in Rome, also due to socio-economic dynamics [7]. Similarly, all Environmental Zones and related EIs have a higher-than-average resident population in the 70–99 age group (lowest value for Trieste/Trieste Wage; highest value for Villaggio Olimpico).

Regarding the context variables, from a socio-economic characterization point of view, all the UZs considered, and the related EIs appear to have a percentage of the population with a low level of education below the average of the Municipality of Rome, with the sole exception of Tufello, which is also one of the areas with the lowest level of education of the entire Municipality of Rome [12].

If we consider the unemployment rate (obtained from the ratio n. unemployed/active population) the lowest value is totaled by the UZ of Trieste (4.52), the highest by the Tufello (10.33). For the EIs, the lowest value for Sacco Pastore (5.45), the highest once again for Tufello (11.72) compared to an average value on the Municipality of Rome of 6.50. Regarding the state of use of the properties, the share of "rent or other titles", which in the census survey also includes Public Residential Building, compared to an average value of 30.11 in Rome, the highest value is obtained by the 4I-Tufello Urban Planning Zone (68.49), the lowest value 4H-Sacco Pastore 24.92. For the EIs: the highest value for Tufello was 77.91, the lowest value for Villaggio Olimpico was 23.21. All the UZs and EIs have a crowded index (total population/surface of the dwellings occupied by at least one resident person) lower than the average (2.53) with the only exception of Tufello (UZ 2.97, EI 3.01). It is good to specify how this result derives from the evaluation of the available residential area to the number of inhabitants, and is not an indicator of urban population density, previously exposed.

As far as the state of conservation of buildings is concerned, we have a heterogeneous situation. The rate of buildings in a poor state of conservation is found in the UZ and EI of Sacco Pastore respectively 44.38 and 42.22, the lowest in the UZ and

EI of the Villaggio Olimpico respectively 4.76 and 0.00, against an average of the City of Rome of 12.57. The survey is influenced by the redevelopment interventions carried out in the context of the Villaggio Olimpico in recent years.

The variable % empty dwellings calculated as Empty dwellings/total dwellings is also heterogeneous: average value Municipality of Rome: 9.42; Aventine UZ: 21.86; Villaggio Olimpico 0.81 and its EIs: San Saba: 17.23; Villaggio Olimpico: 1.22.

Analysing the functional mix, or the relationship between residential buildings on the total of buildings in the area, the lowest values are obtained for the UZ and the related EI of Tufello (respectively: 16.87 and 9.55), higher values for the UZ of the Villaggio Olimpico 50.00 and the Trieste-Salario EI 38.67, compared to an average of the Municipality of Rome of 20.96). All Urban Planning Zones and EIs, with a high residential vocation, have a rate of large buildings (with more than 8 interiors) well above the average of the Municipality of Rome. Likewise, if we consider the buildings built before 1946, we can see that there are UZs that exceed the average of the municipality of Rome: Tufello, Aventino (a.i. San Saba), and Trieste (a.i. Trieste-Salario) and others that are lower: Villaggio Olimpico and Sacco Pastore. The latter two were built in practically a single solution, the first for the 1960 Olympics in Rome, the second during the years between 1946 and 1960, the so-called decades of the building boom in Italy [27], a characteristic that can also be deduced from the extremely compact and uniform fabric of buildings on the EI.

Low, for all areas, are the percentages of buildings built in the years after 1990 (average value: 15.39; UZs/EIs value considered in many cases 0, proof that it is an urban fabric now consolidated). Finally, all the UZs and EIs considered have lower-than-average percentage values of masonry buildings; higher percentage values if, on the other hand, the variable % of reinforced concrete buildings are considered.

3.2 *Walkability Index Measurement*

Unlike the instruments that allow a remote measurement [28–30], the one presented requires a specific training path and above all, a detection carried out directly on site. This represents a limit in terms of necessary resources, but it allows us to know the territories in-depth, through the collection of photographic material, but above all by effectively evaluating the conditions of the contexts, following their paths, and being able to form an idea of any problems, for example, emerged in the inspections presented, about obstacles or general conditions related to more subjective factors, such as pleasantness or perceived security, but that surely make the difference in terms of perception and usability of a context, especially for the most fragile or vulnerable categories of the population.

Figure 2 shows the scores measured in each EI. In general safety and urbanity show low scores, while practicability and pleasureness result more satisfactory, although some exceptions are observed (e.g., Sacco Pastore). In average, this results in a low T-WSI value. This differences in the neighborhood characteristics cause variability

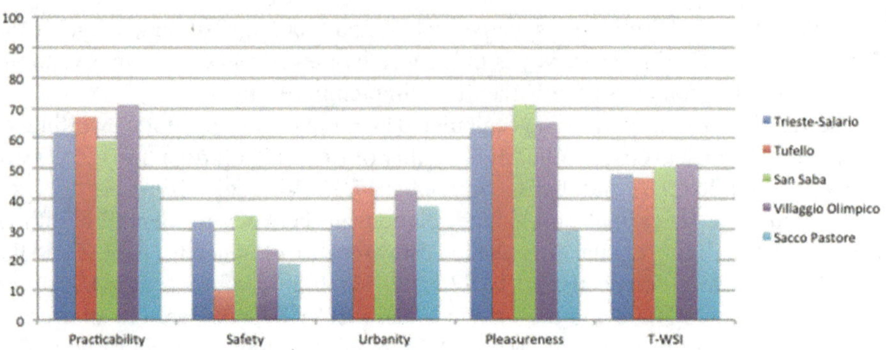

Fig. 2 Walkability level measured in the investigated EI

in terms of spaces usability and attractiveness, contributing to create the basis of the environmental injustice.

These preliminary measurements showed that the main critical issues in terms of unfavourable factors for walking are the obstacles on the sidewalks, in particular the parked cars (Fig. 3a), and the dimensions related to safety, concerning the safety of pedestrian crossings and protection from vehicular speed (Fig. 3b). For this measurement, the item "traffic" was estimated from a direct observation.

These latter factors, as highlighted, are critical not only in the analysed areas identified as more private, but also in the most affluent neighbourhoods, or in any case that presents better indicators regarding the characteristics of the building, such as Trieste-Salario. This figure is consistent with the high accident rate recorded over the years in Rome [31], which can be linked not only to the high number of vehicles in circulation but also to the total absence of safeguards aimed at mitigating their speed. The area with the lowest T-WSI index, however, is Sacco Pastore, especially due to the low scores totalled in terms of walkability (due to the high number of cars parked everywhere), and pleasantness (as also evidenced by the high rate of buildings in poor condition, according to the census survey).

The EIs of San Saba and Villaggio Olimpico have the highest score. These are different contexts from the point of view of urban stratification and the type of project. San Saba has an original nucleus, consisting of lots of small masonry buildings of two or three floors, some isolated and surrounded by green pertaining, others curtain to delimit the road space, and a "nucleus of expansion of buildings and villas of value. Both these souls, the one of ERP birth and the next one of medium–high class, develop around a historical nucleus consisting of the Basilica of San Saba, of great historical and archaeological value [32]. On the other hand, Villaggio Olimpico was created to host the athletes of the 1960 Olympics in Rome and subsequently became an ERP district, preserving the original elements, characterized by in-line or "network" buildings, a very widespread green (although objectively little usable), and, in the centre of the area, two large squares delimited by the long slats of the main buildings. Overall, these two areas have in common the limited height of buildings, a low level

Fig. 3 Some examples of situations detected during the inspections. Row **a**, practicability, row **b**, safety; row **c**, urbanity; row **d**, pleasurableness

of internal traffic, and a good distribution of green, as well as a limited but uniform presence of commercial and public establishments.

4 Conclusion and Future Perspectives

This work aims to present a project contribution, an approach based on the integration of tools, disciplines, and institutions, to transform the urban space, improving usability and ergonomics. The proposed approach, therefore, represents an example of integration between instruments belonging to different disciplines, integrating languages and methodologies with the aim of collective health and well-being. As anticipated in the introduction, this possibility is provided for by the National Prevention Plan and reiterated by the Regional Prevention Plan of the Lazio Region. In addition, the role of ASLs is well defined by the Prime Ministerial Decree of 12 January 2017 on the LEA, Essential Levels of Assistance, which indicates the direct involvement of the same in the definition of urban planning and regulation tools through hygiene and health assessment program and the National Prevention Plan (PNP) 2020–2025, approved by the State Regions Conference on 6 August 2020, which provides for the participation of health professionals in technical tables on Urban Health and support for the definition of Urban Sustainable Mobility Plans (PUMS).

The inter-sectoral nature of the Plan is one of its main strengths and has allowed ASL Roma 1 to develop an integrated intervention model in urban contexts, integrating classic social and health instruments, based on the care of patients, with public health and urban health instruments, which provide for the involvement of communities. Above all, through collaboration with municipal and municipal institutions, responsible for Urban Planning and Mobility, the approach discussed so far can become an institutional instrument, as already happens in other international contexts [33] [the Canadians] precisely for the evaluation of the consolidated urban fabric and the prioritization of structural interventions aimed at urban transformations. In an urban context such as that of Rome, where 58% of travel takes place by private means, and only 21.2% by public means [14], a figure worsened due to the pandemic [34].

After reiterating the importance of the participation of the health sector in the planning of urban environments, attention must be focused on the development of a model that improves both the urban-environmental plan but also the economic and social one. Good urban planning, the improvement of road traffic, the creation of green spaces, pedestrian and bicycle paths and safe paths are among the main effective measures to promote physical activity of people and help reduce the risk of chronic non-communicable diseases (NCD) [35].

The urban environment, in fact, affects health, exposing the population to risk factors linked to an inadequate environment. Everything is related to an incorrect urban development, for example neighborhoods without greenery or places for socializing, which lead citizens to adopt unhealthy behaviors. Phenomena such as a high population density, congested traffic, industrialization expose the population to numerous risks that clearly translate into the spread of NCD, both respiratory and cardiovascular diseases, causing chronic damage to the physical and mental health [36].

These associations mainly concern the most vulnerable or socially disadvantaged groups. In fact, diseases are also linked to implicit factors such as urbanization, environmental policies, population aging and poverty [37]. It is widely recognized that lifestyles are influenced by the social condition and physicality of the city in which one lives [38]. Not everyone in the city has the same opportunities or methods of accessing educational services, health services, public transport, green spaces, and parks [39].

This study, in addition to the current construction, is intended to be a starting point for a future prospect that will improve this field. To this end it is necessary to involve and relate to local institutions, with the aim of implementing and supporting the interventions, as is also the involvement of the community. In this regard, from a multidisciplinary perspective, which wants to favor prevention policies, it would be appropriate to consider, starting from a study on walkability, the importance of investigating issues that concern everyone (such as road safety) and raise awareness among the population, starting projects with schools that promote health for example.

The need to re-imagine the area also leads to reflect on the classic tools of urban planning and public health, with a view to integrating knowledge and skills from different fields. And it is starting from the relationship between built space, social space, and quality of life, that it is necessary to focus the intervention both on terms of study and in-depth analysis and of action aimed at change.

References

1. World Bank Data, Urban Population (% of total population). Available at: https://data.worldbank.org/indicator/SP.URB.TOTL.IN.ZS. Last accessed 28 March 2022
2. World Bank Data, Urban Population Growth (annual %). Available at: https://data.worldbank.org/indicator/SP.URB.TOTL.IN.ZS. Last accessed 28 March 2022
3. CSDH (2008) Closing the gap in a generation: health equity through action on the social determinants of health. In: Final report of the commission on social determinants of health, World Health Organization, Geneva
4. United Nations (2015) Sustainable Development Goals
5. Italian Ministry of Health, National Prevention Plan 2020–2025. Available at: https://www.salute.gov.it/portale/temi/p2_6.jsp?lingua=italiano&id=5772&area=prevenzione&menu=vuoto. Last accessed 28 March 2022
6. Insolera I (2011) Roma Moderna, da Napoleone I al XXI Secolo. In: (1° ed. 1962), Edizione ampliata con la collaborazione di Paolo Berdini, Einaudi, Torino
7. Cesaroni G, Venturi G, Paglione L et al. (2020) Mortality inequalities in Rome: the role of individual education and neighbourhood real estate market. Epidemiol Prev 44(5–6 Suppl 1):31–37. https://doi.org/10.19191/EP20.5-6.S1.P031.071
8. Cacciani L, Bargagli AM, Cesaroni G et al. (2015) Education and mortality in the Rome longitudinal study. In: Dalby AR (ed) PLOS ONE 10(9):e0137576
9. Lelo K ((2017)) Suburbs and fragmentation patterns: the case of Rome. Eurodiv Paper 44
10. D'Eramo M (2017) The not so eternal city. New Left Rev 106:77–103
11. Tocci W (2020) Roma come se, Alla ricerca del futuro per la capitale.Donzelli editore, ISBN: 978-88-5522-038-5
12. Lelo K, Monni S, Tomassi F (2021) Le sette Rome, La capitale delle disuguaglianze raccontata in 29 mappe. Donzelli editore, ISBN: 9788855221597
13. Vineis P, Beagley J, Bisceglia L, et al. (2021) Strategy for primary prevention of non-communicable diseases (NCD) and mitigation of climate change in Italy. J Epidemiol Community Health 1(0):1–8. https://doi.org/10.1136/jech-2020-21572
14. Mobility Report (2020) City of Rome. Rapporto Mobilità 2020–Roma. Available at: https://romamobilita.it/it/media/pubblicazioni/rapporto-mobilita-2020. Last accessed 23 March 2022
15. Urban Sustainable Mobility Plan of the City of Rome. Piano Urbano della Mobilità Sostenibile del Comune di Roma Capitale, 2019. Available at: http://www.urbanistica.comune.roma.it/images/pums-vas/PUMS-ROMA-vol-1.pdf. Last accessed 23 March 2022
16. Knuiman MW, Christian HE, Divitini ML et al. (2014)A longitudinal analysis of the influence of the neighborhood built environment on walking for transportation: the RESIDE study. Am J Epidemiol 180(5):453–461. https://doi.org/10.1093/aje/kwu171
17. Bianchi L, Angelini D, Lacquaniti F (1998) Individual characteristics of human walking mechanics. Pflugers Arch Aug 436(3):343–56. https://doi.org/10.1007/s004240050642
18. Gray JA, Zimmerman JL, Rimmer JH (2012) Built environment instruments for walkability, bikeability, and recreation: disability and universal design relevant? Disabil Health J 5(2):87–101. https://doi.org/10.1016/j.dhjo.2011.12.002
19. National Association of City Transportation Officials (NACTO) (2013) Urban Street Design Guide, Island Press, Washington, USA

20. Capolongo S, Rebecchi A, Dettori M et al. (2018) Healthy design and urban planning strategies, actions, and policy to achieve salutogenic cities. Int J Environ Res Public Health 15:2698
21. Paglione L, Cacciani L, Baglio G, Brandimarte MA et al. Characterising a setting with a high level of informality, integrating national and specialised surveys, administrative and census data. In: Urban health: participatory action-research models contrasting Socioeconomic inequalities in the urban context (2020), Springer. https://doi.org/10.1007/978-3-030-49446-9_6
22. ISTAT, 15° Censimento della popolazione e delle abitazioni 201. Available on: https://www.istat.it/it/censimenti-permanenti/censimenti-precedenti/popolazione-e-abitazioni/popolazione-2011. Last accessed 24 March 2022
23. Appolloni L, Corazza MV, D'Alessandro D (2019) The pleasure of walking: an innovative methodology to assess appropriate walkable performance in urban areas to support transport planning. Sustainability 11(12). https://doi.org/10.3390/su11123467
24. D'Alessandro D, Valeri D, Appolloni L (2020) Reliability of T-WSI to evaluate neighborhoods walkability and its changes over time. Int J Environ Res Public Health 17(21):7709. https://doi.org/10.3390/ijerph17217709
25. Official List and Names of Municipality and Urbanistic Zones of Rome. Roma Capitale. Denominazione Municipi e Zone Urbanistiche. Available on: https://www.comune.roma.it/web-resources/cms/documents/ElencoZ_Urbanistiche_rg_A.pdf. Last accessed 23 March 2022
26. 2020 Statistical Yearbook of Rome. Annuario Statistico 2020–Roma Capitale. Available on https://www.comune.roma.it/web-resources/cms/documents/Annuario_statistico_2020_agg_giugno2021_1.pdf. Last accessed 29 March 2022
27. Secchi B (2005) La città del ventesimo secolo. Editori Laterza, Bari
28. Booth GL, Creatore MI, Luo J et al. (2019) Neighbourhood walkability and the incidence of diabetes: An inverse probability of treatment weighting analysis. J Epidemiol Community Health 73(4):287–294. https://doi.org/10.1136/jech-2018-210510
29. Adhikari B, Delgado-Ron JA, Van den Bosch M et al. (2021) Community design and hypertension: walkability and park access relationships with cardiovascular health. Int J Hyg Environ Health. 237:113820. https://doi.org/10.1016/j.ijheh.2021.113820
30. Lang JJ, Pinault L, Colley RC et al. (2022) Neighbourhood walkability and mortality: findings from a 15-year follow-up of a nationally representative cohort of Canadian adults in urban areas. Environ Int. 161:107141. https://doi.org/10.1016/j.envint.2022.107141
31. Comi A, Polimeni A, Balsamo C (2022) Road accident analysis with data mining approach: evidence from Rome. Transp Res Proc 62:798–805, ISSN 2352-1465. https://doi.org/10.1016/j.trpro.2022.02.099
32. Chung K, Raab L, Schwartz E, Thatte A, Truong S San Saba: L'oasi di Pace. Available on https://aap.cornell.edu/sites/default/files/2010-san-saba-111813.pdf
33. Bulkeley H, Schroeder H, Janda K, Zhao J, Armstrong A, Chu SY, Ghosh S (2011) The role of institutions, governance, and urban planning for mitigation and adaptation. Cities Clim Change: Responding Urgent Agenda 62696:125–59
34. Aletta F, Brinchi S, Carrese S, Gemma A, Guattari C, Mannini L, Patella S (2020) Analysing urban traffic volumes and mapping noise emissions in Rome (Italy) in the context of containment measures for the COVID-19 disease. Noise Mapp 7(1):114–122. https://doi.org/10.1515/noise-2020-0010
35. World Health Organization (2018) Global action plan on physical activity 2018/2030m more active people for healthier world. World Health Organization, Geneva, Switzerland
36. Tartaglia S (2013) Different predictors of quality of life in urban environment. Soc Indic Res 113:1045–1053. https://doi.org/10.1007/s11205-012-0126-5
37. Redman CL, Jones NS (2005) The environmental, social, and health dimensions of urban expansion. Popul Environ 26(6):505–520. http://www.jstor.org/stable/27503943
38. Van Diepen AML, Musterd S (2009) Lifestyles and the city: connecting daily life to urbanity. J Hous and the Built Environ 24:331–345. https://doi.org/10.1007/s10901-009-9150-4
39. Ompad DC, Galea S, Caiaffa WT et al (2007) Social determinants of the health of urban populations: methodologic considerations. J Urban Health 84:42–53. https://doi.org/10.1007/s11524-007-9168-4

Housing and Health in Urban Areas

Daniela D'Alessandro and Letizia Appolloni

Abstract Living environment, and especially dwellings, affect health in several ways end represent a key social determinant of health. The current COVID-19 pandemic has further highlighted its relevance. Factors linked to housing and neighborhood conditions that influence health, can be grouped into broad categories: the health impacts of residential instability; those related to housing internal conditions; the health impacts of context in which dwelling is located; the housing affordability. Many answers to these requirements can be offered by co-housing and social housing and Authors describe same examples from international experiences. These problems nowadays need to be assessed with a multidisciplinary approach, because of the complexity and wideness of its components. To guarantee good health standards it is also necessary to direct political and administrative choices to improve the overall conditions of the neighborhood and of the buildings, and, to dispose of a clear and updated regulatory system, since key factor to ensure health and social justice.

Keywords Housing · Health · Health inequalities · Healthy living spaces · Covid-19 and built environment · Sustainability

1 Introduction

The relationship between health and built environment has long been recognized. Already in the Victorian's age, in England, assuming that an association exist between poor housing and ill-health, significant improvements were obtained clearancing slums and improving sanitation [1]. Similar interventions, realized in many other European countries, Italy included, obtained improvements in the epidemiological profile, reducing the spread of diseases like tuberculosis, cholera, and other transmissible diseases [1, 2].

As the knowledge of illnesses has grown, so has the awareness of the importance of dwelling quality for physical and mental wellbeing [3], and the recent CoViD-19

D. D'Alessandro (✉) · L. Appolloni
Department of Civil Building and Environmental Engineering, Sapienza University of Rome, Rome, Italy
e-mail: daniela.dalessandro@uniroma1.it

A. Battisti et al. (eds.), *Equity in Health and Health Promotion in Urban Areas*,
Green Energy and Technology, https://doi.org/10.1007/978-3-031-16182-7_8

pandemic have further documented its central role [4]. In fact, housing is the foundation for social, psychological, and cultural wellbeing, today like in the past [1, 5]. Poor housing conditions are related to the occurrence of a wide range of typical health problems of the modern societies as accidents, asthma, chronic diseases, psychological distress, and social isolation [6].

Therefore, considering that the world's urban population is expected to double by 2051 and that will require adequate housing solutions, the implementation of policies that pay attention to improve population housing conditions can save lives, prevent disease, increase quality of life, help mitigate climate change, especially for disadvantaged and vulnerable people, reducing injustice and inequalities in health.

It must be underlined that improving housing conditions means many things, since the building related factors influencing health belong to several sectors, from the environmental to the economic, social, and sanitary sector [4].

For example, the **residential instability**, that's to say the residents' impossibility to willingly remain in their homes free from harassment or dispossession, is a pivotal issue. Individuals may move voluntarily for many reasons (e.g., for a new job or a larger home, or even fear of crime) but, in some situations, involuntary displacement could occur, due to inability to afford rents or mortgage payments, eviction or foreclosure, consequences of natural disaster, etc. In the last few years, several catastrophic events, such as floods, tsunamis, earthquakes, landslides, volcanic activities, and heat and cold waves episodes, have occurred around the world, causing many victims [7]. Dwellings should provide a secure shelter from these threats and not permit further harm. Intense land use, climate changes, urbanization, poor building quality, and the spread of informal settlements have increased the frequency and intensity of these tragedies. These events can generate a deterioration of indoor environmental quality even when buildings resist the impact, worsening already poor living conditions, as it may happen in the case of shacks, basements, semi-basements, and garrets [8]. Housing instability is associated with a wide range of physical and mental health problems. Children and adolescents are particularly vulnerable to impacts of residential instability. Wars and natural disasters related to climate change are increasingly a major threat for displacement, as they can instantly damage and destroy massive amounts of housing, causing significant increases in health consequences [3, 4]. The need to guarantee a stable and safe home is specifically indicated among the United Nations' Sustainable Development Goals (SDGs). In particular, the SDG 11.1, expects, by 2030, to ensure access to adequate, safe, and affordable housing for all, and to upgrade slums [9].

At the same time**, housing internal conditions** have a direct impact on health. It is known that thermal wellbeing, lighting, indoor air quality, noise protection, water supply, and waste disposal interfer both psychological and physical health of inhabitants [6, 10]. The exposure to chemical pollutants induces several effects: from airways and mucous membrane irritation (e.g., by VOCs), to irreversibly damages to the brains and nervous systems of children (e.g., lead), but also several chronic diseases and cancer [3, 6, 11]. Substandard housing conditions due to water leaks, poor ventilation, dirty carpets, and pest infestation have been associated with poor health outcomes, most notably those related to allergic sensitization and asthma [3,

4, 6]. Literature shows that the lack of sufficient spaces, not only is related to inadequate indoor air quality, but it affects how and where people prepare and consume food, how they socialize, how they handle household waste and recycling, how they store goods, how much privacy they have for their daily activities (e.g., study, work, play, etc.), to what extent, and how these spaces can adapt to new needs (e.g., isolation, disability), etc. [12]. These are the main reasons why overcrowding interferes with health contributing to the development of a wide range of physical and mental problems. Immigrants and marginalized populations are at higher risk, since they are more likely to live in deteriorate housing stock, outdated infrastructure, lack of maintenance, and in overcrowding shelter; such situation is often exacerbated by unequal power dynamics between landlords and tenants [4]. Furthermore, these people frequently live in semi-basements or garrets, with several environmental problems and higher exposures to several quite a few indoor pollutants (e.g., radon, molds, etc.) [8]. Today several evidences, both on the risks associated with housing deficits and the potential health gains of providing housing or improving conditions inside the home, are available. Many of the studied interventions focus on health impacts, while only a few studies evaluate cost impacts for health systems, payers, or society. More integrated research projects, aimed to carry-out cost-benefits analysis of housing interventions, could add useful information for the decision makers. As Taylor argued [4], these evaluations should consider costs related to social services and the criminal justice system also, since the improvement of the living conditions is generally related to a reduction of crime. Although the health consequences of these situations are today widely recognized at scientific level, they are not adequately protected at legislative level [7], determining a large variability in terms of environmental justice. A neglected issue is related to the change in housing requirements due to the aging of the population, and need for flexible housing solutions, able to adapt to new needs. Not only the elderly has health problems and movement limitations that need for a flexible dwelling; such adaptation is required for many temporary, chronic, and acute conditions, among which are injuries, and genetic, neurodegenerative, autoimmune, cardiovascular, and infectious diseases [7]. The chance of living a healthy life these people is linked to the possibility of using suitable indoor and outdoor spaces, especially at home and the surroundings, to conduct an independent and active life. To ensure that, living spaces ought to be designed for people with functional limitations, guaranteeing at least the activities of daily living (ADLs): bathing, dressing, ambulation, toileting, and feeding. Accessibility for disabled people and safety for fragile people should be merged in new adapted/adaptable housing design.

As the housing internal conditions, the **context in which housing is located** influences health. It includes a broad set of structural, cultural, and functional aspects of the physical and social environment whose impact on the health is difficult to quantify as a whole, but which, nevertheless, exerts a powerful influence on how a society distributes resources among its members and consequently on the health opportunities of the population. The relevant aspects of the "context" can be summarized in the following main elements: physical characteristics of area, culture, and social values, but also governance, social and economic policies.

In terms of health impacts, WHO recognizes the influence that adequate living conditions can have on public health [13]. Air quality, noise, water supply, management and collection of municipal solid waste, transportation, green and blue areas, street lighting, etc. represent features of the built environment directly and indirectly impacting on citizens' health and safety [3, 4]. If well managed these factors contribute to fight also climate changes [14], and their consequences, like natural disasters. Adequate living conditions thus necessitate healthy environments and promoters of active lifestyles [15]. At the same time, to reach sustainable development goals (SDGs) for 2030, a strong synergy among local governance and community is required.

Inequalities across and within cities are one aspect of social injustice in health [16, 17]. Environmental hazards (e.g., waste processing facilities) are mainly located in peripheral areas in which generally live low-income communities. In these contexts, it is easy to find urban voids, abandoned buildings and degraded lots, all conditions related to segregation and to an increased risk of violent assault [18, 19]. Neighborhood segregation is also related to disparities in the access to schools, jobs, and health care; it influences health behaviors and crime [20, 21]. Fear of crime is one of the most significant social problems in cities, negatively affecting people's habits and lifestyle [22]. In general, this type of urban insecurity is related to other uncertainties regarding labor, economic, or social insecurities arising from changes in welfare state policies. As already described, the most severe expression has been found in badly maintained housing estates with large housing blocks, little maintenance, and large public open spaces with unclear management responsibilities [18]. Evidence indicates that remediation programs (e.g., greening lots and remediating doors and windows) or better a true regeneration one, reduce violence and stress and increase physical activity also [17, 18].

Finally, the possibility to have an adequate housing depend on its **affordability**, generally considered as the financial overburden rate resulting from high-cost housing [12]. With house prices and rents rising, the cost of housing can be a burden. This can be measured by the housing cost overburden rate, which shows the share of the population living in a household where total housing costs represent more than 40% of available income. The percentage of population in this condition varies between countries, based mainly on the wealth and social policies of the Country; this percentage increases significantly for tenants renting with market price. In the EU in 2020, 12.3% of the population in cities lived in such a kind of household. The highest housing cost overburden rates in cities were observed in Greece (36.9%), Germany (22.2%) and Denmark (20.3%) [23]. Housing affordability can affect families' ability to make other essential expenses, contributing to the occurrence of physical and mental health problems [6]. Low-income families with difficulty in paying their rent or mortgage or their utility bills are less likely to have a usual source of medical care, are more likely to postpone needed treatment [24] and health-related expenses [3, 4, 25] and are less likely to have resources for children development [21]. Frequently a strategy to reduce high rent burdens is to share housing with someone else, but this solution can lead to overcrowding [4] and to several adverse health effects, like mental problems [6, 26, 27] and infectious diseases [3, 6, 27]. However, other studies could be useful, to understand how people set priorities among basic needs and make decisions in conditions of scarcity.

2 Housing Needs and Possible Answers

As previously reported, today modern housing units have to respond to new needs related to social, economic, demographic and environmental factors. They include: the increase in the average life expectancy of the population, the immigration, the economic crisis, the increase demand for new ways of working (e.g., remote work) and related technological needs, as well as adequate spaces to work and for any needs for isolation, the climate changes [12]. Furthermore, the consequences of the pandemic, and the imminent risk of its repetition, highlight the need to apply a new concept of health, in terms of indoor well-being, to housing policy [24]. The lockdown due to the COVID-19 pandemic showed the importance of housing conditions on people health and well-being, documenting the different distribution of health problems based on housing conditions and underlining the vast inequalities registered in Italy, mainly in metropolitan areas. Scarce quality of part of the housing stock, lack of adequate space, terraces and gardens have contributed to increased stress and aggressivity, especially among the disadvantaged groups. Therefore, the policymakers should consider housing as a major priority for the potential relapses in public health related to it.

In a 2020 study [24] the authors highlight practical ideas and key-solutions to rethink the living spaces, focusing on functional organization of living spaces in the light of the COVID-19 experience, from a healthy, safety and sustainability perspective. Translating the inhabitants' needs into essential characteristics in the post-pandemic home, it is possible to identify numerous requirements: the versatility of the spaces, the larger dimensions, the availability of gardens and balconies/terraces, external views, adequate spaces for studying and work, the presence of bright and well-ventilated environments and with good sound insulation. Another important aspect to increase and optimize social cohesion between the inhabitants in complete safety is the reconsideration and redevelopment of the common areas of condominiums and residential buildings.

The pandemic has also brought to the re-emergence of significant aspects related to living spaces such as, for example, the importance of the house in which you live, the bond that is established with it and the quality of life it guarantees; the existence of an intermediate place between private and public space, a place that re-enhances the concept of community and neighborhood, often set aside in many contemporary cities; the importance of proximity and accessibility at least to services and basic necessities.

Many answers to these requirements can be offered by **co-housing** and social housing, housing solutions, the latter, not much widespread in Italy yet. More in dept, cohousing is a condition in which residents give up a part of their individual housing in favor of the creation of common areas (e.g., recreational areas, playrooms for children, gym, services such as laundries and kitchens, gardens or spaces outdoors) with the aim of social interaction and management economics. Usually, a co-housing project includes from 20 to 40 families who live together as a neighborhood community and manage the common spaces collectively, thus obtaining economic savings and ecological and social benefits.

Social housing refers to sustainable housing, at low costs, which meets the needs of specific categories of people (e.g., young couples, low-income families, the elderly, out-of-home students, and new workers, etc.), that do not find an answer to their needs in the traditional real estate market. The aim is to ensure access to housing for all social categories. This housing solution could prove to be capable of responding to the new demands of the population and the changes that the pandemic has imposed such as, for example, the need to work from home, the sense of loneliness due to isolation, the needs of help people fragile, etc.

An example of co-housing is Marmalade Lane Co-Housing Cambridge [28]. Located in the north of Cambridge, it is a multigenerational and multi-ethnic complex that occupies a lot with 42 independent units. The complex, which covers 8600 square meters, has common areas and services: a vegetable garden, a play area, one for socializing, a waste area, and the Common House with some bedrooms that can be booked by residents to accommodate any guests. Another example of co-housing is the "*senior housing*", who offers an alternative housing solution to the increasing population of the elderly. These are rental accommodation for independent people over the age of 65, in search of safety, comfort, accessibility to services (medical assistance, cleaning services, laundry etc.) and recreational activities. These accommodations guarantee good standards of living and compliance with their needs. These are often active and completely autonomous people, capable of offer their skills to the community. An example of this buildings is the senior cohousing Oosterkade (The Netherlands) [29]. In the building, once the needs relating to the spaces to be shared were identified (gym, laundry, sauna, warehouses, garden, terrace), six independent and private apartments were created. The apartments have been adapted to the wishes and needs of individuals, achieving the right balance between private area and shared spaces.

Some examples of social housing are the Social Housing Carabanchel Ensanche 6 of Madrid [30] and the Social Housing in Lérida [31]. Both proposals are particularly interesting also in terms of inhabitants' well-being, for their typological flexibility. Indoor flexibility of domestic living spaces means the opportunity to rethink the spaces of the house, considering the renewed needs that have arisen especially in the period of physical distancing, with the aim of better satisfying the needs of well-being and hygiene of the indoor environment. The idea of flexibility is not new but was the focus of various studies of engineers and architects during the twentieth century and has produced works of historical significance. Some interesting examples that experiment and implement various types of housing flexibility are the already quoted Social Housing in Carabanchel Ensanche 6 [30] and Social Housing in Lérida [32], but Casa Schroder too [33]. Schröder House [31], built in Utrecht by the Dutch architect Gerrit Rietveld in the 1920s, has been part of the UNESCO World Heritage

Site since 2000. This building is an example of a dynamic open space, in which the rooms can be remodeled according to needs thanks to movable walls and other devices that involve the furnishing elements. The floor plan of Casa Schröder shows a considerable flexibility of the paths and different possible configurations of the domestic environments that can be obtained thanks to the use of movable walls.

In addition to the internal flexibility of the living space, it would be appropriate to focus attention also on the envelope, rethinking the entire layout of the building, including the condominium areas. For example, the flexibility of some spaces, such as the ground floors, the free floors, the basements, (often used as a residence despite not having adequate health and hygiene requirements) should be considered [8], to easily readjust them, if necessary, in order to increase the available spaces for the inhabitants, as in the case of the lockdown, to have a quiet temporary workstation and to maintain social distancing, always considering the specific regulatory requirements.

The ground floors could be used to offer the inhabitants accessible proximity services, always trying to ensure the most of attention in minimizing the negative impacts that functional coexistence can generate. These good practices could help improve the quality of the neighborhood and make the living environment healthier for the inhabitants, in line with the most recent WHO indications [33].

Another issue, re-emphasized after the COVID19 pandemic, is the need of open spaces and of visible and accessible green elements. The role of green spaces in mitigating the impacts of the built environment on the climate and in improving the ecological-climatic conditions of cities and of the buildings themselves is widely documented; green is also associated with a wide range of health benefits, both physical and mental, for all age groups [34]. Even during the pandemic, the presence of green elements and more generally of outdoor spaces played an important role in mental health and the management of emotions [35]. In fact, the benefits that can be drawn from green infrastructures, such as green roofs and walls where the building organization allows it [36], from the strengthening of gardens and condominium spaces, from the presence of green spaces in the proximity, are emphasized.

The greenery offers greater opportunities to practice physical and leisure/recreational activities thus helping to promote well-being and social relationships, as well as reducing the frequency of various pathologies such as coronary heart disease, skeletal disorders, anxiety, depression, diabetes, etc. [37] and encouraging socialities [38]. It also helps to produce a greater sense of belonging and identity and to reduce crime rates [24, 39]. The view of greenery from the windows of a building can have beneficial effects in reducing stress, especially if natural elements or quality landscapes are visible [24, 40, 41] and this can also contribute to accelerating the healing process of patients admitted to nursing homes [42]. Another important element in homes is the presence of balconies or terraces in which it is possible to grow plants or small gardens (therapeutic for the mood), elements that implement the performance and perceptive aspects of confined environments by strengthening the relationship between man and nature [43]. In addition, introducing vegetation into the courtyards of buildings or in the immediate vicinity provides spaces useful for socializing and relaxing [18].

3 Conclusions

Housing is a key determinant for human health. This paper describes some of the critical factors involved in the relationship between housing and health, showing the strict relation between them and social, economic, and environmental conditions; this strict relation explains why it is often difficult to assess the real independent effects of housing conditions alone on health. The COVID-19 pandemic has highlighted housing issues worldwide again, showing the big gap in negative health consequences due to housing conditions, that are mainly hit disadvantaged population [24].

Although some possible solutions have been described, the theme of "housing and health" nowadays needs to be further assessed using a multidisciplinary and transdisciplinary approach in both research and practice [44], because of the complexity and wideness of its components. Transdisciplinary knowledge production has to move beyond conventional research agendas, to address real world concerns, to address societal challenges in many domains that require collective understanding, political commitment, and innovative responses [2]. Actually, there is a transversal need of sharing knowledge, instruments and methods, for all the figures involved in the planning process, and to face up to complex issues like this, whose causes lie beyond the traditional remit of the health sector, it is necessary to share knowledge from many sectors. Therefore, collaborative activities involving professionals trained in different cultural areas need to be further implemented in the next future [2, 4]. At the same time, to guarantee good health standards it is also necessary to dispose of a clear and updated regulatory system, taking into account social justice issues.

In conclusion, building healthy and safe housing is a complex issue and a multisectorial responsibility, achievable only if all relevant players contribute to that, since it needs of policy vision, health data, resources, and technical competences.

References

1. Shaw M (2004) Housing and public health. Annu Rev Public Health 25:397–418. https://doi.org/10.1146/annurev.publhealth.25.101802.123036
2. D'Alessandro D (2020) Urban Public Health, a multidisciplinary approach. In: Battisti A, Marceca M, Iorio S (eds) Urban Health. AIMETA 2019. Green Energy and Technology, Springer, Cham. https://doi.org/10.1007/978-3-030-49446-9_1
3. D'Alessandro D, Appolloni L (2020) Housing and health: an overview. Ann Ig 32(5 Supple 1):17–26. https://doi.org/10.7416/ai.2020.3391
4. Taylor L (2018) Housing and health: an overview of the literature. Health affairs health policy brief. https://doi.org/10.1377/hpb20180313.396577
5. Rolfe S, Garnham L, Godwin J, Anderson I, Seaman P, Donaldson C (2020) Housing as a social determinant of health and wellbeing: developing an empirically-informed realist theoretical framework. BMC Public Health 20(1):1138. https://doi.org/10.1186/s12889-020-09224-0
6. WHO: Housing and Health Guidelines. Geneva: World Health Organization (2018). Available on: https://apps.who.int/iris/bitstream/handle/10665/276001/9789241550376-eng.pdf. Last access 20 June 2022
7. Capasso L, D'Alessandro D (2021) Housing and health: here we go again. Int J Environ Res Public Health 18(22):12060. https://doi.org/10.3390/ijerph182212060

8. Capasso L, Capolongo S, Faggioli A, Petronio MG, D'Alessandro D (2015) Living in a semi-basement in the era of floods. Italian law cause inequalities in health protection. Ann Ig 27(2):502–504. https://doi.org/10.7416/ai.2015.2038
9. United Nations (1991) Office of the United Nations high commissioner for human rights: The Right to Adequate Housing. Fact Sheet n. 21/Rev 1. Available on: https://www.ohchr.org/Documents/Publications/FS21_rev_1_Housing_en.pdf. Last access 25 May 2022
10. D'Alessandro D, Dettori M, Raffo M, Appolloni L (2020) Housing problems in a changing society: regulation and training needs in Italy. Ann Ig 32(5 Supple 1):27–35. https://doi.org/10.7416/ai.2020.3392
11. Braubach M, Jacobs DE, Ormandy D (2011) Environmental burden of disease associated with inadequate housing: a method guide to the quantification of health effects of selected housing risks in the WHO European region. Retrieved from World Health Organization Regional Office for Europe. Available on: http://www.euro.who.int/_data/assets/pdf_file/0017/145511/e95004sum.pdf. Last access 25 May 2022
12. Appolloni L, D'Alessandro D (2021) Housing spaces in nine European Countries: a comparison of dimensional requirements. Int J Environ Res Public Health 18(8):4278. https://doi.org/10.3390/ijerph18084278
13. World Health Organization (WHO): Health as the Pulse of the New Urban Agenda (2016). Available online: http://apps.who.int/iris/bitstream/handle/10665/250367/9789241511445-eng.pdf;jsessionid=07F882D99F1E1AF399B57D5546EEB2BB?sequence=1. Last access 25 May 2022
14. World Health Organization (WHO) International workshop on housing, health and climate change: developing guidance for health protection in the built environment—mitigation and adaptation responses. Available online: http://www.who.int/hia/house_report.pdf. Last access 10 May 2022
15. McMichael AJ (2000) The urban environment and health in a world of increasing globalization: Issues for developing countries. Bull World Health Organ 78(9):1117–1126
16. WHO (2012) Addressing the social determinants of health: the urban dimension and the role of local government. WHO, Institute of Health Equity, University College London, London, UK
17. WHO (2012b) Environmental Health Inequalities in Europe. Assessment report. World Health Organisation, Bonn, Germany
18. Capolongo S, Rebecchi A, Dettori M, Appolloni L, Azara A, Buffoli M, Capasso L, Casuccio A, Oliveri Conti G, D'Amico A, Ferrante M, Moscato U, Oberti I, Paglione L, Restivo V, D'Alessandro D (2018) Healthy design and urban planning strategies, action and policy to chieve salutogenic cities. Int J Environ Res Public Health 15(12):2698. https://doi.org/10.3390/ijerph15122698
19. Branas CC, South E, Kondo MC, Hohl BC, Bourgois P, Wiebe DJ, MacDonald JM (2018) Citywide cluster randomized trial to restore blighted vacant land and its effects on violence, crime, and fear. Proc Natl Acad Sci USA 115(12):2946–2951. https://doi.org/10.1073/pnas.1718503115
20. Iorio S, Salvatori LM, Barnocchi A, Battisti A, Rinaldi A, Marceca M, Ricotta G, Brandimarte AM, Baglio G, Gazzaniga V, Paglione L (2019) Social inequalities in the metropolitan area of Rome. A multidisciplinary analysis of the urban segregation of the "formerly-Bastogi" compound. Ann Ig 31(3):211–229. https://doi.org/10.7416/ai.2019.2284
21. Swope CB, Hernandez D (2019) Housing as a determinant of health equity: a conceptual model. Soc Sci Med 243:112571. https://doi.org/10.1016/j.socscimed.2019.112571
22. Valera S, Guàrdia J (2014) Perceived insecurity and fear of crime in a city with low-crime rates. J Environ Psychol 38:195–205. https://doi.org/10.1016/j.jenvp.2014.02.002
23. LNCS Homepage. https://ec.europa.eu/eurostat/cache/digpub/housing/bloc-2b.html?lang=en. Last access 20 June 2020
24. D'Alessandro D, Gola M, Appolloni L, Dettori M, Fara GM, Rebecchi A, Settimo G, Capolongo S (2020) COVID-19 and living space challenge. Well-being and public health recommendations for a healthy, safe, and sustainable housing. Acta Biomed 91(9-S):61–75. https://doi.org/10.23750/abm.v91i9-S.10115

25. Garnham L, Rolfe S Housing as a social determinant of health: evidence from the housing through social enterpirese study. Glasgow Centre for Population Health. Available online: https://www.gcph.co.uk/assets/0000/7295/Housing_through_social_enterprise_WEB.pdf. Last access 20 Feb 20
26. Jaworsky D, Gadermann A, Duhoux A, Naismith TE, Norena M, To MJ, Palepu A (2016) Residential stability reduces unmet health care needs and emergency department utilization among a cohort of homeless and vulnerably housed persons in Canada. J Urban Health 93(4):666–681. https://doi.org/10.1007/s11524-016-0065-6
27. Suglia SF, Duarte CS, Sandel MT (2011) Housing quality, housing instability, and maternal mental health. J Urban Health 88(6):1105–1116. https://doi.org/10.1007/s11524-011-9587-0
28. LNCS Homepage. http://www.marmaladelane.co.uk. Last access 20 May 2020
29. LNCS Homepage. https://archicollective.com/SENIOR-COHOUSING. Last access 20 May 2020)
30. Sposito C (2012) Identità, Flessibilità e Sostenibilità per un nuovo Social Housing. TECHNE 4:153–159. ISSN online: 2239-0243
31. LNCS Homepage. https://www.rietveldschroderhuis.nl/en. Last access 22 Nov 2021)
32. LNCS Homepage. https://arquitecturaviva.com/works/viviendas-sociales-en-lerida-2#lg=1&slide=1. Last access 22 Nov 2021
33. Bonnefoy X (2007) Inadequate housing and health: an overview. Int J Environ Pollut 30:411–424. https://doi.org/10.1504/IJEP.2007.014819
34. D'Alessandro D, Buffoli M, Capasso L, Fara GM, Rebecchi A, Capolongo S (2015) Green areas and public health: Improving wellbeing and physical activity in the urban context. Epidemiol Prev 39(4 Suppl 1):8–13
35. Pauso S, Borja A, Fleming LE, Gomez-Baggethun E, White MP, Uyarra MC (2021) Contact with blue-green spaces during the COVID-19 pandemic lockdown beneficial for mental health. Sci Total Environ 756:143984. https://doi.org/10.1016/j.scitotenv.2020.143984
36. Buffoli M, Rebecchi A, Gola M, Favotto A, Procopio GP, Capolongo S (2018) Green SOAP. A calculation model for improving outdoor air quality in urban contexts and evaluating the benefits to the population's health status. In: Mondini G, Fattinnanzi E, Oppio A, Bottero M, Stanghellini S (eds) Integrated evaluation for the management of contemporary cities. Green Energy and Technology, Springer, pp 453–467. https://doi.org/10.1007/978-3-319-78271-3_36
37. Maas J, Verheij RA, de Vries S, Spreeuwenberg P, Schellevis FG, Groenewegen PP (2009) Morbidity is related to a green living environment. J Epidemiol Community Health 63:967–973. https://doi.org/10.1136/jech.2008.079038
38. Cohen-Cline H, Turkheimer E, Duncan GE (2015) Access to green space, physical activity and mental health: a twin study. J Epidemiol Community Health 69(6):523–529. https://doi.org/10.1136/jech-2014-204667
39. Kuo FE, Sullivan WC (2001) Aggression and violence in the inner city: effects of environment via mental fatigue. Environ Behav 33(4):543–571. https://doi.org/10.1177/00139160121973124
40. Capolongo S, Rebecchi A, Buffoli M, Appolloni L, Signorelli C, Fara GM, D'Alessandro D (2020) COVID-19 and cities: from urban health strategies to the pandemic challenge. A Decalogue of Public Health opportunities. Acta Bio-Med Atenei Parm 91(2):13–22. https://doi.org/10.23750/abm.v91i2.9615
41. Labib SM, Lindley S, Huck JJ (2020) Spatial dimensions of the influence of urban green-blue spaces on human health: a systematic review. Environ Res 180:108869. https://doi.org/10.1016/j.envres.2019.108869
42. Brambilla A, Rebecchi A, Capolongo S (2019) Evidence based hospital design. A literature review of the recent publications about the EBD impact of built environment on hospital occupants' and organizational outcomes. Ann Ig 31:165–180. https://doi.org/10.7416/ai.2019.2269

43. Berto R, Barbiero G, Pasini M, Unema P (2015) Biophilic design triggers fascination and enhances psychological restoration in the urban environment. J Biourbanism 1:26–35. https://doi.org/10.13140/RG.2.1.2177.496
44. Lawrence RJ (2017) Constancy and change: key issures in housing and health research, 1987–2017. Int J Environ Res Public Health 14(7):763. https://doi.org/10.3390/ijerph14070763

Health, Well-Being, Good Living. Architectural Attempts with Acupuncture-Type Regenerations for Quito, Cairo and the Baghère Region

Patrick Thépot

Abstract The studies carried out for the cities of Quito, Cairo, and the region of Baghère within the master course 'Aedification—Large territories—Cities' at the École Nationale Supérieure d'Architecture de Grenoble raise the question of good living, well-being, and health by relying on punctual architectural proposals that take into consideration the environment on both a large and small scale. The main theme of the three sites is violence against women and all people in precarious situations. For the capital of Ecuador, the northern slope of the Panecillo hill is host to project hypotheses that fit into abandoned buildings with high heritage value. As an extension of these attempts, the opportunity to rethink informal housing through innovative prototypes is inspired by local know-how. For the Egyptian capital, Bab el-Wazir Street is imagined through a new dynamic between social programs and heritage programs for a reinterpretation of vernacular architecture. In the Tanaff valley in Senegal, the small town of Baghère invites reflection through initiatives built for a more peaceful society. In each case, good living, well-being, and health are questioned as a central concern to offer the best possible quality of life to the most disadvantaged people.

Keywords Health · Nature · Precarity · Regeneration · Well-being · Women's conditions

1 Introduction

Health, well-being, and good living must be considered a right for all. From three experimental sites, this right is dedicated to women victims of violence and to people in precarious situations. Projects, which are studies and research, should be considered as "attempts" or "hypotheses". They are both possibilities of realization and tools for collective reflection which participate in architectural tests with a will of punctual regeneration. As in acupuncture, small pricks at strategic points can be

P. Thépot (✉)
MHA Laboratory, EA 7445, École Nationale Supérieure d'Architecture de Grenoble, 38000 Grenoble, France
e-mail: patrick.thepot@hotmail.fr; thepot.p@grenoble.archi.fr

A. Battisti et al. (eds.), *Equity in Health and Health Promotion in Urban Areas*, Green Energy and Technology, https://doi.org/10.1007/978-3-031-16182-7_9

expected to have a beneficial effect in specific places, the consequences of which offer real transformations. The changes that take place are then part of a new equilibrium that resonates simultaneously on several scales, from the building to the territory. In *On the Art of Building in Ten Books* (1991), English translation of the Latin version of *De re aedificatoria* (1485), and about nature in relation to health, the Renaissance architect Leon Battista Alberti offers us: "*But it is clear that in everything Nature thrives on moderation; and what is good health but a moderation composed on fabric of different extremes? The mean is always pleasing*" [1]. Also translated into Italian [2] and French [3] by very similar words, this quotation still asks us today to conduct a cross-reflection on the inseparable relationships that we can have between the environment, architecture, and human behavior. More simply, what Alberti conveys to us is that nature is like health. Nature contains an equilibrium in its manifestations that invites us to consider or reconsider the right measure. We could go further in comparing the translations of each word and say that *measure*, *moderation*, or *medicine* have the same etymological root. That temperament also means to moderate, that it is also the right proportion of the humors in the human body. In the same way that the word *fabric* opens to the inner thought by evoking construction, production, making or know-how to the point of recalling the making of fabric by its texture as well as by its structure in a spatial organization. All these analogies proceed from a reasoning by the spirit to amplify the design processes of the architectural project in gestation. Nature and health thus have similarities, and, in this alliance, they become a fertile source of inspiration for architects. However, health, well-being or the good life can be interpreted in different ways. This is what we will try to measure with the three sites studied.

2 Quito and the Panecillo Hill

The first site is in Quito (Fig. 1). Ecuador was the first country in the world to include the rights of nature in its constitution. Ecuadorian culture has always been strongly oriented towards nature, which it considers the mother of humanity. With more than 2 million inhabitants, Ecuador's capital is located at an altitude of 2800 m. Founded in the sixteenth century by Spanish settlers, the city of Quito today stretches 50 km from its historic center. The Panecillo hill is a continuation of this center. At the bottom of the hill and close to each other, the San Lazaro hospice and the El Sena swimming pool are currently abandoned (Fig. 2). These two buildings with a high heritage value are still waiting to be converted between rehabilitation and extension [4].

For the San Lazaro hospice, a new house for women with different services is recommended. For the El Sena swimming pool, whose main objective is to respond to the problem of the professional reintegration of women, a leisure center, craft production areas and construction workshops to envisage prototypes are taken as hypotheses. Beyond these proposals, all the statistics concerning violence against women are very important in Ecuador and particularly in Quito (Fig. 3).

Fig. 1 The city of Quito and the location of the Panecillo hill

Fig. 2 The situation of the hospice San Lazaro and the swimming pool El Sena

In an interview we conducted with Berenice Cordero, the former Minister of Economic and Social Inclusion in Ecuador recalls the seriousness of the situation. The country suffers from a real lack of protection and consideration for women's rights, health, and safety. On a more positive note, some existing structures are to be followed by their exemplary nature. Several associations are models of temporary accommodation to promote a protective environment with care and security to undertake life projects with psychological support or vocational reintegration training. These models have been studied very carefully to introduce the desired programs.

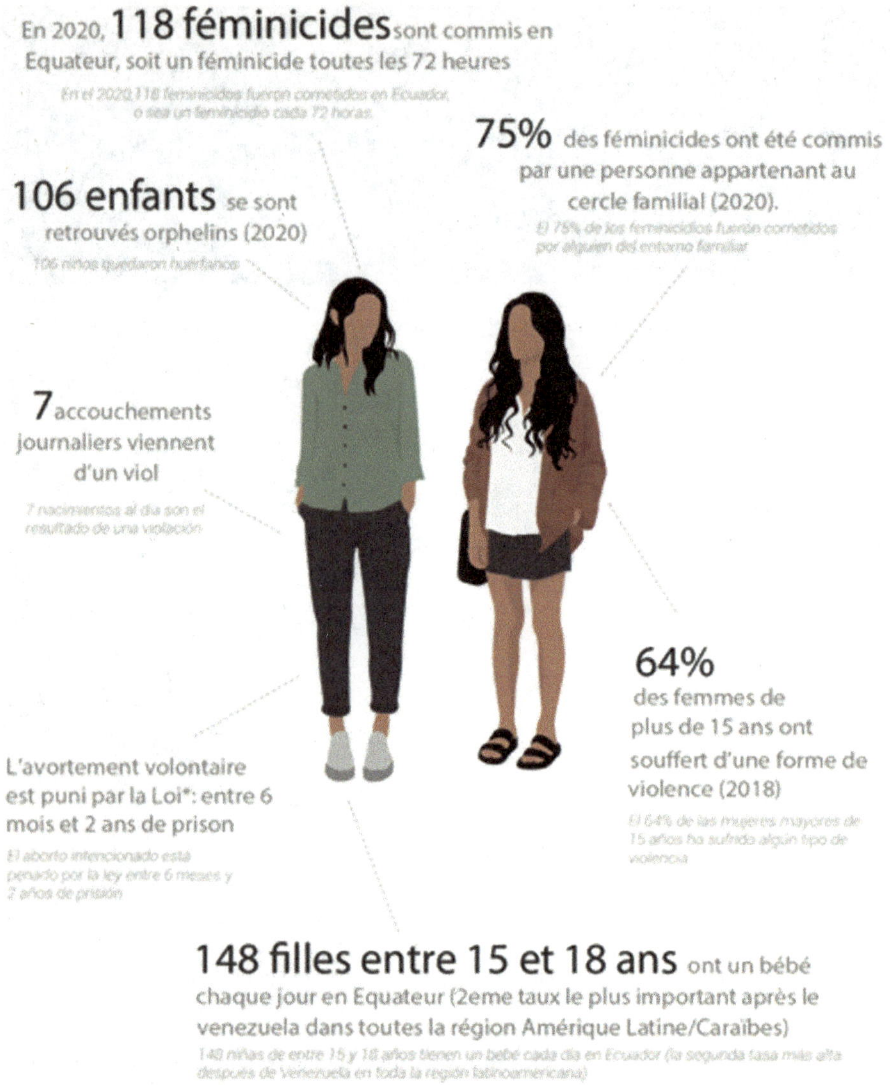

Fig. 3 Statistics on the status of women in Ecuador are alarming

3 The San Lazaro Hospice. A New House for Women with Accommodation, Support, and Public Spaces

Abandoned since 2011, the Hospice San Lazaro constitutes a closed block that is only waiting to be opened in a new relationship with the city (Fig. 4). The most prestigious parts of the building are located along Ambato Street and need rehabilitation (Fig. 5). In the rear part, other buildings of little interest are to be demolished to provide new edifications and a park. The main objective is therefore to open the hospice enclosure and make it possible to cross it (Fig. 6). The rehabilitation of the existing building makes it possible to accommodate women residents with accommodation spaces, regular visitors with support spaces, and occasional visitors with public spaces (Fig. 7). The accommodation spaces are located around the void of one of the courtyards to maintain some privacy (Fig. 8). At the other extremity are the accompanying spaces, which include associative premises, medical care, a nursery for children and workshops. Between these two large spaces, a desacralized chapel allows for the passage of different systems of circulation with independent walkways without crossings (Fig. 9).

Likewise, this former chapel communicates with the central cloister, which becomes a space for everyone (Fig. 10). It is a place of passage and distribution to a restaurant, a museum or to access the private parts receiving new accommodation and workshops that fit into the slope (Fig. 11). The development of this rear part reproduces the spirit of a new cloister in a three-dimensional multiplication (Fig. 12). The accommodations have several typologies with intermediate patios that consider the sunlight that is very important to consider in Ecuador (Figs. 13 and 14). And it is brick that is used as a building material, some of which are perforated to filter light and let air through. The entire spatial proposal for the San Lazaro hospice is defined between intimacy and openness to the city (Fig. 15). From this hospice, we transit to another place, also abandoned, which is the El Sena swimming pool, of which the program is an extension.

Fig. 4 The San Lazaro hospice in its urban context

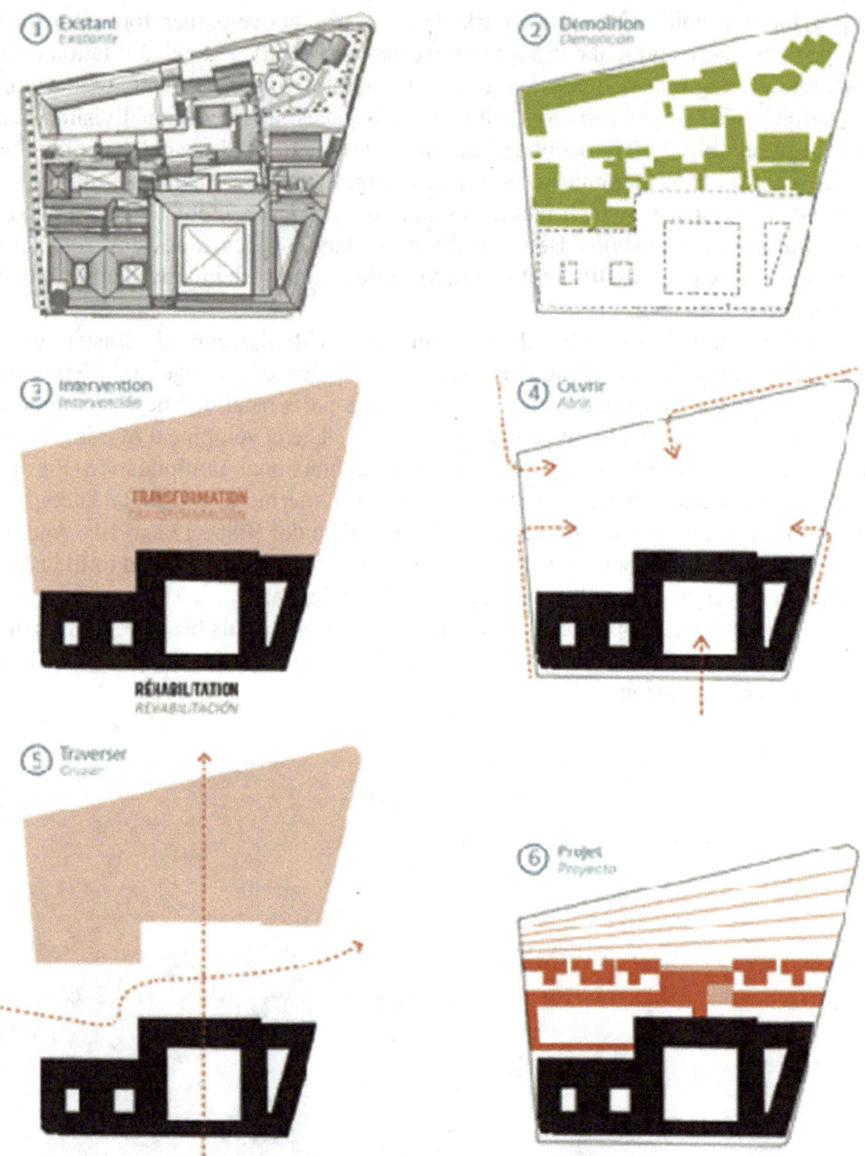

Fig. 5 The existing, the demolitions, the intervention, the openings, the crossings and the project

Fig. 6 The different ways to get to the Hospice San Lazaro from the city

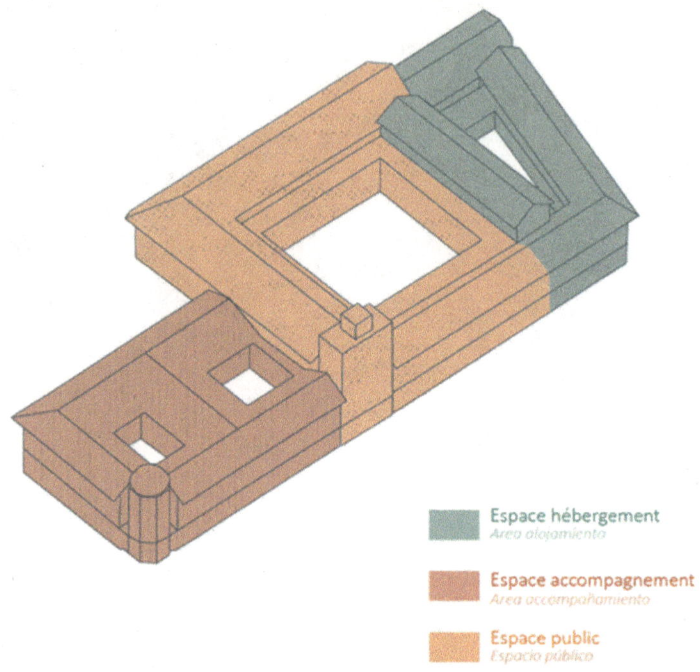

Fig. 7 Rehabilitated areas with accommodation, support and public spaces

Fig. 8 The intimate courtyard of the accommodations

Fig. 9 The old chapel and the circulation crossroads

Fig. 10 The public space

Fig. 11 Rehabilitation and new spaces proposed in relation to the slope

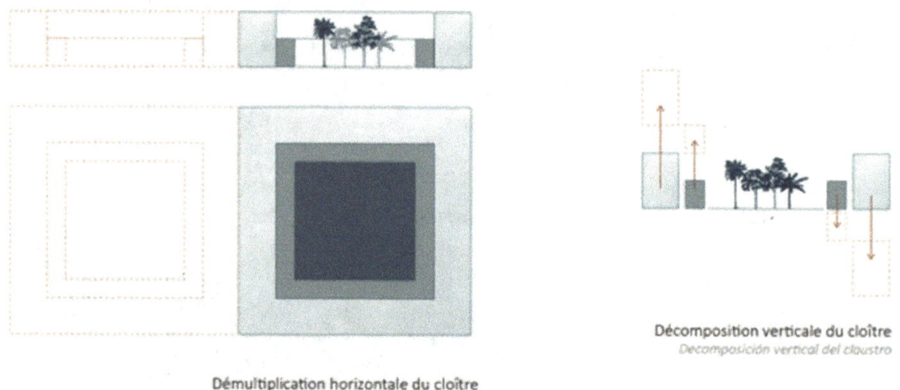

Fig. 12 Demultiplication/decomposition of the cloister space

4 The El Sena Swimming Pool. A Leisure Center, Spaces for Handicrafts, Workshops for the Manufacture of Housing Prototypes for the Poorest People

Built in 1815, the El Sena swimming pool was originally intended for the military and became public in 1938 (Fig. 16). Its activity was abandoned in 1980 and it remains unoccupied today. The program for this former swimming pool includes a public meeting and leisure area, workshops with the sale of handicrafts, and construction workshops for building prototypes or renovating existing houses with local and traditional materials such as Adobe and Bahareque (Figs. 17 and 18). However, the existing state shows very damaged built parts which are destined for demolition (Fig. 19).

As a replacement, new buildings are proposed that take into consideration the rhythms that make up the existing state. These rhythms continue as a weave to

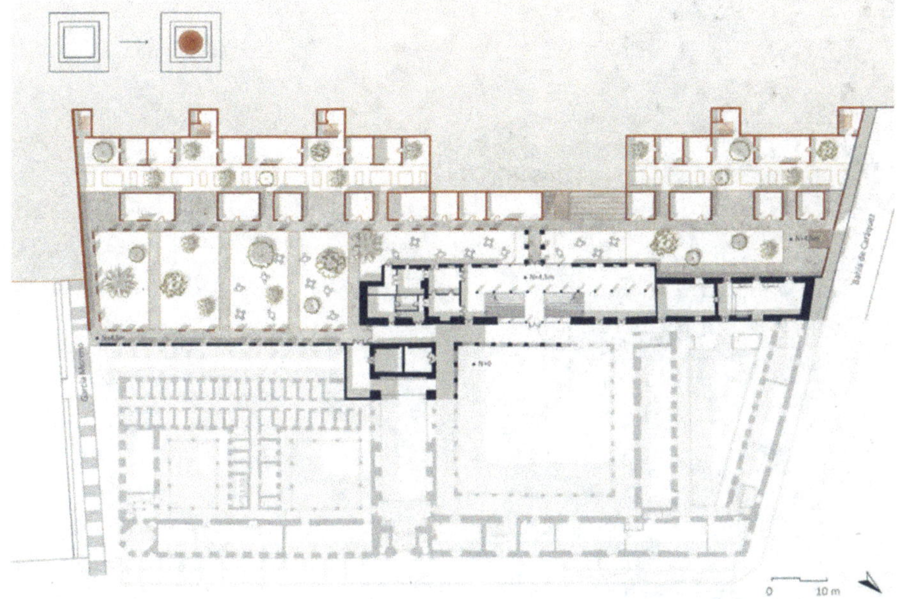

Fig. 13 Plan of the housing, workshops and patios

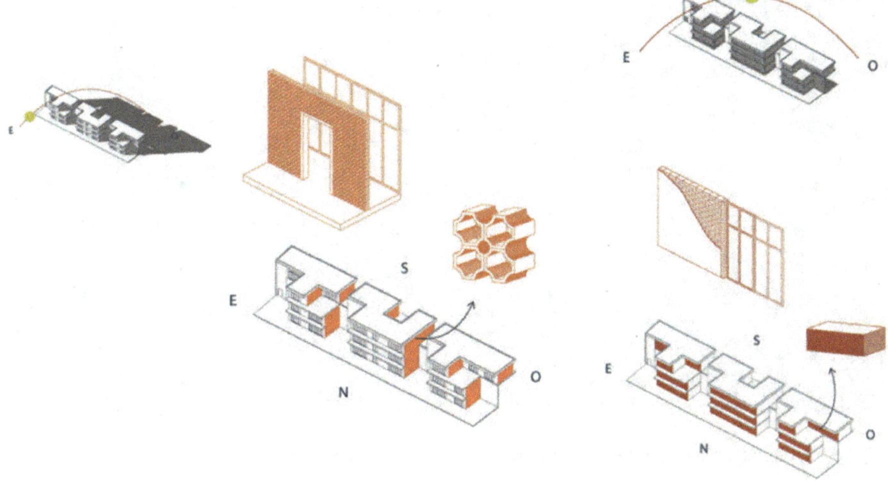

Fig. 14 Materiality and consideration of sunlight

Fig. 15 Prospects between the new and the old, between inside and outside

become a structure and the whole remains connected to the city in three phases that are inscribed in the slope (Figs. 20 and 21). The lower part is the entertainment area. The middle part is dedicated to crafts and in the upper part are the workshops for building with local resources. These workshops are divided into different areas according to their activities. On one side is located the prefabrication of everything made of wood, including the frames for the Bahareque (Figs. 22 and 23). And the other

Fig. 16 The activity of the swimming pool after 1938 and the current state

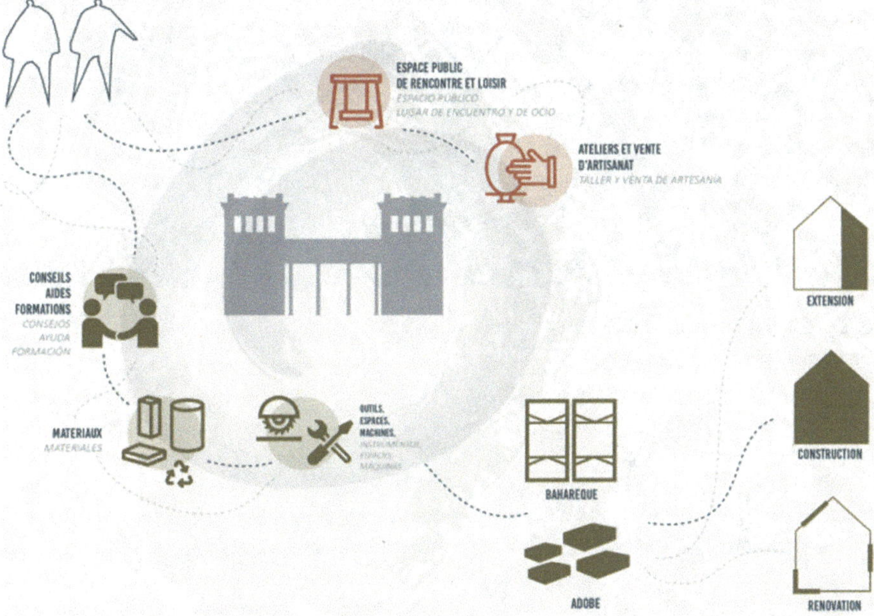

Fig. 17 Principles and strategies of interventions

side is intended for the manufacture of everything made of earth for the preparation of prototypes (Fig. 24). The two workshops together allow for the manufacture of prototypes made of local materials and know-how. In their design, each prototype is imagined as an anti-seismic and expandable unit that adapts to its environment (Fig. 25). Considering sunlight and air circulation (Fig. 26), all the constructive assemblies were studied in detail (Fig. 27) with enough freedom for these prototypes to find a place on the slopes of the Panecillo hill in response to the lack of housing, in a climate of well-being, for the most deprived (Fig. 28). To conclude on the city of Quito, these experiments make it possible to give new life to historical buildings. And through their programs, they offer protective structures for women without separating

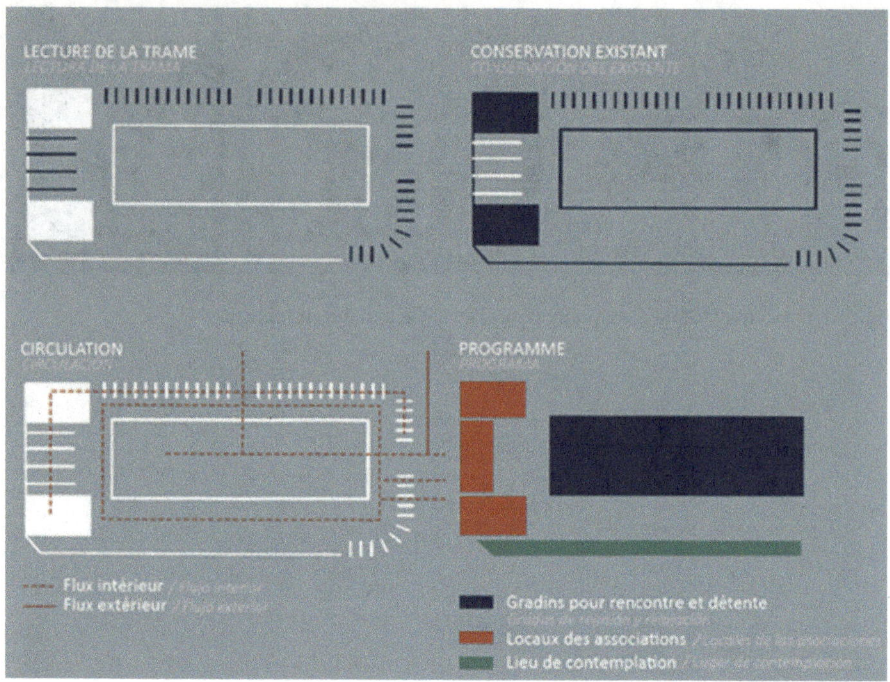

Fig. 18 Spatial intervention schemes

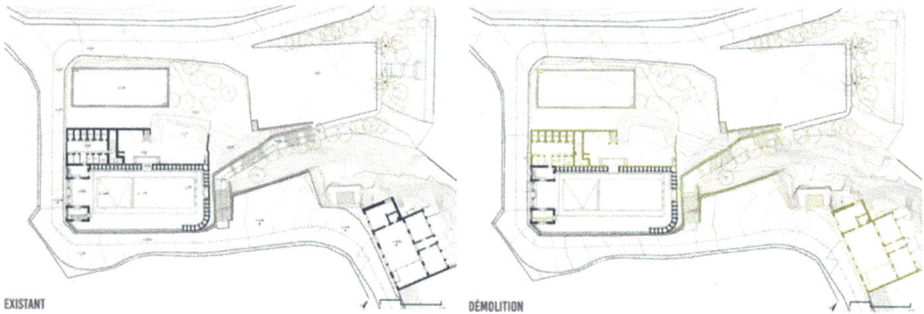

Fig. 19 Existing condition and demolition proposals

them from a social framework that is important to maintain so that they can regain their dignity.

Fig. 20 The three phases of intervention as they relate to the slope

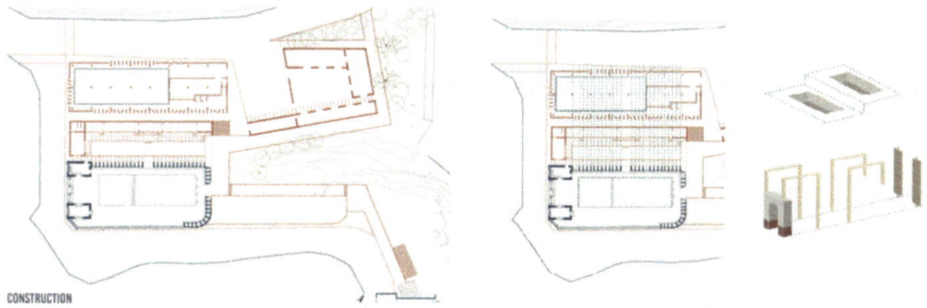

Fig. 21 New edifications and the consideration of the rhythms of the existing state

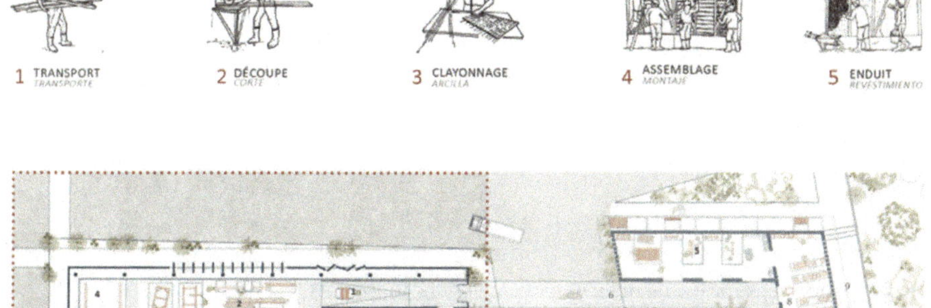

Fig. 22 Workshops for the prefabrication of wooden frames

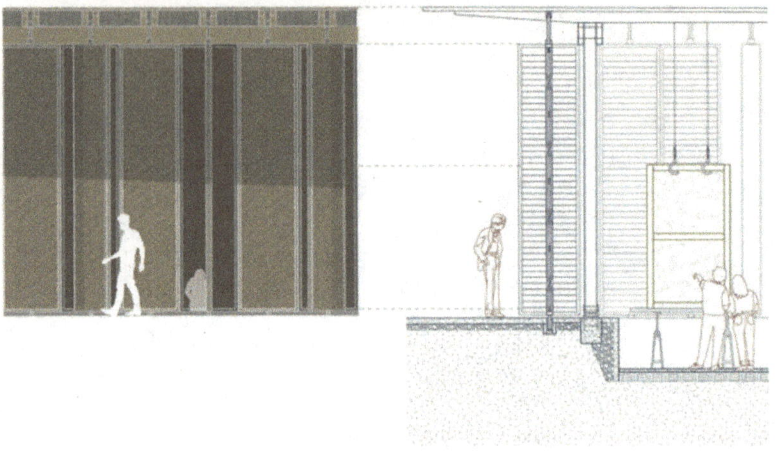

Fig. 23 Elevation and section, detail of the workshops

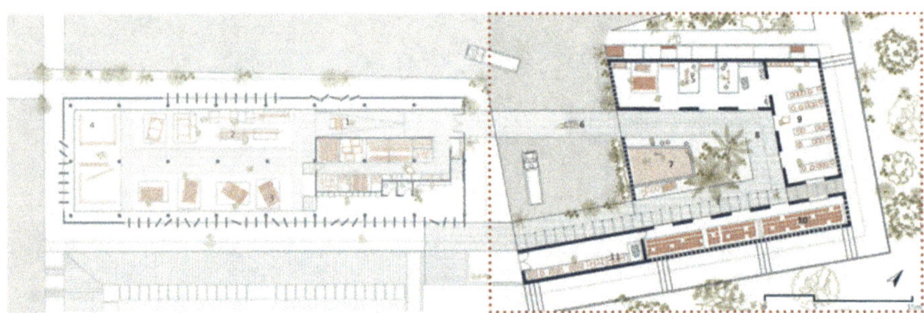

Fig. 24 Workshops for the manufacture of clay bricks for prototypes

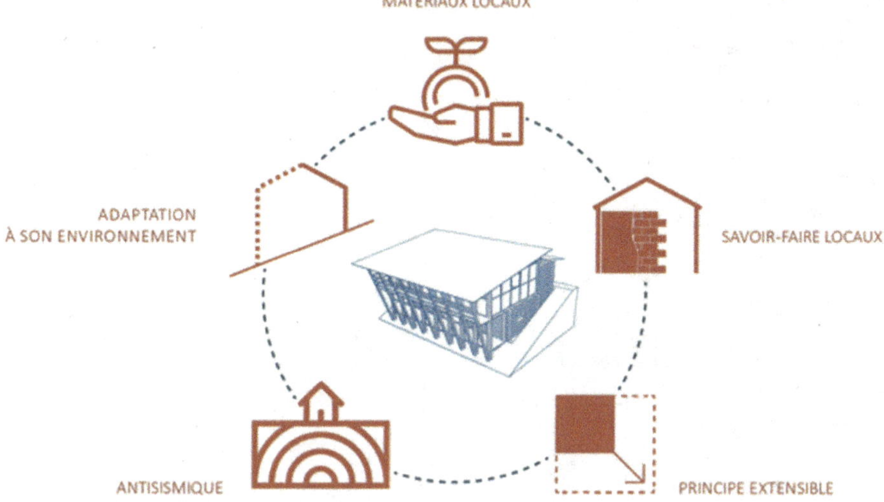

Fig. 25 Schemes of the principles taken into account for the development of a prototype

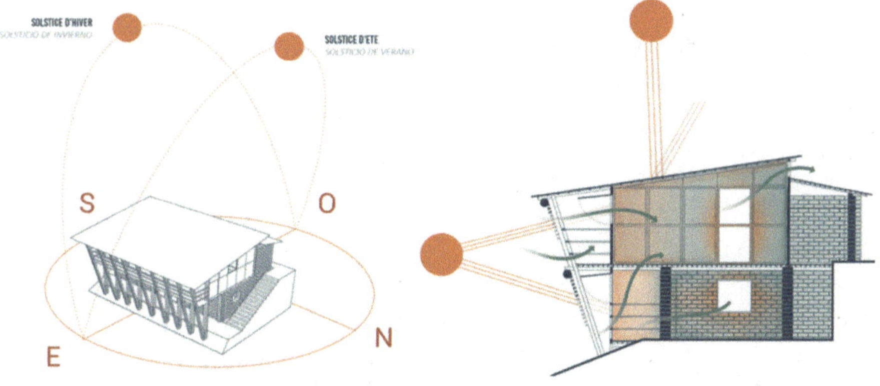

Fig. 26 The relationship between sunlight, materiality and spatiality

5 Bab El-Wazir Street in Cairo. A Look at the Spontaneous to Study the Good Life. A Social Centre for Women and a Dispensary

The city of Cairo is a megalopolis with an imperiled historical center and Bab el-Wazir Street belongs to this ancient center [5]. Forgotten and neglected by the public authorities, this street is a little more than 1 km long with a steep declivity. In its everyday appropriation, it is occupied by particularly interesting spontaneous

Fig. 27 Detailed section of a prototype

Fig. 28 Testing the prototypes on the Panecillo hill

situations (Fig. 29). To study the effervescence of these arrangements, representations drawn from in situ surveys were used to better show the relationships between spatiality, appropriation, mobility, or fixed situations that occur in everyday life.

By drawing and measuring, it is possible to understand what protects, what is attractive, what is comfortable (Figs. 30 and 31). Based on these instructive considerations, several architectural proposals were considered, including a social center for women to alleviate difficult situations (Fig. 32).

As in Quito, the condition of women in Cairo is very difficult to live with. This first proposal is located on an unoccupied site that is currently closed off by a wall. The development of the programs considers the activity observed in the street with a transition made by small shops (Fig. 33). These shops act as a filter and proceed from a cooling intention and a winding principle to access the distribution of internal spaces.

Fig. 29 The spontaneous occupation of the street

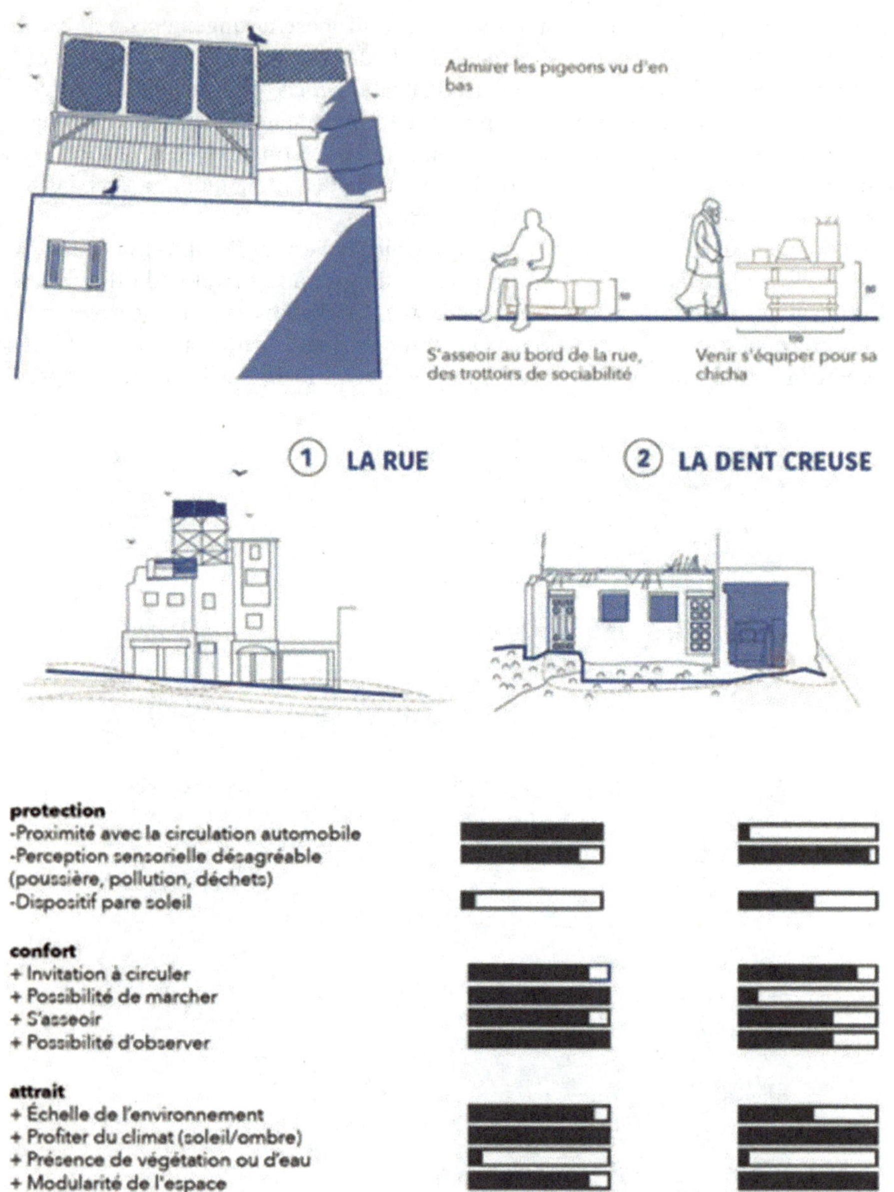

Fig. 30 Protection, comfort, attractiveness, and measures

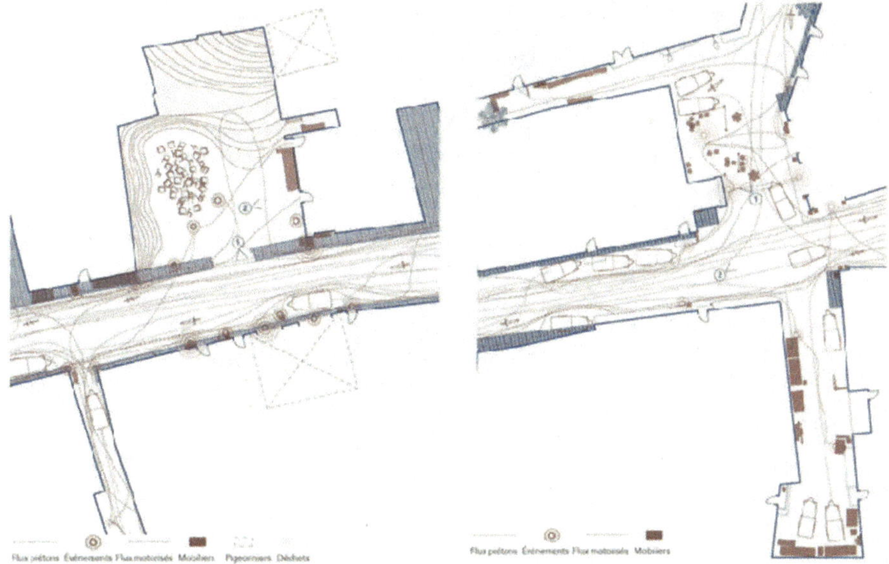

Fig. 31 Drawings of everyday situations

The different functions revolve around a central courtyard that allows air movement and light to enter (Figs. 34 and 35). The materiality of the building is based on local and traditional techniques. Brick, stone, lime, marble, limestone, and wood are used to reinterpret contemporary vernacular architecture. The ensemble presents two constructive variants, one in brick, the other in stone, to test the composition of the building in its spatiality (Fig. 36).

The second proposal is a dispensary to respond to the lack of this type of activity in this part of the city. Its location is mainly degraded (Fig. 37). The buildings surrounding the unbuilt space are very fragile. The proposed structure plays a dual role, that of consolidating the existing with detailed constructive principles and at the same time being able to accommodate new spaces that will remedy a medical deficiency (Figs. 38, 39 and 40). To conclude on Bab el Wazir Street, by considering women in difficulty and people waiting for care, it is possible to give this neglected part of the historic center a new dynamic which takes into consideration traditional construction techniques but also the spontaneous to correctly apprehend the good life of the public space.

Fig. 32 Location of the women's social center and the dispensary

6 Baghère and Its Region. A Women's House and Accompanying Buildings to Reconsider Environmental, Social, and Mental Ecology

The last site studied is on the African continent [6]. The Baghère region is in the south/western part of Senegal, and it is again a women's house and accompanying buildings that are planned. The site lies along the Casamance River and consists of forests, tree cultivation and agriculture (Fig. 41). The whole of this territory presents the problem of three distinct and indissociable ecologies. The environment, the social and the mental are the major axes of reflection for this very poorly urbanized area (Fig. 42). This lack of urbanity should not be overlooked, as the problems encountered

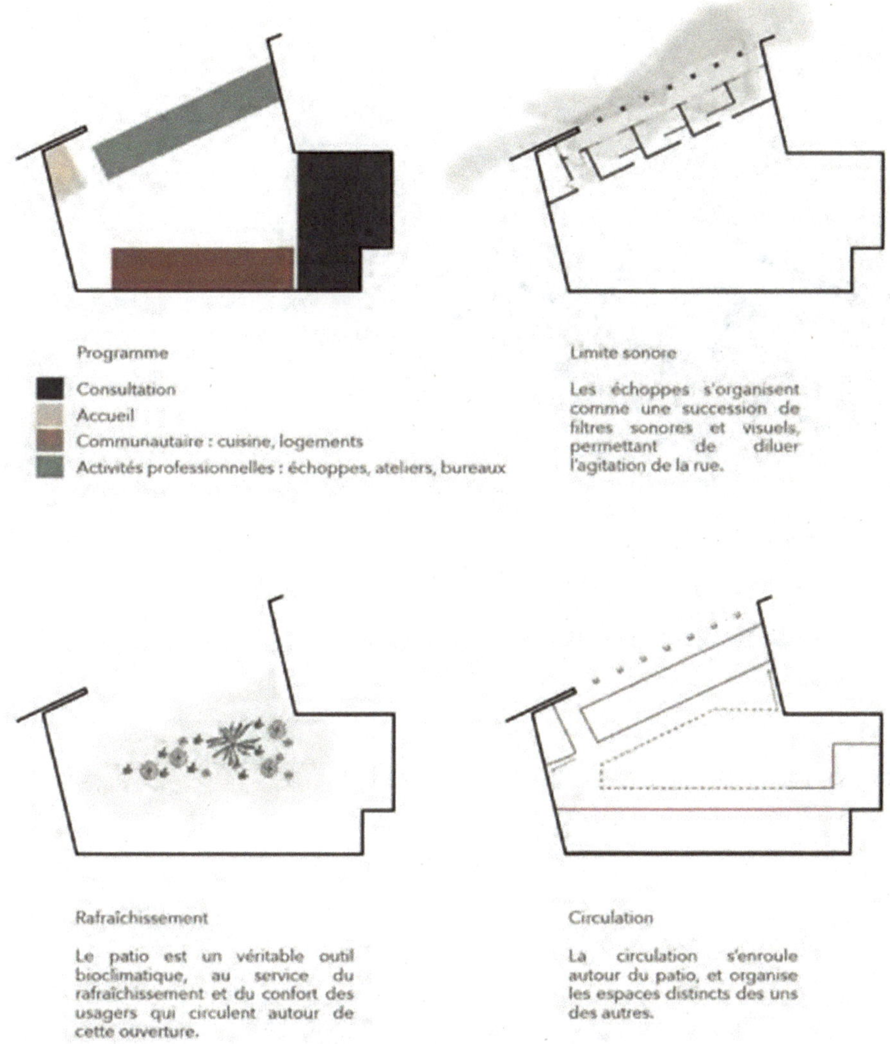

Fig. 33 Main characteristics of the social center

in this case study can be transposed to another scale to regenerate much denser urban areas. With the presence of a main and secondary roads as a starting point, the project hypotheses aim to counter the effects of climate change in a sustainable manner and are subdivided into a waste recycling center, small shops, packaging of products, a refuge for women and the reinforcement of school infrastructures (Fig. 43).

All these edifications revolve around the women's house, which becomes the heart of it. This house contains various services which are articulated around a courtyard with an internal circulation to distribute the covered spaces (Figs. 44, 45, 46, 47 and

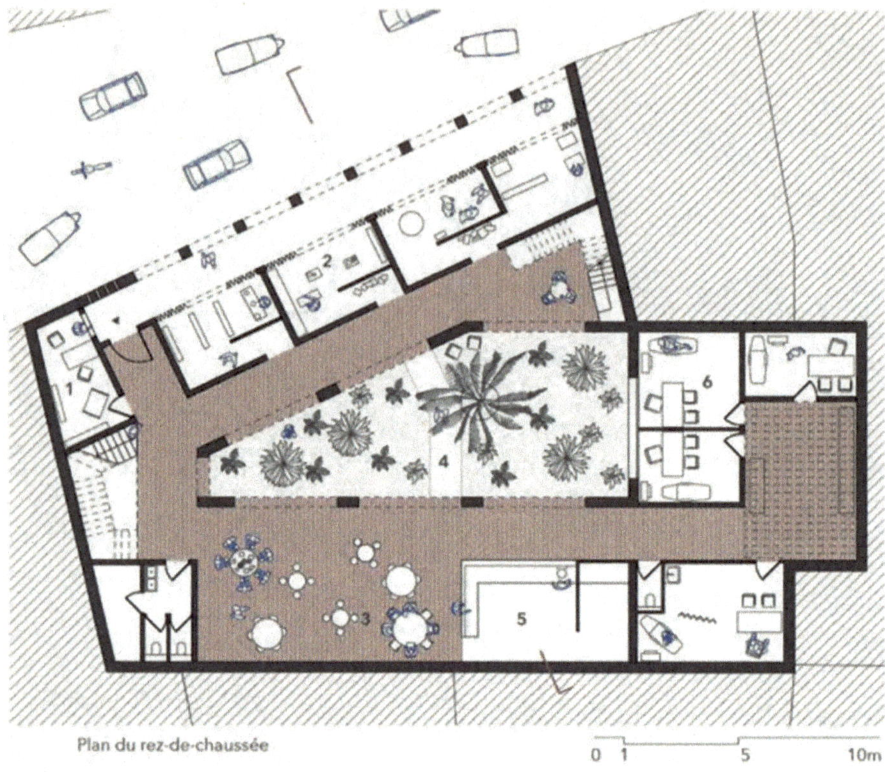

Fig. 34 Plan of the ground floor of the women's social center

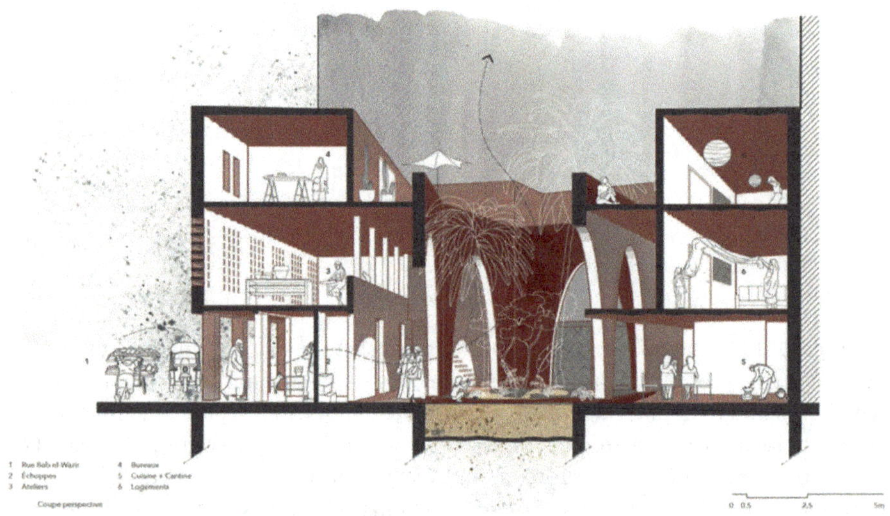

Fig. 35 Prospect of the women's social center and its main spatial characteristics

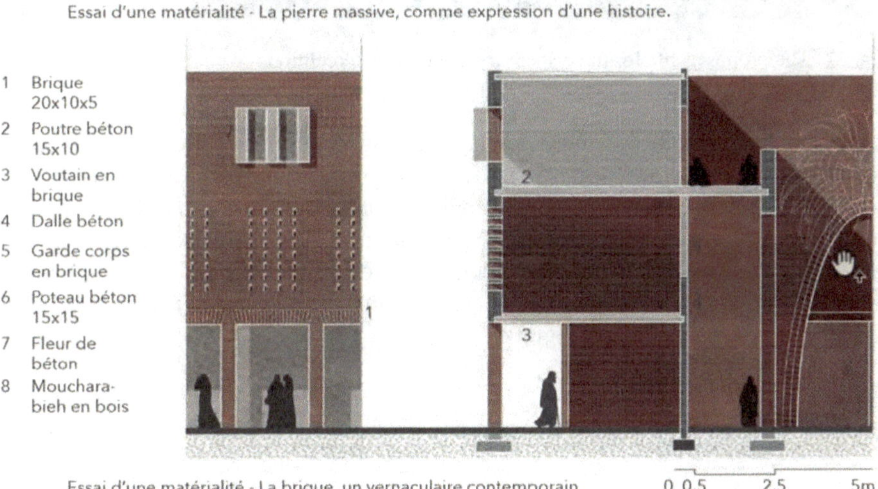

Fig. 36 Two possibilities of materiality, stone and brick

48). The exterior is surrounded by cultivable areas and a tree that provides a place for discussion. Very close to this main building, a women's refuge is built on a raised platform with a protected intimate area, a shared, sheltered courtyard and intimate spaces for sleeping (Fig. 49).

Between the shops and production (Fig. 50), which are gathering places, a Warka Tower transforms air into water. This tower can produce more than a hundred liters of water per year, which seems small but essential in this part of the world. Concerning the school complex, existing buildings are given new platforms, new roofs, new protected passages. And all these protections provide shadows to improve the well-being of everyone (Fig. 51).

These architectural reflections are very simple in their attention. They are based on local strategies to respond to large-scale problems. The proposed changes tend

Fig. 37 The proposed site for the dispensary, the existing condition

towards gender equality, better access to education and the preservation of biodiversity. These transformations include a waste recycling network, a freshwater network associated with small shops and packaging. And the practice of permaculture responds to the problem of the salinization of the Casamance River. All these systems are at the service of the women whose daily lives are linked to agriculture in the region. And all these principles can be multiplied to regenerate other places on the scale of this territory (Fig. 52).

7 Conclusion

Whether we are in Quito, Cairo or the Baghère region, all these proposals show and demonstrate the importance of finding the right equilibrium when developing architectural project hypotheses. An equilibrium that is inspired by Alberti's thought when he compares nature to health in response to citizens in difficulty. And by analogy with these edifying words, the project hypotheses developed on the three sites have all the will to be modest while keeping a strength that lies in the impacts they generate. This gives us the opportunity to recall that the word modest also has the same etymological root as the words measure, moderation or medicine. Thus, with intentions that are necessarily only architectural, it is possible to put into action a measured equilibrium between the natural, the artificial and the human for a common well-being that nevertheless remains in constant movement.

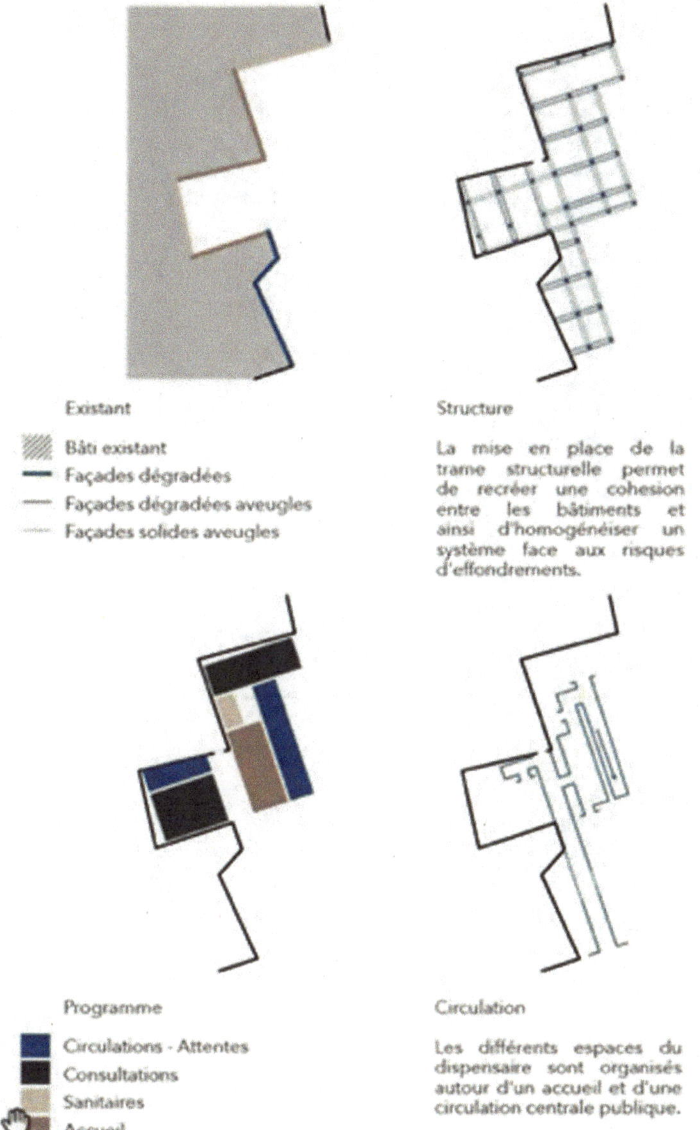

Fig. 38 Existing, structure, programme and circulation

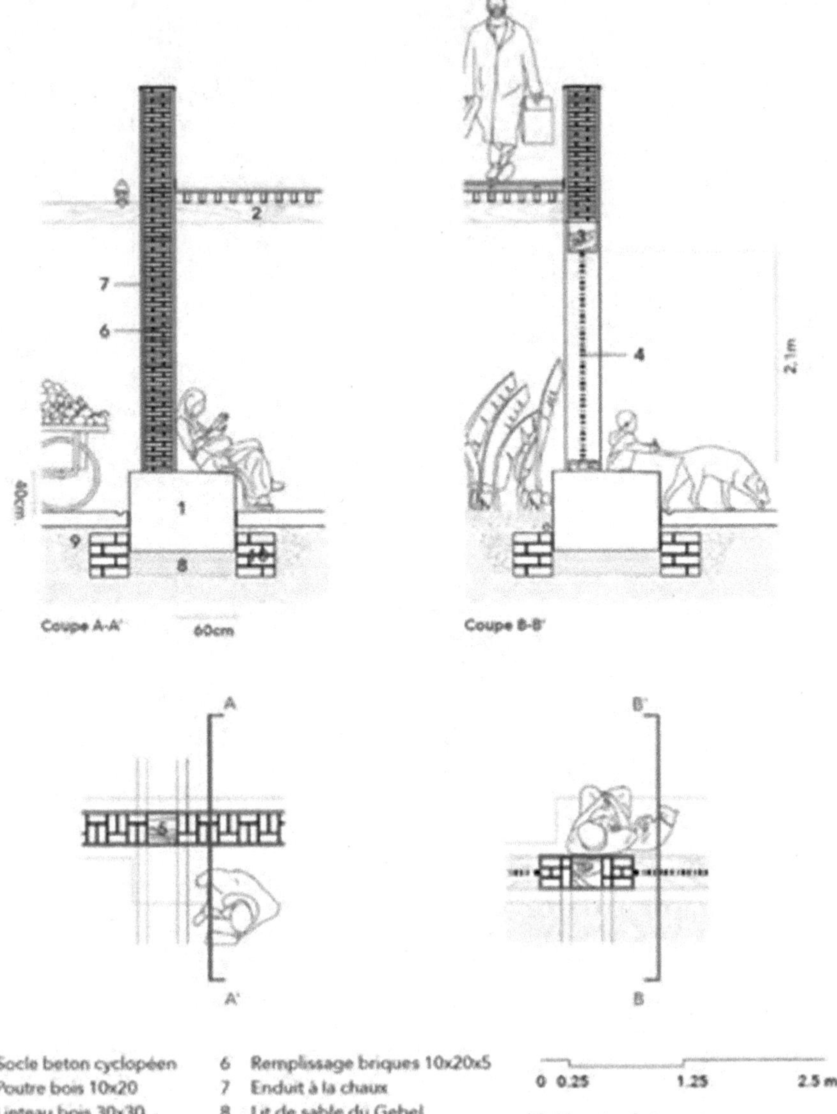

Fig. 39 Constructive details

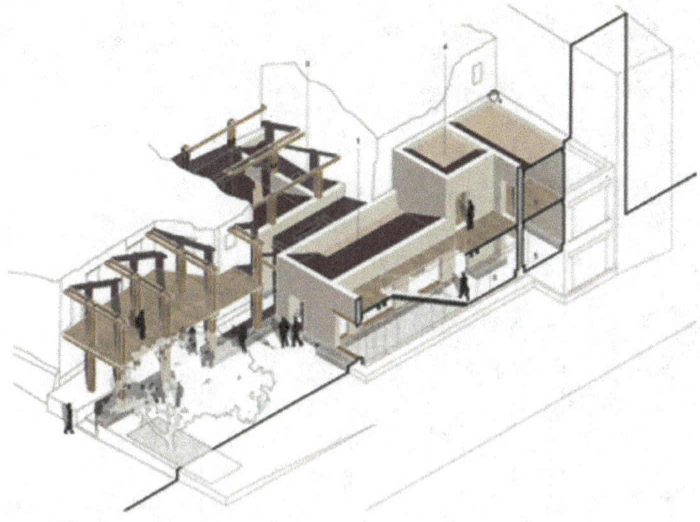

Fig. 40 Axonometric view of the dispensary, a double consolidation

Fig. 41 The Casamance River and the situation of Baghère

Fig. 42 The environment, the social, the mental. Three axes of reflection for ecology

Fig. 43 The women's house and accompanying buildings

Fig. 44 The women's house in its environment

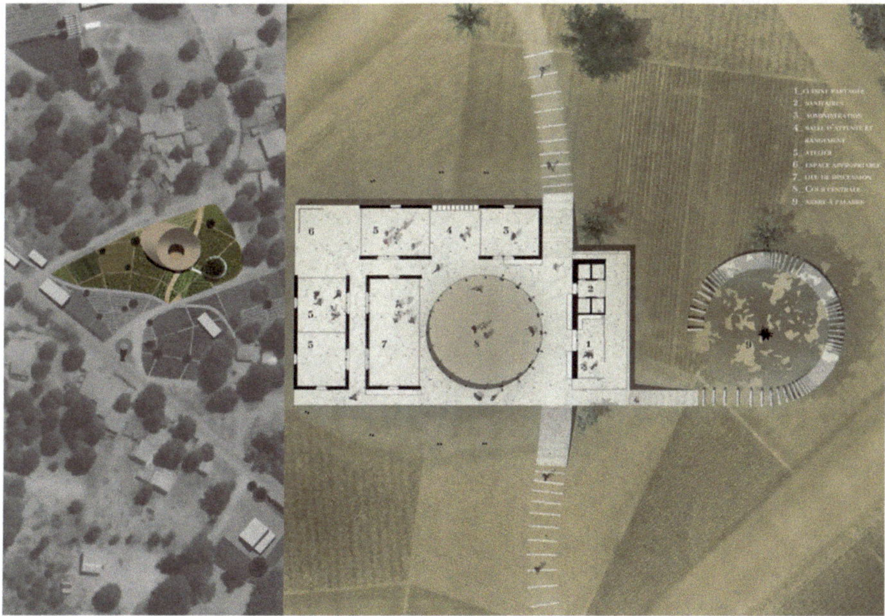

Fig. 45 General and detailed plan of the house for women

Fig. 46 View from the entrance of the house for women

Fig. 47 The section

Fig. 48 View from the central courtyard

Fig. 49 The women's refuge and its protected areas

Fig. 50 View of the outdoor meeting spaces

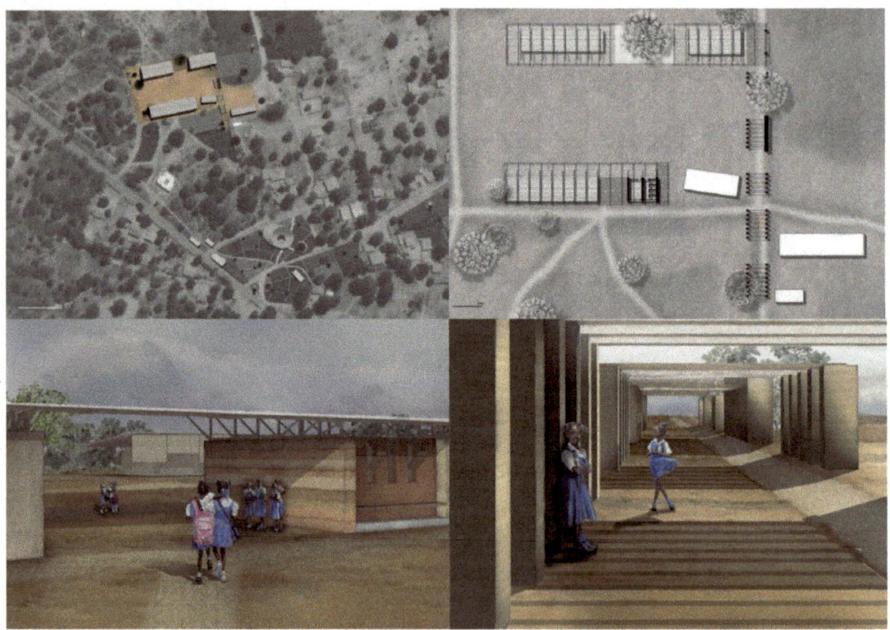

Fig. 51 The existing school complex receives new platforms, new roofs and protected walkways

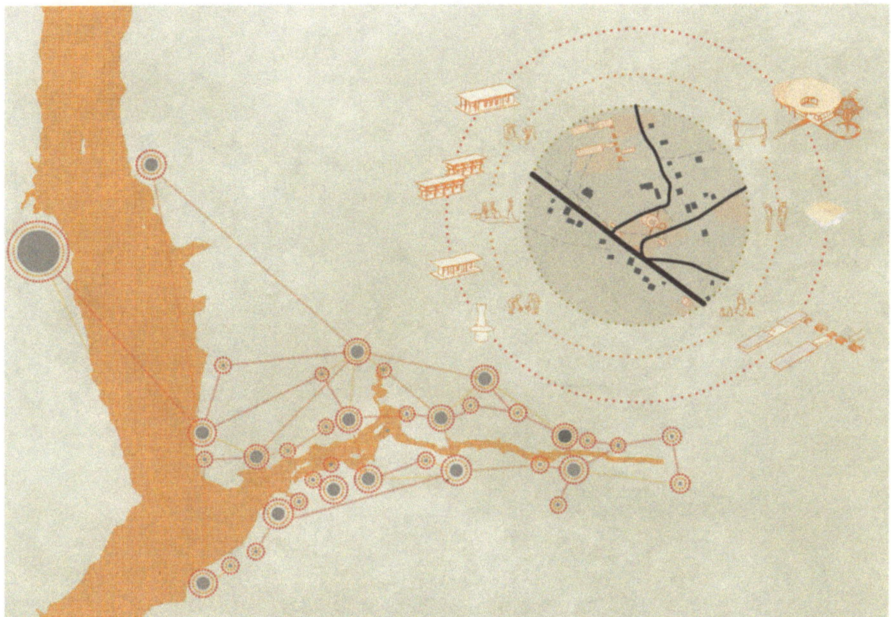

Fig. 52 Schemes of the proposals at the Baghère and territorial scales

References

1. Alberti LB (1991) On the art of building in ten books, translated by Rykwert J, Leach N, Tavernor R, p. 130, The MIT Press
2. Alberti LB (1966) L'architettura. Traduzione di Giovanni Orlandi. Edizioni Il Polifilo, Milano, pp 368–369. Translation of the quote into Italian: « Del resto è noto che la natura in tutte le sue manifestazioni preferisce il giusto mezzo: la buona salute stessa consiste nell'intreccio e nel contemperamento di fattori diversi, ove la via di mezzo è sempre la piu gradita ». In Leon Battista Alberti, L'architettura, libro V, Opere di carattere particulare. Original quote in Latin: « Sed palam est naturam in re omni gaudere temperamento; quin et sanitas ipsa haud aliud est quam complexi, ex quibus constet temperamentum; et mediocria semper delectant ». In Leonis Baptistae Alberti, De re aedificatoria, de singulorum operibus, liber quintus
3. Alberti LB (2004) L'art d'édifier. Traduction Pierre Caye et Françoise Choay, p 239, Éditions du Seuil. Translation of the quote into French: « Il est évident qu'en toutes choses la nature aime la juste mesure; davantage, la santé elle-même n'est rien d'autre qu'une composition d'éléments d'où naît sa juste mesure; car la modération plaît toujours ». In livre V, Édifices destinés aux catégories particulières de citoyens, chapitre 8
4. Giroux E, Perrot F, Schneider V, Virolle M (2021) Quito: Réinclure la colline du Panecillo, vers une réactivation de son patrimoine remarquable. End of studies projects, Director of studies Thépot P, co-direction Llorca N, Vaca V, UISEK ARQ
5. Aimonetto L, Barre N, Boinay G (2020) Le Caire: Vers une transition post-urbaine. End of studies projects, Director of studies Thépot, P
6. Sahy C, Yahouni M (2021) Sénégal, la Vallée de Tanaff: Réflexions multi-scalaires au service d'abris d'initiatives pour les populations rurales. End of studies projects, Director of studies Thépot, P

We for Us: Collective Action in the Favelas During the Pandemic

Sonia Fleury

Abstract "We for Us" is the motto used by activists of social movements and urban collectives from favelas and peripheries in Brazil. The motto demarcates that, in the absence of public policies, the residents need to organize themselves to supply collective services and means of consumption necessary for their well-being in the territory. The COVID-19 pandemic that devastated and transformed the world from 2020 onward found Brazil amid a process of dismantling the state apparatus in charge of public policies that transform rights-in-law into rights-in-exercise. The existence of the national health system (SUS) is considered the most democratic and inclusive policy built after democratization in Brazil. But its renewed base of social support and successful institutionalization and development of state capacities were unable to sufficiently serve the populations in favelas and peripheries to face the health, economic, and social crisis caused by the pandemic. Community organizations reacted to this situation by mobilizing internal and external resources. Many actions took place as part of the biopolitics of resistance, based on mobilization and social organization in collective measures aimed at compensating the government's omission. Other initiatives were developed as part of insurgent citizenship, claiming the protection of rights and demanding the government's effort to meet the population's needs.

Keywords Favelas · National health system · SUS · Brazil · Collective · Actions · Pandemic

1 Introduction

Social movement activists and urban collectives in favelas and peripheries in Brazil use the motto "We for Us" to stress community self-organization to obtain collective services and means of consumption in the absence of public policies in a territory. The history of favelas is marked by resistance to the erasure of identity, culture, and

S. Fleury (✉)
Center for Strategic Studies/FIOCRUZ, Dictionary of Favelas Marielle Franco
Wikifavelas.Com.Br, Rio de Janeiro, Brazil
e-mail: prof.soniafleury@gmail.com

A. Battisti et al. (eds.), *Equity in Health and Health Promotion in Urban Areas*, Green Energy and Technology, https://doi.org/10.1007/978-3-031-16182-7_10

knowledge of black populations and immigrants from the country's poorest regions searching for better living conditions. It is also a history of collective construction of urban space through cooperation and residents' organizations that fight for their demands in the relationship with governments and political representatives and a long tradition of daily vicinity solidarity and solidarity with strangers during frequent catastrophic events [1].

Even with the predominant feeling among older residents that they produced that part of the city (their neighborhood, their favela), they do not feel they share the condition of citizenship, the sense of belonging to the political community of citizens [2]. Urban property and housing policies push the poorest population to distant areas or areas with more difficult urbanization, such as the hills of Rio de Janeiro, public or vacant lands on which precarious housing has been built without urban infrastructure [3, 4].

The state produces both the legal city and the territory of illegalism [5]—the favelas and peripheries—the favelas and peripheries—where the very construction of order is a product of negotiation between residents, or an order imposed by armed drug dealers and militia. The populations inhabiting such territories are often subjected to state violence (with threats of removal and police incursions that disrespect human and civil rights), the violence and discretion of the armed groups that dominate the territory, and the symbolic violence that manifests as discrimination and prejudice against these residents.

However, the permanent feeling of precariousness and vulnerability did not prevent favelas from having exponential growth in recent decades. In 2018, 15.2% of the Brazilian population lived in these areas, spread all over the country. The largest concentration of favelas is in the Southeast region (the richest of the country, including the cities of São Paulo and Rio de Janeiro), where the ten largest favelas are located. According to the 2010 Census, the favela of Heliópolis in the city of São Paulo had 41,000 residents and the favela in Rocinha, Rio de Janeiro, had 69,000 residents. The population living in these territories in São Paulo summed more than 2 million, and in Rio de Janeiro, almost 1.4 million. The census showed that 11,425,644 people lived in favelas and peripheries—called by the Brazilian Institute of Geography and Statistics "subnormal agglomerations"—in the country. The average monthly income was below the minimum wage. Comparatively, this number surpassed the entire population of Portugal and was three times greater than that of Uruguay. It is essential to mention that the 2010 Census offers an outdated picture, but it is still cited since the current government canceled the census scheduled to be held in 2020. As there is no comparable data from the census to analyze the period, this study uses data produced more recently by private organizations.,

The Instituto Locomotiva, in partnership with Data Favela and the Central Única de Favelas [6], found that, in 2021, favela residents represented 8% of the Brazilian population, with the majority of this population in the Southeast. In relative terms, in the cities of the poorest regions, in the North and Northeast regions, the people living in favelas represent more than half of the residents of the capitals, such as Belém do Pará (54.48%). The same organizations conducted the research "Economy of Favelas—Income and Consumption in Brazilian Favelas," where they identified that 67% of favela residents are black, while in Brazil, black people count 55% of the population; women are head of 49% of households, and the total amount of resources moved by favela residents reached BRL 119.8 billion in the year [7]. Such data show the social and economic dimension of favelas in Brazil and the geopolitics of urban exclusion with evident intersectionality with poverty, gender, and race.

The social inclusion policies implemented from 2000 onward included the recovery of the minimum wage, income transfer to families registered in extreme poverty, quota policies for access to public institutions of higher education, student financing to enter private higher education institutions, personal credit for low-income families, urbanization policies in some favelas, homeownership policy for the low-income population, expansion of primary healthcare and education network, among others. As a result, Brazil is not one of the poorest countries but is well known as one of the most unequal. Although such policies were insufficient to address the issue of inequality as required, they certainly changed the structure of social stratification, reducing misery and poverty. Recently, the financial globalization and the predominance of austerity economic policies worldwide have increased the concentration of income in the wealthiest 1% of the population. Brazil has not been immune to this phenomenon. Therefore, poverty reduction and income concentration co-occurred for a short period until frustrated expectations of social mobility and consumption exploded in large urban demonstrations in 2013 [1]

The critical political instability that followed the 2013 demonstrations, and the economic decline partly stemming from the fall in commodity prices, were appropriated by the most conservative political forces—bankers, mainstream media, members of parliament, judges, neo-Pentecostal pastors, foreign companies, and governments. These forces sponsored the impeachment of President Dilma Rousseff and the arrest of former President Lula da Silva, preventing him from running for the 2018 presidential election. Instead of the traditional coups that predominated in Latin America, this process of de-democratization was a lawfare. Inspired by the Italian experience of Mani Pulite, the fight against corruption forced the replacement of the political group in government by its contenders. With the impeachment, the deterioration of the social protection network under implementation since the 1988 Federal Constitution began and deepened in 2018, with the election of President Jair Bolsonaro and the performance of an authoritarian populist government.

The COVID-19 pandemic that devastated and transformed the world from 2020 onward began in Brazil amidst the dismantling of the state apparatus and public policies responsible for transforming rights-in-law into rights-in-exercise. The national health system (SUS) was not enough to ensure that the favela and periphery populations were sufficiently served in the face of the health, economic, and social crisis caused by the pandemic. SUS is considered the most democratic and inclusive policy built after democratization in Brazil because of its successful development of state capacities. According to data from the Brazilian Institute of Geography and Statistics -IBGE, severe food insecurity occurred in 10.3 million Brazilian homes between 2017 and 2018. Almost 5% of the Brazilian population returned to living with hunger, while 36.7% of households had some degree of food insecurity during the period.

Once again, the favela and peripheral populations had to mobilize collective actions, as in the motto "We for Us," creating innovative ways to face the pandemic and overcome the absence of public policies. The second section of this article analyzes the trajectory of SUS, from creation and institutionalization up to the challenges facing the COVID pandemic. In the third section, we explain collective action in favelas due to recent subjectivation and organization processes resulting from social and cultural changes. In the fourth section, we deal with the symbolic and material disputes in the face of the pandemic. Finally, we present the final considerations.

2 Building Democracy and the Right to Health in Brazil

The social movements engaged in the overthrow of the military dictatorship were highly active in the 1970s–1980s, associating popular demands in the areas of urban reform, health reform, and the fight against poverty and misery with the struggle for a democratic regime to assure civil, political, and social rights. The proposal to build a democratic society sought to affirm the principles of equity and social justice "to establish rights as parameters in the reorganization of the economy and society" [8].

The formed public space spread the notion of the "right to have rights," and the struggles for citizenship became the unifying banner of different political, economic, cultural, environmental, and social demands. Even though the new unionism vigorously propelled the struggle for democracy, the expansion of citizenship as a public space and legal-institutional construction that materializes the correlation of forces in a given society proved to be fundamental for the agglutination of urban struggles.

One of the major movements that emerged during this period was the sanitary movement, which formulated and promoted sanitary reform [9]. It was composed of intellectuals and health professionals, inspired by Gramsci—concerning the struggle for hegemony, essential in changing the correction of forces—and in the teachings of Poulantzas—on how disputes for power cross the state and not only society. After all, it is about the construction of the political subject or the **Subjectivation dimension of the reform process**. Thus, the sanitary movement was able to build:

- a field of knowledge, collective health, considering health as a social practice, subject to social determinants;
- a social organization led by institutions that produce, unite and disseminate a new health conscience (such as CEBES [10] and ABRASCO [11]), with a social base in permanent expansion and renewal;
- an original political and sectoral political project, the sanitary reform, which was inspired by the Italian sanitary reform but without a social base of the labor movement; in the British National Health Service, even in the absence of a centrally organized public service network; and in the Cuban model of mobilization of community health workers, even though Brazil was under a coercive and demobilizing regime;

- an architecture of participation, social control, and co-management became a model for other public policies. This arrangement started with the 8th National Health Conference in 1986, a crescent discussion process with the election of delegates that culminated in a national assembly with more than three thousand participants, encompassing government and civil society representatives [12].

All this civic mobilization was conveyed to the National Constituent Assembly, adopting a bottom-up participatory model. The 1988 Federal Constitution instated the aspirations for social democracy in the constitutional text, especially in Title 8 (Social Order) [13].

For the first time, a set of rights encompassing social, environmental, cultural, and protective rights to specific groups -as indigenous people, children, and the older population—was brought together under social justice. Also noteworthy was creating the social security system with its specific budget, including retirement and pension schemes and health and social assistance.

The section in the constitution that addresses health care had innovative characteristics compared to the previous situation in the country since the right to health was guaranteed only to workers employed in the formal labor market (therefore, a contractual right). As a result, workers with legal contracts had access to rehabilitative hospital medicine. At the same time, the rest of the population lacked the right to health care and only got a care in philanthropic institutions and the precarious facilities network of the Ministry of Health and state and local governments' health departments.

The 1988 Constitution considered:

- health as a right for all and a duty of the state;
- an enlarged concept of health assured by a set of social and economic policies aimed at risk reduction and universal and equal access to actions for promotion, protection, and recovery;
- integral attention and equity in the access and use of services;
- all health services have public relevance and must be regulated, supervised, and controlled by public authorities;
- the organization of health actions and services in a regionalized and hierarchical network, decentralized and with a single direction in each sphere of government, with comprehensive care and priority for health promotion.
- community participation at all levels of government. Subsequently, was the creation of sectorial councils aimed at social accountability and co-management, conferences aimed at mobilizing and forming political will, and inter-management commissions, or instances of agreement and negotiation of conflicts between federative entities.

In other words, the constitution offered the design of the national health system (SUS), lately installed by common law. It is about the legal and normative construction of health as a universal and integral social right—**the dimension of the constitutionalization of the reform process**.

From the 1990s onward, the third dimension of the reform process began with creating and implementing SUS. **This dimension was institutionalization.**

The proposal of a universal health system benefited from the timing of the reform associated with the macro-phenomena of the democratic transition. It also helped precede the economic crisis (which explains its generous nature regarding universality and comprehensive health care). However, institutionalization took place in a different context, with significant financial constraints resulting from inflation and austerity measures imposed by dependence on loans from the International Monetary Fund and the World Bank. This restriction implied a reduction in social spending, the impediment of public investment, and restraining the expansion of state capabilities. Thus, public policies were framed in this period by the clash of forces in opposite directions: on the one hand, social pressure to expand coverage and ensure constitutional rights, and, on the other hand, the economic pressure to limit public spending and reducing the role of the state.

The dominance of neoliberalism in the 1990s shifted the political field from organized civil society to philanthropy, from collective movements to entrepreneurial competitive individualism, and from government to the market. Measures were taken to facilitate privatization and contracting out third-party providers to deliver social services in line with the establishment of public spending ceilings with salaries of government officials. Thus, the health area, which was already heavily dependent on the hospital supply of the private sector since the military regime, also started to contract services for the management and provision of services in health care units.

In addition to these political priorities, in line with the hegemony of neoliberalism, the restriction on financing the health sector was the principal and constant economic obstacle to the improvement, expansion, and qualification of SUS. Countries with universal health systems, such as Canada, Spain, and the United Kingdom, invested 7.7%, 6.5%, and 7.9% of GDP in 2015, respectively, while Brazil invested only 3.8% in its national health system. Even in comparison with Latin American countries, such as Argentina and Chile, whose per capita public expenditure on health is, respectively, USD 993 and 1157 ppp, in Brazil, per capita expenditure was only USD 595 ppp in 2015 [14]. More expressive data is public spending per capita per day, estimated at BRL 3.79 in 2019, around the value of one dollar at the time. More expressive data is public spending per capita per day, estimated at BRL 3.79 in 2019, around the value of one dollar.

When the system faces increasing demand and permanent underfunding, the burden ends up weighing more on subnational governments, where health care takes place, despite the national tax burden being disproportionately divided between levels of government with a high concentration in the federal government. For example, in 1991, the composition of SUS funding was 73% from the federal government, 15% from states, and 12% from municipalities. In contrast, in 2019, the federal government contributed 43% of the funding, the states 25%, and the cities 32% [15]. The distortions in fiscal federalism concerning health increase regional inequalities since municipalities and regions with fewer resources are not sufficiently benefited by transfers from the federal government.

After the impeachment of President Rousseff in 2016, a constitutional amendment was enacted, establishing a ceiling to public spending for 20 years. Thus, the historical pattern of underfunding of health became a pattern of de-funding, which implies the reduction of funds assigned to health. As they were already insufficient, universality and comprehensiveness of care are unfeasible for a long time [16].

Despite this adverse situation, SUS experienced significant advances driven by the reform coalition that acquired new characteristics over time. With the cooling of popular and union movements in recent decades, the most critical actors defending SUS became municipal and state health managers, besides the vast range of health professionals. Social movements were also present, participating in health councils and conferences, in large national campaigns to protect rights, and networking between the National Congress and the Federal Supreme Court in defense of measures that favored increasing funding, regulating the private sector, and keeping rights.

One outstanding achievement occurred through reversing the model focused on curative care around the hospital facility (legacy of social security medicine), toward a preventive care model, with the primary health care units (PHC) as the gateway to SUS entry. PHC units work in the most deprived territories with a multidisciplinary family health team and community health agents. In addition to being a fundamental part of the change in the health care model, it proved to be essential for social inclusion. The mere universalization principle was not enough to reach all the vulnerable populations alone, and many continue to be excluded from social protection. Such efforts were reflected in traditional health indicators, such as the increase in life expectancy, which in 1988 was 69.7 years and reached 73.1 years in 2011, and the decrease in infant mortality, which fell from 53.7 per thousand live births in 1990 to 21.17 per thousand live births in 2009. The volume of care in 2011 is also significant, such as the completion of two million births, mobile emergency service assistance to 111 million people, and care to 101.3 million people by 32,000 family health teams [17]. More recently, it has been estimated that the 41,000 multidisciplinary teams serve 130 million Brazilians [18].

Even with significant advances in SUS management and services, considerable inequalities in access and use persist, especially in secondary and tertiary care. The poorest populations, living in peripheral and poorer regions, suffer from problems such as queues at services, lack of professionals in specialties, and delays in receiving surgeries. Perhaps the most significant expression of **the counter-right to health** is the pilgrimage of patients from one health unit to another in search of care. In these cases, the health system does not take responsibility for providing care when demanded in one of its facilities [12]. Although care in PHC units, with the work of family health teams and community health agents, has generated better proximity and reception of users to SUS, the lack of better resources and the low-resolution capacity are obstacles to meeting demands.

According to the 2019 National Health Survey, only 27.9% of Brazilians have a private health plan. While in the wealthiest state, São Paulo, insurance coverage rises to 38.4% of the population, in poorer regions, as in the case of state of Maranhão, only 5% of the inhabitants contracted private health plans [19]. Therefore, SUS serves more than 70% of outpatient and hospital treatment inhabitants. The entire population benefits from epidemiological surveillance, health surveillance, and vaccination coverage.

The COVID-19 pandemic has placed an enormous burden on healthcare systems worldwide, especially those with chronic underfunding problems and poor distribution of the service network. The initial lack of knowledge about the virus and the disease, the high rates of contagion, and the absence of vaccines brought insecurity to the world population. In Brazil, the strong impact on the hospital structure led to the channeling of extraordinary resources to expand the supply of beds in intensive care units, many of them in temporary units, not permanently incorporated into the network. The high dependence on imported inputs placed the country in a situation of extreme vulnerability due to the intense process of deindustrialization that took place in the national production of drugs and equipment. The inequalities in the distribution of hospital equipment between regions, municipalities, and urban areas materialized the cruel and dramatic face of unfairness in the country.

This situation was profoundly augmented by the denialist position of President Bolsonaro over the severity of the pandemic and the continuous dissemination of fake news by the government regarding possible harm from vaccines. Also, the insistence on disseminating the propaganda of treatments without any scientific evidence. Finally, the national government permanently opposed the subnational authorities who decreed social distancing measures. During the pandemic, the president dismissed two health ministers who disagreed with his guidelines and placed a paratrooper general as minister of health, who militarized the ministry, placing military personnel in crucial command positions of health policy. The ministry of health failed to play a role in coordinating SUS, ignoring the instances of participation and agreement, breaking with the model of cooperative federalism that had been in place. Instead, federalism of confrontation replaced the previous relationship among the health system players in a permanent clash between the president and state governors that had taken the lead in combating the pandemic. The results are counted in the number of deaths that in 2022 exceed 650 thousand, placing Brazil among the ten countries with the highest mortality from COVID-19. At the beginning of the pandemic, studies indicated the catastrophic national situation:

Brazil recorded, proportionally to its total population, more deaths from COVID-19 in 2020 than 89.3% of the other 178 countries, with data compiled by the WHO. However, when these records are adjusted to the population distribution by age group and sex in each country, the Brazilian result becomes worse than 94.9% of the same 178 countries. [20].

Despite the underreporting, comparative data presented on the Our World in Data website in March 2021 show that Brazil, with 2.7% of the world population, concentrated more than 11% of COVID-19 deaths worldwide [21].

The Parliamentary Commission of Inquiry installed in the Senate that investigated possible crimes committed by the federal government in the face of the pandemic heard experts who said that about 400,000 deaths could have been avoided if the government had not postponed the purchase of the vaccine for almost a year [22].

Furthermore, an academic study on rights in the pandemic concludes that there was a deliberate federal government strategy to spread COVID-19 [23].

Until the vaccine's arrival in January 2021—which, despite being boycotted by the federal government, had broad support from the population—the measures recommended by the subnational authorities were non-pharmacological, including social distancing and prophylactic hygiene measures. The emphasis on hospitalization led to the initial closure of PHC units, followed by precarious operating conditions of these services, with a lack of personal protective equipment, a lack of protocols and standards of care, and a lack of professionals and supplies, medicines, and facilities such as internet for the provision of teleservice.

As the PHC units with the family health teams and community health agents are located in favelas and the periphery and have direct contact with their inhabitants, this lack of priority was felt in the abandonment of the population by public authorities.

With little information, living in overcrowded environments, and being unable to follow recommendations such as buying hand sanitizer, stocking up on food, or working from home, favela residents were the primary victims of the SARS–CoV–2 in Brazil. In addition, the drastic reduction in the income of informal workers caused by isolation measures and the loss of domestic or commercial jobs brought hunger to the favela and periphery populations.

The government launched an emergency financial compensation for the neediest population only after the first year of the pandemic. Still, there was no definition of policies aimed at the specificity of the favela populations' living conditions. The public authorities did not implement specific measures to address, in an integrated way, problems of food insecurity, population concentration, housing deficit, lack of regular water supply, lack of Internet access, or financial incapacity to keep the population connected. Neither overcomes the difficulties of reporting cases of contamination and deaths in these regions (not rarely dominated by drug dealers and militia).

COVID-19 has exacerbated structural inequalities of race, income, and place of residence, as evidenced by a study on mortality from COVID-19 in the city of São Paulo, the largest in Latin America. The study found that the average age of death could vary by up to 23 years, separating wealthier neighborhoods and the city outskirts. According to the 2021 Inequality Map [24]:

We showed that black and mixed individuals observed mortality rates 81% and 45% higher than white individuals, respectively, and disparities were more pronounced in the young/adult population [25].

The poorest women, in general black, were also most affected by the pandemic as they are responsible for reproductive work in domestic services and paid care—working in health services and at home performing unpaid work (family care). In addition, they saw increased domestic violence (and difficulties in denouncing the aggression) and obstacles to accessing prenatal and gynecology services [26].

Health, being multi-determined, does not depend only or mainly on SUS services, with the most vulnerable populations being those subject to the worst living, housing, and working conditions. The pandemic has disrupted the precarious economic situation of favela residents, with the loss of jobs, income, and precarious work. Even with the support of health institutions and professionals, the absence of effective political leadership in the face of the pandemic in the favelas left residents feeling that they needed to act.

Once again, the "We for Us" motto is imposed. "We felt abandoned as if we were not Brazilians. Forgotten," says Gilson Rodrigues, representative of the residents of Favela de Paraisópolis, the second largest in the city of São Paulo [27]. Faced with the pandemic's health, economic, and social crises, favela residents decided to organize and act together to cope with the dramatic situation, mobilizing partners and filling the void left by a government that makes them invisible.

3 Subjectivation, Organization, and Collective Action in Favelas

For over a century since the first favelas began to form on the hills and slopes of the city of Rio de Janeiro, the population in these territories had to organize themselves. Not only to build their houses but also to access essential services such as water, electricity, sanitation, and waste collection. This community organization began to gain strength and prominence in the public debate, mainly by creating the first associations of favela residents in the 1940s. It took place in an urban modernization context due to favelados (people living in favelas) reactions to proposals to remove favelas to areas far from the city center. This associative dynamic has variations both over time and from one territory to another, in a movement that includes losses and gains. Machado da Silva [28] called this movement "negotiated control":

> The relationship of collective organizations of favela residents with public authorities, politicians, supralocal organizations [3]. and the broader favela movement has changed throughout its history. It changes according to local and national political conjunctures and the internal and specific dynamics of each of these locations. The ability of these associations to make demands, their organizational autonomy, their cooperation with state policies, the level of repression of their activities, etc., have always depended on a correlation of forces that took place in a highly politically unfavorable environment for these social groups. Nevertheless, they continued to exist [29].

However, throughout its history, the favela was seen through the lens of the "favela problem" [28]. It varied over time from the idea of a cyst to be extirpated from the modernizing urban landscape, passing through the symbology of the favela as a space of material and moral disorder, until the more recent language of the urban violence due to the domination of drug dealers and militia [30]. These changes replaced the language of rights precariously in force at the beginning of the recent democratic construction.

Some theoretical keys must be activated to understand the persistence and meaning of the "favela problem and favelado stigma." They are the concepts of necropolitics, permanent transience, and the biopolitics of precariousness and scarcity.

Mbembe [31]. resumed Fanon's studies on the characteristics of colonial domination. He states that it implies a division of space into compartments, the definition of internal borders based on the principle of reciprocal exclusivity. He added control, surveillance, separation, and also seclusion. However, Mbembe goes beyond Foucault's notion of biopower and relates this idea to the concepts of state of exception and state of siege as the normative basis of the right to kill. It states that the absolute absence of law comes from denying any common bond between the conqueror and the native [31]. Necropolitics concerns defining who matters and who does not, who is disposable and who is not. [31]. In other words, it is necessary to construct the "other" as unequal and undesirable so that there is a moral justification to make them disposable in the eyes of the government.

Rolnick finds that despite the differences between favelas in the same country and the world, "they have in common the fact that they constitute zones of indeterminacy between legal/illegal, planned/unplanned, formal/informal, inside/outside the market, presence/absence of the state" [32]. Contrary to the current voice that the state does not reach these territories, the author states that favelas are strongly constituted and mediated by the state. The state establishes the definition of illegality or tolerates it, or even when unblocking legal and administrative impossibilities for the recognition of the existence of the settlement and the incorporation of popular demands through public policies.

Leite [33], based on Foucault, introduces the concept of biopolitics of precariousness. It describes how government policies and agencies have been deepening the historical poverty in which the lower classes live during the pandemic in Brazil. It is concerned with governmentality [34] or managing the population by taking its life as an object and producing consistent subjectivity. To this end, Freire understands scarcity as a form of government constituted by actions that produce and reproduce the idea that existing public resources are "limited" and "scarce." Thus, their distribution and use dynamics become dependent on priorities and the balance between individual needs and collective policies [35].

It is necessary to understand the abovementioned processes that work to subordinate favela populations, removing their possibility of speaking or being heard. Thus, preventing them from being recognized as subjects with demands to be met [36] and interdicting redistribution [37]. In short, they are impeding constituting themselves as a subject. Fleury [38] sees that the constitution of the subject configures an action that affirms autonomy and conscience within a framework that they did not choose. Inside this tension between social determination and the affirmation of individual and group freedom is the place of the subject's constitution. For Arendt [39], the foundations of the human condition are observed in the relationship between discourse and action because there is the subject's place. Therefore, if the discursive appropriation is the foundation of the human condition, the prohibition of discourse deprives individuals of their condition as actors and the possibility of inclusion in a relational symbolic order constituted by a web of acts and words. Therefore, the constitution of subjects of action and their social insertion necessarily passes through the possibility of rescuing their discursive capacity.

The signifier favelas/favelados was historically associated with the Brazilian social literature on the urban issue, the territories and residents identified by the negative pole of the normal versus pathological, modern versus archaic, inclusion versus exclusion, legal versus illegal, center versus periphery, citizen versus marginal mass, among others. In other words, identity is socially constructed from the equivalence with lack, disorder, and illegal issues, such as the absence of rights, culture, and property, in short, at the margins of the community of citizens. Such stereotypes of neediness and violence are strongly emphasized and reproduced daily by the commercial media.

However, it is necessary to observe the changes in the centuries-old organization of favela populations in search of infrastructure improvements, initially in the form of the residents' association. Recently, the political arena in the favelas has become more complex with the presence of the state through community agents, the growing role of external political actors involved in projects carried out by non-profit organizations, and the dispute between drug dealers and militia to control the favelas organizations and territories. As a result, associations in the favelas were transmuted into less hierarchical and more plural local organizations, giving rise to a myriad of cultural collectives that carry out both aesthetic and political interventions. They aim to symbolically re-signify the social meaning of the places occupied in the cultural and political life of the city.

Even recognizing that one can only speak of favelas in the plural, considering their diversity, there is a recent phenomenon identified as the increase in the self-esteem of young residents. They are connected in networks with social movements, using information technologies to problematize racial identity, class, and gender issues with greater participation in political parties and elections. This phenomenon identified by D'Andrea [40] as the emergence of the peripheral subject, is about the positive affirmation of the identity of part of the youth from favelas and peripheries, built around the polarization between needs and powers, a place from which they debate through cultural and aesthetic manifestations, issues of class, race, and gender. Such problems appear in different struggles and cultural forms, in an aesthetic production of their own, mostly collectivized: hip-hop and funk, poetry, dance battles of slams and passinho (Brazilian dance), and video production.

The material basis of this transformation is rooted in the affirmative policies that democratized the access of the poor, black, and indigenous people to higher education. This way, overcoming the tradition of the Brazilian university as a reproducer of economic and political elites. Today, we find a new generation of university students and professionals who live in favelas and the periphery. We also find museums, cultural centers, and other devices that support knowledge socialization, an active alternative media that disputes meanings and information dissemination.

Understanding the role of political groups, leaders, and social movements in the construction of society is essential, especially concerning the dispute around universal rights. Amid collective actions, one can point out the buildings of counterpowers, ways of being where there is space for horizontal practices, and constant innovation. For example, in a study on Brazilian favelas, Holston [41] indicates that the peripheries were becoming denser due to a disjunctive democracy, which provoked part of the population to insurgent citizenship.

> Living passes, in many cases, through the collective organization – which takes the city as the object of its claims – in an attempt to demand rights and denounce injustices and violations. In short, collective movements indicate objective possibilities of transformation, social recreation, reconfiguration, and rearrangements of life, including the institutional dimension of the state [42].

Otherwise, it would not be possible to understand how favelas organized themselves to face the pandemic: mobilizing internal and external resources, developing partnerships with universities and scientific institutions, preparing government action plans, producing new technologies and innovative means of communication, producing and disseminating knowledge, and creating territorial management instruments. Collective action is preceded by the process of subjectivation—the actor as the subject in action—and can only be understood from the recognition of the existence of university students and cultural centers in the favelas, the enthusiasm of artistic collectives, the growing awareness of the favela as power rather than just a place of need, the existence of countless groups dedicated to alternative communication in the favelas.

Fleury and Menezes [43] identified different types of organizations developed to fight the pandemic, considering the heterogeneity of favelas concerning previous organizational experiences. Some already had a history of struggles, consolidated leaders and organizations, external partnerships, and greater capacity to mobilize resources and vocalization. In contrast, others showed more significant institutional and political weakness, although they reacted by creating organizations to face the impact of the pandemic on community life.

The degree of institutionalization and connection can be an important indicator of social capital, involving relationships of trust and resources accumulated in community organizations. However, the degree of institutionalization should not be confused with the level of politicization. Any mobilization has strong political potential, whether from a political subject organized before the action or from a context of urgency that requires effort in which the actor is formed as a political subject. In other words, the political subject is constituted in the web of relationships these actions mobilize.

Considering the differences in connecting, formalization, scope, visibility, and the previous experience of these community organizations, it was possible to identify actions that could be presented in a continuum that varies according to the forms of organization, such as (a) crises offices (quite structured and connecting many organizations, focused on fighting the pandemic); (b) multiple actions, but not unified in the same territory; (c) punctual and less institutionalized actions [43].

The organization and action developed showed that, even in a health and economic crisis, there are potentialities and capacities in the territory that can be mobilized by social relations and by the web of relationships and external supports. Moreover, solidarity between favelas is also vital, providing the redistribution of collected resources and knowledge transmission.

Fleury and Menezes [43] identified the following predominant forms of collective action developed in the fight against the pandemic: the guarantee of subsistence; community communication; prevention; mapping and production of data on incidence and mortality; meeting demands and criticizing the government; the presentation of community action plans.

All these actions, even simple measures or relief, are also political. They require the construction of action strategies and consensus-building: mobilizing resources, building alliances, forming new leaderships, and breaking the selective barriers of knowledge. However, some of them are more directly focused on political incidence, whether in denunciation, judicialization, or the construction of action plans. Defense of the right to life and healthcare shapes the content and form of political action in all of them.

4 Pandemic: Reframing, Symbolic Disputes, and Materials

Most collective actions developed during the pandemic in favelas and peripheries tried to reframe symbolic disputes. Others were related to the mobilization of resources and territorial management, and more still were developed in knowledge production and new technologies.

4.1 Reframing the Pandemic: From Symbolic Disputes to Action Plans

Community media have already played a leading role in many movements over the last decade, tensioning narratives about the peripheries and favelas in large Brazilian cities. Not only in well-known newspapers, such as Jornal Voz das Comunidades, produced and distributed in the favela Complexo do Alemão, or Maré de Notícias, in Complexo da Maré (both in Rio de Janeiro), but also through the internet, through social networks of leaders and residents or in progressive media spaces. In addition, community radio stations and different communication vehicles give the reality of favelas and peripheries new interlocutors, reaching a larger audience inside and outside their territories. They work to question narratives prevailing in the mainstream media, which, in most cases, build the image of the favela and the favelados as violent, criminal, poor, or stressing the absence of the state.

Through their voices, in an increasingly broad and capillary way, favelados and residents of peripheries dispute their memory and place in the city, overcoming stereotypes and representing the full power of their history and struggle. It is precisely within these narrative and discourse disputes that favela residents are constituted, criticizing, and identifying with the statements in which they are framed. Therefore, community communication has been critical in building and connecting social movements and the public arena. In the current context of crisis, in favelas and peripheries, the activity to face the pandemic has been enhanced by access to communication networks and technologies. Through them, political actors disseminate information on prevention through videos, audios, and booklets, make complaints, requests for support, and connections between favelas and collectives for prevention actions. And, of course, to increasingly produce opinion articles, research, and data concerned with representing the favela through their practices in the political field and the scientific field. Several analyses and proposals have been built through the network, shared in community newspapers by their actors, or echoed in mass media newspapers through some of their representatives.

The 'Marielle Franco' Favela Dictionary [44] is an initiative started based on the need of favela residents to express their stories, aiming at the decolonization of knowledge [45, 46]. It brought together a set of materials, news, actions, and analyses regarding the reality of the peripheries and favelas to support the dissemination, connection, and coping with the pandemic. In the "Coronavirus in the favelas" section [47], ten pages collect and share different content from different vehicles, actors, and motivations In the "Coronavirus in the favelas" section ten pages collect and share different content from different vehicles, actors, and motivations.

At the beginning of the pandemic, in March 2020, when public bodies were still seeking to position themselves on measures to protect the Brazilian population from the new coronavirus, favela leaders and collectives were already connecting and thinking about its impacts on territories. The favela movements are leading actors in the historic struggle for fundamental rights, and, recognizing the reality of their daily lives, they anticipated the need for a community organization. For the leaders who began to organize themselves early on, the certainty is that when the pandemic arrived in the favelas, it would deepen the pre-existing structural inequalities. This discourse demonstrates that beyond the current health crisis, the political aspect of framing favelas is still marked by "a lack of support"—even if, through community connection, people create new proposals for the transformation of the city and the society.

Opinion articles and calls from favela residents [48] began to circulate in the second half of March 2020, pointing out the inequalities and the different impacts that the pandemic could have on the populations of the favelas. Among the most cited were race, class, and gender inequalities that historically reproduce rights violations. They are related to infrastructures such as lack of basic sanitation, housing, access to water and health equipment, precarious work, and (in)security. This is due to the constant criminalization and marginalization of favela youth through police operations and the incarceration of black men and women.

The political positioning of this narrative indicates a special place for those who live in risky situations and their neighbors and relatives to speak and identify vulnerability as an expression of class dominance. These discourses are distinguished from the treatment given by the commercial media in their content and the discursive interaction they propose to establish.

Therefore, the debate about the "democratic virus" that framed the discourses of the mainstream media (the virus does not choose whom to contaminate) becomes increasingly problematized. In territories where the state and assistance do not reach, the virus inevitably causes greater lethality if there are no adequate and effective policies that consider the conditions of favelas and peripheries. An article published in Portal Geledés frames the discussion from a racial perspective, denouncing that the lack of data disaggregated by color/race in Brazil may neglect the perception of the impact of the pandemic on the black population they already neglect other diseases. The majority of people in vulnerability in Brazil are black and mixed color, living in the streets, in precarious houses, or are serving time in prison, which shows the structural racism in the country. In countries marked by inequality, racism is a social determinant of health, as racism crosses the black people's conditions of death and life.

Faced with the repercussion of complaints and action programs, working with community and academic networks, the representation of the pandemic from the favelas (and favelados) is taking a different frame. Discourses take the form of political action, constituting, through their placement, political subjects. The materials collected by the 'Marielle Franco' Favela's Dictionary demonstrate this path and the meanings of action that reframe the pandemic itself in this reality. For example, 79 entities, networks, collectives, and civil society movements—including the 'Marielle Franco' Favela's Dictionary—the National Forum for Urban Reform published/forwarded a political document proposing urgent measures to combat the new coronavirus in the various peripheries of the country, from the perspective of the right to the city and social justice. The document brings a series of proposals, divided into 13 fronts, which include: the elaboration of emergency plans by municipalities, states, and the federal government; guaranteeing access to hygiene and food equipment and services; guaranteeing access to essential services for the promotion and universalization of sanitation; financial assistance to low-income families; strengthening community actions and spaces for social participation; information and communication campaigns; the promotion of mobility; the universal right to quality public health, with the strengthening of SUS; security of tenure and right to housing; solidarity with the homeless population, offering quality shelters; the end of the militarization policy in communities; a COVID-19 prevention policy in prisons; and a new fair, democratic, and sustainable economic policy. It is important to note that public policy agenda is demanded by society, and the connection between different actors in networks and networks of networks gradually becomes denser.

Another proposal, also launched in May, brought together leaders from different favelas and Universities to develop an action plan to fight COVID-19 in the favelas and peripheries. The document suggested that 13 prevention actions, medical care, and social support prevent new infections and reduce the impact of the pandemic on favela residents. In other words, it recognized the necessary prevention and communication actions, with support for the "Se Liga no Corona" campaign, by Fiocruz-RJ. Also, it required an organization of teleservices for health, protecting the vulnerable and those most exposed to the virus, such as essential service workers. Additionally, it demanded the disinfection of public roads in the favelas, and the implementation of exclusive COVID-19 care centers in the favelas, using public spaces, such as schools, and actions to strengthen primary health and social assistance units.

Therefore, through actors and collective mobilization, it was possible to reframe the reality of the pandemic in favelas and peripheries (and cities) through actions for rights and the incorporation of their discourses in research, articles, and public documents. Through their task of (re)framing the pandemic and favelas, discourses constitute a field of dispute in the institutional sphere, causing specific influences on political reality, and even enabling institutional changes [49, 50]. It is important to remember that discourses are part of the context they develop. They are thus part of an updated trajectory, especially in health, political, and economic crises. Under these conditions, political subjects—those who enunciate the discourse—not only pre-exist as a condition for its enunciation but also re-signify their identities and coalitions.

4.2 Production of Knowledge and Technologies

The possibilities of containing the spread of the new coronavirus depend on knowledge about the virus incidence and development in each location. One of the ways medical and health authorities indicated to understand the dynamics of the pandemic is through mass testing. However, Brazil is one of the countries that performed the minor tests, with an average of 63,200 tests per million inhabitants—placing it in the 64th position [51].

In this configuration, social, territorial, and racial markers constitute a cut-off line that informs who will have access to tests and acceptable forms of treatment and who will only obtain precarious care. The selectivity of the information collection and dissemination and the lack of transparency in disseminating data on the new coronavirus in these territories generated great distrust and concern in the leaders who came together to seek a solution. Activists and community leaders consider the precariousness and inadequacy of the data produced by government agencies as discriminatory political action. Furthermore, based on the biopolitics of scarcity increased the risks of contagion and deaths for the populations of the favelas and prevented the planning of adequate protection and prevention actions.

In the face of this reality, activists and collectives from favelas and peripheries, working with health workers and research institutions, organized themselves to build community panels—actions to map cases and elaborate specific policies for these territories. Such activities use new technologies and pre-existing networks in the favelas for diagnostic and prevention measures, such as, for example, in the constitution of panels and campaigns [52]. According to the authors.

> It is possible to say that these panels seek to twist the regime of truth [53] that constitutes and authorizes the true discourse on the new coronavirus in Rio de Janeiro. In this sense, they are presented as a practical-discursive effort to make the pandemic visible in the favelas, to validate certain statements and practices about the sanitary and health emergency in these locations.

Other authors analyze the practice of urban collectives from the perspective of counter-hegemony, understanding how social media were used as a space to fight the virus and support the insurgency. Thus, creating content, information, and research material on COVID-19 in their communities and establishing partnerships with institutions to expand their claims [54].

The network of residents and health professionals was responsible for inserting the favela and the favelados into the scientific debate about producing data on the new coronavirus pandemic. Initiatives such as Voz das Comunidades, in Complexo do Alemão, and Redes da Maré, in Complexo da Maré, started to organize the data collected by family health units and community agents to build panels to monitor cases in favelas and peripheries. It was a response to complaints regarding data collection on suspected cases, confirmed cases, and deaths, given the scarcity of tests for all territories in Rio de Janeiro.

Therefore, different collectives and territories created their methodologies to monitor and quantify the reality of the virus in their population—an example is the Santa Marta Against COVID-19 campaign, which created an internal form for residents. Therefore, residents began disputing data and statistics of the pandemic, building another image of the reality of facing the disease and the rights violations. Faced with these initiatives, the Comunidades Catalisadoras (catalytic communities) (ComCat) organization [55], which has supported favela mobilizers in their struggles for twenty years, developed a partnership with dozens of other collectives and organizations, and created the Painel Unificador COVID-19 nas Favelas (unifying panel of COVID-19 in favelas.) The panel's main objective is to support prevention efforts carried out by community movements, inform their neighbors and press for necessary public policies, and provide a more accurate view of the impact of the pandemic on favelas. In addition, Fundação Oswaldo Cruz—FIOCRUZ, through Fiocruz's COVID-19 Observatory, started to produce monthly newsletters Radar COVID-19 mas Favelas, seeking to systematize, analyze, and disseminate information about the health situation in the territories. In other words, in addition to community communication, the discourses built essential political strategies to fight for citizenship rights in the favelas and peripheries, possible through their different actors' representation and political networks.

In addition to producing the methodology and building the information-producing network, and disseminating community panels with epidemiological data, other innovations were created by residents, such as the preventive sanitation technology developed by residents of Morro Santa Marta. They were able to identify the appropriate chemical solutions and mobilize support to purchase supplies and equipment for disinfecting the streets and alleys. This technology was later disseminated through training residents of other favelas favelas [56].

4.3 *Territorial Management, Resource Mobilization, and Political Incidence*

In all the favelas, there was mobilization to obtain resources to buy basic food packages and distribute them in the territory. In addition to an intense internal and external communication process, this involved the development of logistics for storage and the definition, based on a close relationship with the residents, of the criteria and priorities for the distribution of food. As a result, many have created community kitchens and distributed meals. In addition, they had to develop measures to disseminate information and materials for prevention, distribute sanitizing hand-gel, collective water storage, aid those infected to isolate from the rest of the population, and remove residents who died in their homes.

The second-largest favela in São Paulo, Paraisópolis, has become an exemplary case in mobilizing resources and managing the territory in fighting the pandemic. Led by Gilson Rodrigues, the residents organized themselves to mobilize resources to purchase basic food packages, hire ambulances, seek support from the state government to use closed public schools, and manage the territory. Street representatives were chosen who were called presidents and became responsible for up to 50 families each. The presidents define the deliveries of basic food packages, call ambulances for those who need them, and refer those who need the care to shelter homes.

Having managed to mobilize financial support from entrepreneurs, they started distributing the basic food packages, meals, and masks. They hired health professionals and three ambulances to assist the residents and created shelter homes for people in need of isolation and special care in the school space provided by the government. Volunteer first-aiders were trained while other volunteers began to spread information based on scientific evidence to a population confused by the fake news that the government disseminated on social networks.

However, territories with community organizations already active before the pandemic witnessed a deterioration in the institutions' political mobilization. For example, this phenomenon was observed in the region of Grajaú Faz, in São Paulo. Political work was demobilized. It connected community leaders, sociocultural collectives, local organizations, health workers, education, and social assistance in a political construction of popular education, discussion, and defense of public policies. The government was not the actor responsible for mobilizing the community to fight against the pandemic in Brazil, particularly in these territories. The actors working in this direction were professionals (civil servants and others) in health, education, and social assistance, who maintained a strong connection with the peripheral populations. Many initiatives had the participation of professionals, social organizations, and scientific institutions, creating organizations to offer legal, social, and psychological support to victims of the disease and their families [57].

5 Final Considerations

The pandemic brought great social insecurity, causing a health crisis of unusual proportions, which unfolded into global economic, political, and humanitarian crises. However, coping with the pandemic depended on the political guidelines of governments, the scientific, technical, and institutional resources available, and the political priorities adopted.

In Brazil, in addition to the devastation caused by the pandemic, factors such as prolonged exclusionary urbanization led to the proliferation and population density of favelas and peripheries in territories lacking essential public infrastructure services. The pandemic accentuated inequalities when faced with an economy in crisis, with a high rate of unemployment and informal work, a process of deindustrialization and dependence on inputs, and prolonged underfunding of the social protection services network.

However, the national health system (SUS), the result of civil society struggles as part of the democratization process consolidated in the last 30 years amid austerity policies, has been an essential factor in improving health indicators and access to services. Although inequalities in access have been reduced by strengthening primary health care, many gaps persist in the distribution of more complex or better-quality services, mainly affecting the poorest population. Nonetheless, SUS was considered the main instrument to face the pandemic, avoiding a more significant number of unnecessary deaths in a context in which the president minimized the severity of the pandemic and disseminated false information about treatment.

Even with subnational governments taking the lead in combating the pandemic, the isolation and hygiene measures propagated did not consider the reality of favela and periphery residents, whose precarious situation and unemployment manifested as food insecurity and increased misery.

Community organizations reacted to this situation by mobilizing internal and external resources. Many actions took place as part of the biopolitics of resistance, based on mobilization and social organization in collectives that sought to compensate for the omission of public power. Others developed as part of insurgent citizenship, claimed citizenship rights and demanded public power attention to meet demands and needs.

At the root of this collective action, the historical process involved residents' associations, cultural collectives, universities, scientific institutions, community media, and volunteers. As a result, the social construction of the universal right to health was indelibly inscribed as part of a democratic society. In the same way, the permanent mobilization of workers and health institutions around the principles of the health reform consolidated a web of partnerships and connections with community organizations that could be mobilized and strengthened in the face of the pandemic.

Undoubtedly, the leading actor is the population, transforming itself into an increasingly active peripheral political subject, capable of developing collective actions for disputes over meanings and reframing the pandemic. They use community media, dissemination of information, mobilization of resources and partnerships, production of knowledge and technologies, territorial management, and the construction of public action plans.

References

1. Fleury S, Pinho C (2018) Authoritarian governments and the corrosion of the social protection network in Brazil. In: Revista katálysis, vol. 21(1), 29–42. ISSN-E 1982-0259
2. Fischer B (2008) A poverty of rights: citizenship and inequality in twenty century Rio De Janeiro. Stanford University Press, California
3. Leeds A., Leeds E (1978) A sociologia do brasil urbano. Rio De Janeiro, Zahar Editores
4. Machado Da Silva L (2016) A. Fazendo A Cidade: Trabalho, Moradia E vida local entre as camadas populares urbanas. Rio De Janeiro, Mórula
5. https://wikifavelas.com.br/index.php/GENI_(Grupo_de_Estudos_dos_Novos_Ilegalismos)
6. https://www.cufa.org.br/
7. Pandemia nas favelas, https://ilocomotiva.com.br/estudos/. Last accessed 20 May 2022, Pandemic in the favelas
8. Telles V (2006) Sociedade civil, direitos E Espaços Públicos. In: Fleury S (org.) Democracia, Descentralização E desenvolvimento: Brasil & Espanha. Rio De Janeiro, Fgv Editora, pp 397–416
9. Berlinguer G, Fleury Teixeira S, Wagner G (1988) Reforma Sanitária: Itália e Brasil. São Paulo, Rio De Janeiro, Hucitec/Cebes
10. CEBES—Centro Brasileiro de Estudos de Saúde https://cebes.org.br/
11. ABRASCO—Associação Brasileira de Saúde Coletiva, https://www.abrasco.org.br/site/
12. Fleury S (2011) Desigualdades Injustas: O Contradireito A Saúde. Psicologia E Sociedade 23:45–52
13. http://www.cfess.org.br/pdf/legislacao_constituicao_federal.pdf
14. https://www.who.int/data/gho/data/indicators
15. Aragão E, Funcia EF (2021) O Sus E As Políticas De Austeridade: O Brasil Na Contramão Mesmo Após A Crise Gerada Pela Pandemia Da Covid-19. In: Revista Brasileira De Planejamento E Orçamento, Brasília, vol. 11(01), pp 49–61
16. Servo L, Santos M, Vieira F (2021) Sá E Benevides, R. Financiamento Do Sus E Covid-19: Histórico, Participações Federativas. In: Saúde debate 44, Spe4 (2021)
17. http://www.ccs.saude.gov.br/sus/numeros-saude.php5n
18. Giovanella L (2019) De Alma-Ata A Astana. Atenção Primária À Saúde E Sistemas Universais De Saúde: compromisso indissociável E direito humano fundamental. In: Cad. Saúde Pública, vol. 35(3), E00012219 (2019)
19. IBGE (2019) Pesquisa Nacional De Saúde, Brasil
20. Hecksher M (2021) Mortalidade Por Covid-19 E Queda Do Emprego No Brasil E No Mundo. In: Nota Técnica, Ipea, Brasília
21. https://ourworldindata.org/
22. Senado Federal (2021) Relatório Da Cpi Da Covi-19, Brasíl
23. Cepedisa/Conectas, Direitos Na Pandemia. Boletim Direitos Na Pandemia, n. 1- 10. (2020–2021)
24. https://www.nossasaopaulo.org.br/wp-content/uploads/2021/10/Mapa-Da-Desigualdade-2021_Mapas.pdf
25. Ribeiro K et al (2021) Social inequalities and covid-19 mortality in the city of Sao Paulo. In: Brazil international journal of epidemiology, pp 732–742 (2021), https://doi.org/10.1093/ije/dyab022, Last accessed 28 Feb 2021

26. Reis AP et al (2020) Desigualdades De Gênero E Raça Na Pandemia De Covid-19: Implicações Para O Controle No Brasil. In: Saúde debate, vol. 44(4), 324–340. Rio De Janeiro
27. https://outraspalavras.net/outrasmidias/nos-por-nos-uniao-na-periferia-contra-a-covid/
28. Machado Da Silvia L (2002) A continuidade do "Problema Da Favela". In: Lippi L (Org.). Cidade: História E Desafios. Rio De Janeiro, Fgv Editora
29. Rocha L (2013) Uma Favela Diferente Das Outras. Rio De Janeiro, Quartet Editora/Faperj
30. Machado Da Silva L (2010) A. "Violência Urbana", Segurança Pública E Favelas—O Caso Do Rio De Janeiro. Cadernos CRH, Salvador, vol. 23(59), 283–300
31. Mbembe A (2018) Necropolítica, n. 1. São Paulo, Edições
32. Rolnick R (2015) Guerra Dos Lugares: A Colonização Da Terra E Da Moradia Na Era Das Finanças. São Paulo, Boitempo
33. Leite M (2020) Biopolítica Da Precariedade Em Tempos De Pandemia. In: Dilemas: Revista De Estudos De Conflito E Controle Social. Rio De Janeiro, Reflexões Na Pandemia (2020)
34. Foucault M (2010) Ditos E Escritos. In: Estratégia Poder-Saber, vol. 4 (1980–1998). Forense Universitária, Rio De Janeiro
35. Freire L (2019) A Gestão Da Escassez: Uma Etnografia Da Administração De Litígios De Saúde Em Tempos De 'Crise', Tese (Doutorado Em Antropologia), Museu Nacional, Universidade Federal Do Rio De Janeiro. Rio De Janeiro
36. Honneth A (2003) Redistribution as recognition: a response to nancy fraser in participation. In: Fraser N, Honneth A (Eds) Redistribution or recognition? A political-philosophical exchange. London, Verso, pp 110–197
37. Fraser N (2009) Social justice in the age of identity politics: redistribution, recognition, and participation. In: Fraser N, Honneth A (eds) Redistribution or recognition? a political-philosophical exchange. Verso, London, pp 7–109
38. Fleury S (2010) Socialismo E Democracia: O Lugar Do Sujeito In Fleury E Lobato. In: Participação, Democracia E Saúde. Rio De Janeiro, Cebes, pp 24–46
39. Arendt H (1993) A Condição Humana. In: Forense Universitária, 6ª edn., São Paulo, pp 31–34
40. D'Andrea T (2020) Contribuições para a defino dos conceitos periferia, sujeitas E Sujeitos Periféricos, vol. 39(01). Cebrap, São Paulo, pp 19–36
41. Holston J (2008) Insurgent Citizenship: Disjunctions of Democracy and Modernity in Brazil. New Jersey: Princeton University Press
42. Genro T (1996) O Novo Espaço Público, 21 Teses Para A Criação De Uma Política Democrática E Socialista. Folha De São Paulo
43. Fleury S, Menezes P (2020) Pandemia nas favelas: Entre Carências E Potências. In: Saúde Em Debate, vol. 44(4), Dezembro, pp 267–280
44. The 'Marielle Franco' Favela Dictionary is a public access online platform gathering knoweldge on favelas and periphery (www.wikifavelas.com.br), hosted in Fundação Oswaldo Cruz
45. Fleury S, Menezes P (2022) Memória Como Direito À Cidade: Dicionário De Favelas Marielle Franco. In: Estudos Históricos Rio De Janeiro, vol. 35(76), pp 309–335
46. Fleury S, Polycarpo C, Menezes P, Fornazin M (2022) The challenge of decolonizing knowledge: The Marielle Franco Favela Dictionary El Desafío De La Descolonización Del Conocimiento. In: El Diccionario De Favelas Marielle Franco, Salud Colectiva, vol. 18, edn. 3850
47. This section is highlighted in the 'Marielle Franco' Favela Dictionary and has ten linked pages, including the page analyzed in this article. Last access on 27 Apr 2022, https://wikifavelas.com.br/index.php?title=Coronav%C3%ADrus_nas_favelas
48. All content mentioned in this excerpt is on the page Análises e Propostas sobre a Realidade do Coronavírus nas Favelas (analysis and proposals on the reality of the coronavirus in favelas). The content was last accessed on 27 Apr 2022, available at: https://wikifavelas.com.br/index.php/An%C3%A1lises_e_propostas_sobre_a_realidade_do_coronav%C3%ADrus_nas_favelas
49. Schmidt VA (2008) Discursive institutionalism: The explanatory power of ideas and discourse. Annu Rev Polit Sci 11:303–326
50. Schmidt VA (2010) Taking ideas and discourse seriously: explaining change through discursive institutionalism as the fourth 'new institutionalism'. In: European political science review, vol. 2(1), pp 1–25

51. https://www.metropoles.com/brasil/brasil-e-2o-pais-com-mais-casos-de-covid-19-e-64o-em-numero-de-testes
52. Menezes P, Magalhães A, Silva C (2021) Painéis comunitários: a disputa pela verdade da pandemia nas favelas cariocas community panels: the dispute for the truth of the pandemic in Rio's Favelas. In: Horizonte Antropológico, vol. 27(59), Porto Alegre, pp 109–128
53. Foucault M (2006) Ditos E Escritos. In: Ética, Sexualidade, Política, Tradução Inês Autran Dourado Barbosa, vol. 8, edn. 2. Rio De Janeiro, Forense Universitária
54. Furtado L, Furtado L (2021) Urban collectives and social media: promoting insurgency to cope with Covid-19. In: Informal Settlements, Oculum, Revista De Arquitetura E Urbanismo, vol. 18. Ensaios, Campinas, E215136
55. Catalytic Communities, CatComm. Solutions, Communities, Networks, Favelas, Social Media
56. https://wikifavelas.com.br/index.php/Sanitization_of_Santa_Marta
57. https://outraspalavras.net/outrasmidias/alem-das-urnas-a-politica-cotidiana-nas-periferias/

Empower Shack Housing

Alfredo Brillembourg

Abstract For much of the past 20 years, our research and design work has primarily concerned relatively discrete interventions: individual structures, from the vertical gym to collective housing; connective tissue, such as the Metro cable car; and neighborhoods, like Khayelitsha in South Africa. But all the while, we were thinking and talking about the city, about what participatory urbanism might mean and be in the twenty-first century. The rigid separation of formal and informal, planned and ad hoc, wealth and poverty, makes no sense to us. Those distinctions are inherently unstable politically, economically, and geographically; marginalization is a social and physical phenomenon, a kind of illness afflicting the civic body. The disconnect between formal and informal has at least two root causes. One is organic: cities grow outward, like the ripples in a pond when one drops a pebble in the middle. Like the ripples, the encircling neighborhoods grow weaker and less coherent the farther they are from the center. The other cause follows the law of unintended consequences: infrastructure, especially transportation, creates barriers between the haves and the have-nots, in the interest of improving vehicular movement. Even where public transportation and pedestrian bridges provide access across highways and six-lane boulevards, neighborhoods are still cut off from one another, preventing mingling and sharing.

Keywords Social architecture · Public space · Housing rights · Informal settlements · Global South

1 Introduction

Where do we stand today when it comes to alternative conceptions of urbanization? What are the forces vis-à-vis the political beliefs and frameworks that inform contemporary roles and models for architectural practice? Since the tail-end of the 1990's one can witness a growing frustration of a generation of architects and

A. Brillembourg (✉)
Urban-Think Tank Design Group, New York, USA
e-mail: brillembourg@uttdesign.com

A. Battisti et al. (eds.), *Equity in Health and Health Promotion in Urban Areas*, Green Energy and Technology, https://doi.org/10.1007/978-3-031-16182-7_11

spatial practitioners, who are no longer willing to accept the truism and conventional understanding of the architect as the sole power, who is in charge of space.

This essay[1] is neither, as they say, a conventional story about an architect's involvement in an informal settlement nor a typical observation. It is about a particular project undertaken under the specific circumstances of Khayelitsha. This is not to suggest that this process was without challenges; as Bret Stephens wrote in The New York Times, *"If you find writing easy, you're doing it wrong"* [1].

We, as Urban-Think Tank, have spent a long time thinking of how our work in South Africa has contributed to advancing the ideas around upgrading communities. With this essay, we attempt to contextualize our work and offer readers arguments about what we call "advanced reblocking of informal communities" in South Africa. We also want to share ideas about architecture, cities, and the role of the architect in addressing the inequities that beset societies everywhere.

The question of how the architect can—and perhaps should—be a public intellectual does not need to be discussed. Incremental housing and informality are already popular concepts in the scholarship [2]. But do the principles that have emerged through research make a difference so far? Do the various theories translate into transformative practice? And, most importantly, are we architects just talking to one another, failing to engage with practical realities?

One answer is clear: we need to escape the special interests of the housing development corporations, whose purposes focus narrowly on economic goals and shareholder expectations. The provision of housing must be addressed in the context of regional development, including employment opportunities, services, transportation, and the like [3]. By yielding to the limited perspective imposed by market forces, architects fail to consider the roles of growing urbanization, limited resources, and the vulnerabilities of the populations, whom they think they are serving.

In the 2011 SLUM LAB magazine, we dealt with global urbanization and its effects on various populations. However, we were not alone in arguing for a new urbanism that links theories and solutions to the truth on the ground: some architects and scholars like Teddy Cruz, Christian Schmidt, Neil Brenner, and Andres Lepik have also taken up the dialogue since the 2000s. Nor is incremental housing a new preoccupation; Le Corbusier dealt with this concept in his Domino House prototype in 1915 [4]. The German architects Martin Wagner [5] and Henry Klumb [6] brought the principle of piecemeal growth to North America when they immigrated to the United States just before World War II. By the early 1950s, architects and planners across Latin America were exploring the possibilities that incremental development offered to financially constrained local governments facing housing shortages [7].

One of the most commendable examples of a housing program subsidized by the government took shape in Peru in 1968, with an initiative known as the PREVI (Programa Experimental de Vivienda) Project [8]. Funded by the United Nations and organized by Peter Land, a British architect and intellectual who had come to Peru

[1] This essay was written, in collaboration with Tord Isdal and Ayca Beygo as contributing researchers, in the first-person plural narrative. It refers to the Urban-Think Tank team in the given timeline.

to teach and work, PREVI became the cynosure of social housing experimentation globally. Renowned practices of architects like Aldo van Eyck, Fumihiko Maki, Charles Correa, George Candilis, Atelier 5, James Stirling, and many others eagerly participated [9]. PREVI's appearance on the architectural scene was timely: it was seen as the realization of the 60's vision of a social utopia. But two factors doomed its role as a widespread influence. First, shortly after PREVI's establishment, celebrity architecture became the profession's obsession, and architects started losing interest in the design and construction of social housing projects [10]. Second, following a military coup and the regime change, the Peruvian government ended the PREVI experiment in 1974, having built just 500 units which were only one-third of the initial target.

Nevertheless, PREVI remains a worthy example of the benefits of international and interdisciplinary collaboration among architects and of architects with governmental entities and the UN. Our experience shows that a still broader and deeper perspective is essential. As urbanists like Edward Soja and David Harvey and urban anthropologists like Henri Lefebvre have all argued, the creation of urban space is far more complex and dynamic than the creation of houses alone [11]. Architects must engage with the social sciences to understand all the forces and processes at play to ensure that their efforts result in genuine and long-term benefits for the people they hope to serve [12].

2 Power to the People

2.1 Discordia Concors[2]

It took nearly 50 years for South Africa to abandon the official principle of apartheid, though it had dominated black/white relations ever since the first white settlers arrived. In 1990, the ban on the African National Congress (ANC) was repealed and, after 27 years of incarceration, Nelson Mandela was released from prison [13]. It took another five years of negotiations and transitional politics, disrupted by violence and riots, for a new constitution to be ratified, giving equal status to all South Africans on paper, if not always in fact.

Among others, housing rights were also codified in the new constitution. However, declaration and implementation took place often years apart, and the euphoria of 1994—the year of Mandela's election as President—did not translate into action [14]. One of the new government's initiatives was the establishment of the National Reconstruction and Development Programme (RDP) [15] for public housing, which aimed to provide one million low-cost houses within the first five years of its founding [16]. There has, to be sure, been some progress: variations of the RDP model became the centerpiece of the country's approach to the housing crisis, and some 2.8 million

[2] A rhetorical device in which opposites are juxtaposed so that the contrast between them is striking.

houses have been built since 1994. Nevertheless, there are approximately 10 million people, 25.6% of the urban population, who still live in 3400 informal settlements in South Africa [17]. The housing shortage across the country amounts to more than 2 million homes [18].

2.2 It's a Question of Perspective

In 2012, we were invited to participate in the Design Indaba Conference in Cape Town, a gathering of international talent and expertise.[3] The presentations and discussions tended to present a rosy picture of accomplishment with respect to the intersection of design, in its broadest sense, conditions in the townships, and the urgent need for enormous quantities of decent housing. However, when asked if the participants had ever been to the informal settlements, the answer was a resounding no.

Urban-Think Tank's investigation and research principle in a new locale is usually to start on the ground. During the conference, however, arose the possibility of a bird's-eye view—a helicopter ride along the coast toward the scenic Cape Point. Ravi Naidoo, the creator of Design Indaba, reluctant at first, due to the bureaucratic and security issues, finally agreed and enabled us to fly over the Cape Flats, to photograph and film the acres and acres of shacks.

After that flight, we spent several days meeting residents and community leaders in the Philippi township, accompanied by Andy Bolnick, architect and founder of the NGO Ikhayalami ("my home" in Zulu). Bolnick was working on post-disaster reconstruction in a small area of the township called Sheffield Road, implementing a "blocking-out" scheme.

2.3 Blocking-Out, Basic and Advanced

"Blocking-out" describes a design and implementation process pioneered by the NGO Ikhayalami and Slum Dwellers International [19]. All phases of the process—from identification of need, to design and implementation—are led by the community and organized networks of the urban poor, supported by NGOs and in partnership with the state.

The scheme involved the reconfiguration of an informal settlement into a more rationalized spatial layout, which allowed the creation of demarcated pathways or roads, public and semi-public spaces, and emergency services access. This facilitated the provision of infrastructure and result in enhanced circulation, greater safety, access to basic services, and, above all, the recognized "right-to-remain" legal status for squatter communities. The approach has been acknowledged by an international

[3] The Design Indaba Conference "brings together people using design and innovation to create a better world." (http://www.designindaba.com).

audience as "best practice" [20], supported and endorsed by thousands of shack dwellers connected to the Informal Settlement Network.

In its implementation, blocking-out consisted of the physical dismantling of individual shacks, which were then either replaced with an upgraded model or reassembled according to the improved and agreed-upon urban scheme. Residents opting for an upgraded shack had a range of prototypes offered by Ikhayalami from which to choose, depending on their financial means.

Walking up and down Sheffield Road, we understood the enormous potential of the innovative blocking-out scheme. Accordingly, it raised the question of whether there was a more powerful upgrading strategy that could begin by building lasting foundations for a future city.

Then we saw it: a double-story shack one resident had built haphazardly for himself. What if this initiative could be replicated over a broad area? By replacing the existing one-story shacks with a two-story prototype, we could reduce the private footprint of each unit, freeing up the land for public space, firebreaks, and basic infrastructure.

We asked the resident what had motivated him and why his neighbors had not followed his example. "*So I could open up a shop on the ground floor*," he explained, adding, "*but the sandy ground made it very difficult to construct a two-story dwelling out of tin and wood.*"

Focusing on our inquiries and research, we asked other two-story-shack owners/builders what lacked in their homes and whether they, too, might benefit from a ground-level shop in a two-story house. What they needed, they told us, was a way of expanding their houses to accommodate growing families. The notion of the nuclear family is an anomaly in South Africa [21]; families can consist of ten or more people, typically living in a six to twenty square meter shack [22].

The solution we found was to design a blocking-out unit that would be double-storied and possibly involve new structural techniques and materials, allowing residents to upgrade their homes safely. In conjunction with Ikhayalami, we developed the concept of Advanced Blocking-Out and the Empower Shack respectively.

While it is based on the two-story unit, we did not believe in the one-size-fits-all design; instead, the scheme accounted for the varying needs and aspirations of the residents. They decided whether larger shacks reduce their footprint, or whether all households maintain the same amount of floor area they occupied prior to blocking-out. During the design process, the community weighed in with whether each unit should include yard space in the form of courtyards. Construction materials were provided at a subsidized cost and included walls for a structure that covered an area of up to twenty square meters. Families who have bigger shacks needed to make their own plans for enlargements if they wanted to exceed this limit. The option of upgrading to a two-story shack in a cluster of row houses increased the density and enabled the flexibility necessary for multiple configurations of the units.

The Empower Shack solution had three goals: to increase the housing density to improve the urban environment and the community's living standards; to create incentives such that all participation is voluntary; and to consolidate community resources—time, land, and income—for a successful outcome.

2.4 BT Section C

We asked Bolnick if she knew of a place where we could try to implement the new blocking-out strategy that could serve as an example of the first double-storied shack upgrade. She pointed us to Khayelitsha, meaning “our new home” in Xhosa [23], located about 29 km from Cape Town, and particularly to the area known as the BT-Section, which is a part of Site C. The site was ideal for our purposes a mix of local initiative and governmental neglect. On one hand, it had a lively street-life and community-based economy: people sold fruits and vegetables or second-hand furniture and clothing; they provided child-care; they fixed cars. There were taverns, houses—more properly rooms—of worship, clubs for youth and for senior citizens. On the other hand, it was very crowded more than 280 individuals occupied about 4000 sq m.

The shacks they have built with found materials were of poor quality and were distributed helter-skelter throughout the site in a nearly impenetrable maze. There was no basic infrastructure or services; flash fires and flooding were persistent environmental threats, and residents were at risk of predatory violence [24]. They suffered from unemployment and Cape Town was a long and costly taxi ride away hence the small businesses tucked into nearly every shack [24]. In other words, this was a place where the Empower Shack’s innovations could be an effective game-changer. But first, we had to make our idea real: the concept could be proved best inside the building.

We set up a ten-day workshop founded on a design brief we drafted with Ikhayalami and accompanied by materials that presented such overarching issues as the socio-political context, local tendencies, practices, and capacities of community engagement.

Shortly after the workshop we and Ikhayalami were able to secure a private grant to subsidize the materials for a two-story shack prototype.

2.5 Test Case: Phumezo’s Shack

Phumezo, the community leader, had already expressed interest in testing the prototype. The one-story shack he had built in 1987 needed major repairs, and his wife and two daughters were pressing him for additional space. In December 2013, Phumezo became the Empower Shack’s first client.

Phumezo and his family were able to contribute some of their savings to cover expenses beyond those subsidized by the grant, and on short notice, our team began to adapt our still-evolving prototype designs to fit within scheduling and budgetary constraints. We successfully petitioned the Anti-Land Invasion Division of the City of Cape Town to approve the project, despite their usual misgivings about any construction in BT that appeared to be permanent. After three intensive days working with Ikhayalami, we prepared a simplified design and construction plan for a shack.

Over a period of four days, a team of four to six people, composed of regular Ikhayalami builders, ISN representatives, local activists, and Phumezo, assembled the latter's eye-opening new two-story shack. Pillars were dug sixty centimeters down into the sand and held together with a dry concrete mix, allowing the foundations to be set after the floor components were installed. Melvyn, the foreman, improvised excellent solutions for unexpected conditions, such as the slanting topology of the site and the presence of concrete slabs beneath the topsoil. The backbone of the house was a basic module of eleven and a half square meters. Scrap treated timber was used to reinforce the footers and the floor plane, and to allow for thinner floorboards between joints. Clip-lock panels were trimmed, and windows cut to customize the design according to Phumezo's requirements. Stairs around the back of the shack allowed for outdoor access to the top level. Neighbors, passing drivers, and pedestrians walking down Maphongwana Avenue congregated around the site, fascinated by the unusual structure. Our group fielded multiple inquiries about the construction process and the parties involved.

The built project inspired leaders in BT to discuss a community-wide blocking-out plan. Phumezo aligned local political forces and used his new shack as an example to start pushing for a neighborhood-upgrading project. Our ambition with the Empower Shack was not to deliver a finished product or a definitive solution, but rather facilitate a process and build a methodology that could be scaled and replicated.

2.6 *Getting from One to Many*

Thus far, after shaping some essential principles to build a prototype, we could assemble Phumezo's shack in a single day. That was a significant feature, because any site left vacant for more than 24 h would almost certainly be squatted by newcomers. The building components were lightweight enough to be manageable by just two people and relatively little skill or experience was required for the construction; local labor could build a sturdy structure. The raised platform enabled sanitation services to be upgraded easily since pipes could be connected through the gap between the ground and the platform. We also conceived a plan in which clusters of shacks were arranged so as to share a basic bathroom unit among them; shacks could install their own bathrooms once the residents have the financial means to do so.

2.7 *Financing and Subsidies*

Finances. Money. Funds. More than almost anything else, this is the missing or misshapen cog in the machinery of housing for the informal settlements [25]. Township residents do not have access to commercial lending, though in some instances there is the equivalent of a local credit union where they can stash their savings for a meager interest. Absent a loan, residents have to build in increments. Rather than building the home they really need, they pay off the loan in increments as money becomes available. This, certainly, makes the ease of expansion absolutely essential to any design.

We proposed that, as community members accepted homes of the new dimensions, they would receive subsidized contributions to the cost of their new houses, in exchange for freeing up land. This idea of binding the housing subsidy to shack sizes created a great deal of interest in the BT community and ensured their participation, which, in turn, led to the Land Release Credit (LRC). With the LRC, each resident received 500 ZAR per square meter of land that was contributed to the project as a credit towards the cost of the upgraded home. Each household was allocated at least thirty-five square meters having access to the minimum units.

As a concept, subsidized social housing goes back to almost 100 years. The extensive social housing program in Vienna, initiated in the 1920s, is still very much alive: sixty percent of all Viennese households live in subsidized apartments, of which 220,000 are in council housing [26].

There is an implicit challenge in setting up subsidized housing: one must determine the conditions of the subsidy. While South Africa has a variety of housing programs, most of them, like the Breaking new ground initiative, have a per-head subsidy [27]. In this program, the government would give a lump sum amount (160,573 rands in 2017) to qualifying households. The problem with a per capita subsidy scheme is that they support a single-solution project that yields monolithic housing blocks [28]. The alternative could be an income support or co-pay program, in which the government would match the household's contribution. The matching contribution could take various forms, such as tax abatement or subsidized loan rates. The Empower Shack project makes use of both types of subsidies. The residents could pay about 100 dollars a month over eight years if there were a bank that would mortgage the houses and pay for the full value of the house over time. For purposes of the pilot project, we invented a scheme in which residents would pay only ten to twenty percent of the value of the house and thirty percent would be subsidized by the Land Release Credit, while the remaining fifty percent was to be subsidized by private foundation donations.

2.8 Ideas and Obstacles

The next question was how to make this prototype available to the sixty-eight families living in BT South. Cities all over the world, including Cape Town and its sprawl, suffer from prioritizing private space over the collective [29]. The solutions aren't easy to implement. At one point, we proposed a house in which the ground floor was partially allocated to a deck for an outside living space, the virtue of which is only realized if the deck overlooks a street or courtyard in other words, responds to the scale of the collective. A great idea, one might think, except that the majority of South Africans would rather enclose those few square meters (as seen all along the N2 highway) [29]. And not only South Africans: one must remember that the residents of Sidi Othmane, in Casablanca, filled in their balconies to create additional rooms [30].

The aversion to a shared domain remained an obstacle to community-building in Cape Town [29]. Eventually, we would hope, some version of the advanced blocking-out scheme, implemented as a test case, could incorporate communal, shared spaces in such a way as to make them desirable and sought-after. In the shorter term, our goal became the establishment of a knowledge base of contemporary building practices in South Africa—including details on pricing, weight, and dimensions—that could inform the second phase of the design process. By testing different combinations of components, we wanted to identify and promulgate an overarching modular system for the housing unit. It could leverage the availability and economy of prefabricated industry-standard materials while offering a variety of unit sizes to meet spatial requirements in an efficient way. We understood that we needed to find a middle ground, but we were navigating between the large urban dense blocks and the sprawling identical RDP housing. Either solution led to some form of a lifeless ghetto effectively just another sort of slum. We took a third way.

3 The Power of the Collective

3.1 Participation

Independent action, as has been observed in the barrios of Caracas, produces an exceedingly dense and static urbanization [31]. On the other hand, with the help of a collective, it was possible to obtain a better neighborhood by creating individual houses and communal streets where the houses join together. In an area of 4263 sq m, a built space with seventy-two shacks covered an area of 2500 sq m; what remained was 1500 sq m of open space. Reconfiguring the shacks into tightly packed row houses would yield more than 2100 sq m of open space, while improving thermal performance, ventilation quality, public–private distinction, and passive security.

A core principle of blocking-out is that the community is involved in all aspects of the project. Indeed, we have always insisted on participation in our projects by the people who were directly affected. This had everything to do with our belief that the residents of a favela or barrio or township knew best what they needed and came up with solutions and techniques singularly appropriate to their circumstances. Typically, nothing taught in schools of architecture or learned through practice touches on these issues [32]. What equally important is the context: townships and barrios are informal settlements, but they come into being as a result of location-specific issues and cultures.

Our research team mapped the complex mechanisms of informal dwellings of sixty-eight families in the neighborhood of BT North, Site C, Khayelitsha, and revealed the spatial and financial potential that could be unleashed. We reached the conclusion that a participatory system of community leaders, NGOs, and architects could reorganize the whole process of developing and rationalizing these settlements from the inside out and without displacing any individuals.

There were three main agents: The leaders of the community, the men and the women whose strength of character and initiative are widely acknowledged, who could organize the sixty-eight households. They also had the skills and experience either to build a house as bricklayers, carpenters, and other construction workers or to manage a project. Lastly, the state, associated with the land proprietors, could permit the development of occupied land in order to extract economic advantage and generate permanent housing.

Although BT residents had no legal claim to the land they occupied, they had user rights over that land (Section 25 (5) of the South African Constitution). It was possible for the government to dislodge them, however, the consequences could be fraught and difficult to handle. This gave everyone involved in the Khayelitsha project the confidence to proceed as though permanence were assured. To help the community grasp the process we proposed and the outcome we anticipated, we invented games, using woodblocks, to illustrate the land redistribution.

Community involvement was not just a matter of consultation to ensure that individual and collective hopes and needs are accounted for; it required investment and a degree of sacrifice of short-term personal or familial objectives for the long-term benefit of the whole. How, exactly, this would work was complicated by conditions in our test area. An initial survey of the BT population showed that the distribution of land and money were both quite skewed: a small percentage of the population controlled a large part of the total occupied area; a different but equally small population held the majority of the jobs that paid well and thus the larger income pool. Given this disparity in resources among the individual shack-dwellers, our group needed to come up with a scheme that would enable all residents to contribute according to their means admittedly a variation on Marx's "*from each according to his ability, to each according to his needs*" the recipient, in our case, being the community [33].

Our solution was to enlist the help of our colleagues from Information Architecture field to see if we could digitize the urban upgrade methodology. It could enable us to maximize user input and transparency, afford opportunities for replicability and, ultimately, scalability. With this collaboration, which we called Preferential City Making, we set about designing the computational tools that would offer planners, the community, and city decision-makers a powerful interface to synthesize multi-user preferences in response to the socio-spatial dynamics of in-situ urban development. Over the course of the building project, we developed the tools to allow the automatic generation of urban layout scenarios based on individual preferences (neighbor, location, and unit size preferences based on micro-finance affordability); community preferences (existing street networks, public spaces, additional rental stock); and municipal planning frameworks (plot sizes, street widths, proximity to existing infrastructure, zoning, and urban use mix). Taking these tools to the public, we developed an online 3D environment that allows residents to view and register feedback on particular layouts and offers real-time data projections to planners for decision-making support. This included public–private land split, projected and potential number of units, building costs, and infrastructure investment. In addition, customized heat maps visualized pre-defined performance indicators (security, street unit accessibility, fire risk, proximity to infrastructure, visual corridors, surveillance, and frequency of interaction).

The economist Alejandro de Soto asserted at the United Nations Roundtable on Urbanization in 2002: "*In the face of the ineffectiveness of the legal system, people resort to extra-legal situations to finance housing projects.*" In other words, waiting for permission or action from the state leads only to inertia; when transformative power rises from the individual to the collective, the neighborhood, the community, and on up the ladder, the state, eventually, is largely disempowered.

On the face of it, this does not look like an equitable substitute for the government's promise of a subsidized single-family home set on an individual lot. But the township residents know only too well how far that promise is from reality. If and when they might acquire such housing, it would be unacceptably distant from their community [34]; and the waiting list for this housing—about whose existence no one was confident—can be up to 18 years long [35]. Under the circumstances, the bird-in-hand principle exerts a powerful incentive.

3.2 (Em) Power

When we arrived in South Africa, many organizations and individuals had already long been working toward the same objectives that inform our efforts. For years, the South African Federation of Urban and Rural Poor has been empowering the disenfranchised to teach themselves, help themselves, and develop their homes and communities themselves [36]. The Federation's projects have enabled hundreds of communities to establish savings schemes and vehicles for social change. These kinds of collaboration and knowledge-sharing across disciplines and perspectives are at the heart of our work as well. A good idea does not care where it comes from, and it is always exciting to find that someone else has been considering an idea that accords perfectly with our thinking.

The availability and distribution of power are at crisis level in South Africa [37]. As the country's economy has continued to industrialize, and more communities have gained access to the electrical grid, demand for energy has increased. This increase in demand, as well as the lack of investment in infrastructure, has pushed South Africa's grid to its limits, resulting in planned black-outs, euphemistically called "load-shedding" [37]. Currently, load-shedding leaves many areas without power for up to two hours, three days a week [38]. This is more than a major inconvenience: people at all economic strata are increasingly dependent on mobile phones and Internet access for every facet of their lives; and the absence of reliable and adequate power threatens the South African economy and is a significant disincentive to international investment [39].

Our research, analysis, and modeling showed us that for any unit-based solar component to be viable, the prototype roofs would have to be scaled up to a significant level from the beginning. A typical shack in Khayelitsha has enough roof area to generate 4000 kilowatt-hours (kWh) of electricity in a year. This is almost ten times the free quota provided to families by the government, and more than the average informal dwelling uses, enabling the shacks to become net energy producers [40].

The virtues of our scheme seemed obvious. The system would provide township-dwellers with enough power for their needs, generate income even beyond the immediate shack-building costs, and, by diversifying Cape Town's energy resources, address the crisis of energy insufficiency. We also believed that everyone, from the poor to the state itself, would come to see that the combination of a renewable energy source with a feed-in tariff program would be a viable and sustainable solution for the immediate and long term.

4 Conclusion

We shall not cease from exploration
And the end of all our exploring
Will be to arrive where we started
And know the place for the first time [41]

Our experience in the townships has persuaded us that the incremental scheme for building housing is the only feasible approach, given the residents' financial constraints. When residents invest their savings, bit by bit, in their homes, the pride of ownership would be a potent and meaningful contributor to community stability. The obstacles of this process are inevitable. However we started working with the Legal Resource Center of South Africa and the City of Cape Town on customized bridge contracts called "fit-for-purpose" certificates. These will allow residents to occupy the units we have designed even though these homes do not yet meet all the current building codes. Fortunately, the City of Cape Town recognizes the disconnect between the laws governing legal habitation and the lived experience of the great majority of the population. The task at hand is to make changes to the building codes and to the requirements for a certificate of occupancy in order to address the housing crisis and lower the threshold for homeownership.

We were under no illusions that this project was, or should be, about architects coming to the rescue of a family, community, or an urban condition. Indeed, it is exactly that paternalistic, "we know best" attitude that underlies the typical failed urban renewal schemes. But we believe firmly that design in general and architecture in particular have the potential—and the obligation—to contribute to positive social change. The challenging dynamics shaping everyday realities in Khayelitsha and other informal settlements across South Africa are largely systemic. To be able to address the quality of life and access to opportunities of township, residents must operate simultaneously on a number of levels; changes to the built environment are part of that equation, but at the same time the real change cannot be achieved in isolation. As a research program and evolving design process, the Empower Shack project still has some distance to travel. However, looking ahead to the next phase of a new prototype that would be developed in collaboration with industry partners, we can already see the catalytic value for a potential change.

References

1. Stephens B (2017) Opinion|Tips for aspiring Op-Ed writers. The New York Times (26 Aug 2017). Retrieved from https://www.nytimes.com/2017/08/25/opinion/tips-for-aspiring-op-ed-writers.html
2. Van Noorloos F, Cirolia LR, Friendly A, Jukur S, Schramm S, Steel G, Valenzuela L (2019) Incremental housing as a node for intersecting flows of city-making: rethinking the housing shortage in the global South. Environ Urbanization 32(1):37–54. Retrieved from https://doi.org/10.1177/0956247819887679
3. Maidment-Blundell L (2020) Infrastructure, place making and sustainability. Places for People, 1–62
4. Aureli PV (2014) The Dom-ino problem: questioning the architecture of domestic space. Log 30:153–168
5. Hellgardt M (1987) Martin Wagner: the work of building in the era of its technical reproduction. Constr Hist 3:95–114
6. Hitchcock HR (1955) Latin American architecture since 1945 (Exhibition Catalogue). Museum of Modern Art (1955)
7. Greene M, Rojas E (2008) Incremental construction: a strategy to facilitate access to housing. Environ Urbanization 20(1):89–108 (2008). Retrieved from https://doi.org/10.1177/0956247808089150
8. Salas J, Lucas P (2012) The validity of PREVI, Lima, Peru, forty years on. Open House Int 37(1):6–15 (2012). Retrieved from https://doi.org/10.1108/ohi-01-2012-b0002
9. Land P (2015) The experimental housing project (PREVI), Lima—design and technology in a new neighborhood. University of Los Andes in Bogota (Uniandes)
10. Saval N (2018) Philip Johnson, the man who made architecture amoral. The New Yorker (December 12 Dec 2018). Retrieved from https://www.newyorker.com/culture/dept-of-design/philip-johnson-the-man-who-made-architecture-amoral
11. Iossifova D, Doll CNH, Gasparatos A (2017) Defining the Urban: Interdisciplinary and professional perspectives (1st ed.). Routledge
12. Karim F (2018) The routledge companion to architecture and social engagement (1st ed.). Routledge
13. The End of Apartheid. US Department of State (2009). Retrieved 8 Dec 2021, from https://2001-2009.state.gov/r/pa/ho/time/pcw/98678.htm
14. The Nelson Mandela Presidency—1994 to 1999. South African History Online (2015). Retrieved from https://www.sahistory.org.za/article/nelson-mandela-presidency-1994-1999
15. O'Malley PO (n.d.) The reconstruction and development programme (RDP)—The O'Malley Archives. Nelson Mandela—O'Malley (n.d.). Retrieved from https://omalley.nelsonmandela.org/omalley/index.php/site/q/03lv02039/04lv02103/05lv02120/06lv02126.htm
16. Moolla R, Kotze N, Block L (2011) Housing satisfaction and quality of life in RDP houses in Braamfischerville, Soweto: A South African case study. Urbani Izziv 22(01):138–143. Retrieved from https://doi.org/10.5379/urbani-izziv-en-2011-22-01-005
17. Population living in slums (% of urban population). The World Bank IBRD IDA Data (2018). Retrieved from https://data.worldbank.org/indicator/EN.POP.SLUM.UR.ZS

18. Harsch EH (2013) Winding path to decent housing for South Africa's poor. Africa Renewal (19 Dec 2013). Retrieved from https://www.un.org/africarenewal/web-features/winding-path-decent-housing-south-africa%E2%80%99s-poor#:%7E:text=Housing%20backlog&text=Although%20the%20Department%20of%20Human,in%20dire%20need%20of%20houses
19. Adam F (2014) Townships in South Africa: can design help solve the housing crisis? The Guardian (14 May 2014). Retrieved from https://www.theguardian.com/global-development-professionals-network/2014/may/14/south-africa-cape-town-slum-housing
20. The initiative "Empower-Shack" on the longlist of 2018 RIBA. Institute of Science, Technology and Policy. ETH Zurich (2017). Retrieved from https://istp.ethz.ch/news/2017/12/the-initiative-empower-shack-2018-riba-prize.html
21. Hall K, Mokomane Z (2018) South African Child Gauge 2018. In: The shape of children's families and households: a demographic overview. Amsterdam University Press, pp 32–45
22. Slovo J (2014) Cape town: Sustainable low-income settlement densification in well located areas. UK aid from the UK Department for International Development (DFID), Department for Energy & Climate Change (DECC), & Engineering & Physical Science Research Council (EPSRC) (Mar 2014). Retrieved from https://www.sustainable.org.za/uploads/files/file79.pdf
23. Raper PE (2004) New dictionary of South African place names. Jonathan Ball
24. Cichello PL, Mncube L, Oosthuizen M, Poswell L (2011) Economists versus the street: Comparative viewpoints on barriers to self-employment in Khayelitsha, South Africa. SSRN Electron J. Retrieved from https://doi.org/10.2139/ssrn.2184230
25. Shand W, Colenbrander S, Mitlin D, Weru J, Ratanachaichan N, Neureiter K, Patel S, Satterthwaite D (2017) Enabling private investment in informal settlements: exploring the potential for community finance. Infrastruct Cities Econ Devel (July 2017). Retrieved from https://pubs.iied.org/sites/default/files/pdfs/migrate/G04180.pdf
26. Reinprecht C (2014) Social housing in Austria. Soc Hous Eur 61–73 (2014). Retrieved from https://doi.org/10.1002/9781118412367.ch4
27. Sustainable Human Settlements—Breaking new ground. South African Government. (n.d.). Retrieved from https://www.gov.za/about-government/sustainable-human-settlements-breaking-new-ground
28. Smith DM (2003) The apartheid city and beyond. Taylor & Francis
29. Landman K (2006) Privatising public space in post-apartheid South African cities through neighbourhood enclosures. Geo J 66(1–2):133–146 (2006). Retrieved from https://doi.org/10.1007/s10708-006-9020-5
30. Ferrante A, Mochi G, Gulli R, Cattani E (2011) Retrofitting and adaptability in urban areas. Procedia Eng 21:795–804 (2011). Retrieved from https://doi.org/10.1016/j.proeng.2011.11.2080
31. Hernández F, Kellett P, Allen LK (2012)Rethinking the informal city: critical perspectives from Latin America (Remapping Cultural History, 11) (1st ed.). Berghahn Books (2012)
32. O'Donnell KM (n.d.) As architecture education faces a shift, how will our communities fit in? The American Institute of Architects (n.d.). Retrieved from https://www.aia.org/articles/6108507-as-architecture-education-faces-a-shift-ho.
33. Bovens L, Lutz A (2019) "From Each according to Ability; To Each according to Needs." Hist Polit Econ 51(2):237–257. Retrieved from https://doi.org/10.1215/00182702-7368848
34. Lall SV, van den Brink R, Leresche KM, Dasgupta B (2008) Subsidized housing and access to land in South African cities. 1–29
35. Dugard J (2020) Staircase or safety net? Examining the meaning and functioning of RDP house ownership among beneficiaries: a case study of Klapmuts, Stellenbosch. Law, Democracy Devel 24 (2020). Retrieved from https://doi.org/10.17159/2077-4907/2020/ldd.v24.9
36. Tshishonga NS (2020) Housing citizenship through the federation of urban poor in South Africa. Megacities Rapid Urbanization 413–432 (2020). Retrieved from https://doi.org/10.4018/978-1-5225-9276-1.ch021
37. Agbenyo Folly K (2021) Competition and restructuring of the South African electricity market. Local Electricity Markets 355–366 (2021). Retrieved from https://doi.org/10.1016/b978-0-12-820074-2.00002-2

38. Pheto B (2021) Eskom says 2-hour power cuts, but city power says it will stick to 4 hours. TimesLIVE (19 Jan 2021). Retrieved from https://www.timeslive.co.za/news/south-africa/2021-01-19-eskom-says-2-hour-power-cuts-but-city-power-says-it-will-stick-to-4-hours/
39. Nathan M (2020) Foreign investors blame BEE, Eskom for staying away. BizNews.Com. (2020, Nov13). Retrieved from https://www.biznews.com/global-investing/2020/11/12/eskom-4
40. FAQ's (2021) Department: energy. Republic of South Africa. Department: mineral resource and energy, Republic of South Africa (2021). Retrieved from http://www.energy.gov.za/files/faqs/faqs_freebasic.html
41. Eliot TS (1942) Little gidding. Faber and Faber (1942)

Measuring Disability Among Migrant People in Urban Area

Marco Tofani, Anna Berardi, Giovanni Galeoto, Giovanni Fabbrini, Antonella Conte, and Donatella Valente

Abstract Good health for All is one of the main targets of the Sustainable Development Goals, ensuring quality of care for all people, including of course people with disability. Migrants with disability represent an invisible group of individuals who are forced to leave their countries. Data on refugees and asylum seekers with disability are lacking. They have poor access to rehabilitation health services, but in Italy there are law and policies to guarantee healthcare. The lack of standardized assessment of vulnerability represents the main barrier to organize specific service within the community involving migrants them-selves and institutions. National stakeholders are urgently called to cooperate for removing barrier to rehabilitation and assistive technology for refugees with disability. Main actions should be considered health literacy and empowerment of migrants, collecting data on health, disability and assistive technology, and organize community-based rehabilitation programs.

Keywords Migrants · Refugees · Disability · Urban health · Rehabilitation

1 Background

At the end of 2020, the United Nations High Commissioner for Refugees (UNHCR) reported that there were 26.4 million refugees and 48 million internally displaced persons worldwide due to conflict [1]. Results of the World Report on Disability rindicate that about 15% of the world's population lives with some form of disability [2]. However, various international organizations and the European Union have critically highlighted the lack of data on disability in the migrant population.

Refugees with disabilities represent an underserved group of individuals who are forced to leave their countries in particularly disadvantaged situations [3]. Refugees

M. Tofani (✉) · A. Berardi · G. Galeoto · G. Fabbrini · A. Conte · D. Valente
Department of Human Neurosciences, Sapienza University of Rome, Rome, Italy
e-mail: marco.tofani@uniroma1.it

G. Galeoto · G. Fabbrini · A. Conte · D. Valente
Neuromed IRCCS, Pozzili, Italy

A. Battisti et al. (eds.), *Equity in Health and Health Promotion in Urban Areas*, Green Energy and Technology, https://doi.org/10.1007/978-3-031-16182-7_12

and asylum seekers with disabilities face multiple and intersecting forms of discrimination, have worse health outcomes, and experience greater difficulties accessing higher levels of education, as well as the labor market. Moreover, with specific regard to health, they do not receive the healthcare services they need, and about half of people with disabilities cannot afford healthcare [4]. However, addressing the needs of migrants with disabilities is fundamental for the achievement of the global sustainable development agenda [5], specifically goal # 3, which calls for the development of good practices that guarantee good health and well-being for everyone. Data on migration and disability must be uniformly collected since they are needed to inform the health policy actions of individual countries. In order to monitor progress on the 2030 agenda, the international community unfortunately relies on disaggregated data on both disability and migration status. The statistical inclusion of data on migrants with disabilities is crucial to allow migrants full and equal participation in society. Statistical data on migrants can enable inclusive disability policies and practices, as well as programs that result in better accommodation and access to critical services and reduce marginalization and discrimination [6].

1.1 Healthcare Service and Policies for Refugees and Asylum Seekers in Italy

In 1995, the Dini decree contained norms that guaranteed health assistance to even non-regular immigrants. However, the decree was not converted into law, and in the end guaranteed assistance to only 200,000 regularized persons [7].

In 1998, the "Napolitano-Turco" law attempted to regulate immigration by encouraging regular immigration. The regular immigrant is characterized by a series of steps towards the acquisition of the rights of the "plenoiure" citizen, including rights to family reunification, health, and education. The illegal immigrant, in contrast, is subject to expulsion from the State.

In 2002, the Bossi-Fini law n.189/2002 determined a more restrictive policy. The residence permit was linked with the work contract and became more difficult to obtain. Expulsion was made easier and detention in centers of temporary stay was extended from 30 to 60 days.

In April 2008, a national survey to ascertain the types of services provided in order to guarantee healthcare revealed considerable differences among regions and limited access to healthcare by the immigrant population. Moreover, within the same regional territory and between regions, there were different interpretations of the rules regarding healthcare access for migrant populations that undermined the principles of universal and equitable care. In December 2012, to guarantee immigrant populations on the national territory adequate access to treatment and healthcare, as provided for by the LEA, the permanent conference for relations between the State, regions, and the autonomous provinces of Trento and Bolzano stipulated guidelines for the correct application of healthcare regulations for the foreign population by Italian regions and autonomous provinces [8].

1.2 Reception Centers for Refugees and Asylum Seekers

National policies for hosting refugees and asylum seekers in Italy have changed rapidly [8]. In 2001, the ANCI (National Association of Italian Municipalities), UNHCR, and the Italian Ministry of the Interior signed a memorandum of understanding to establish the PNA (National Asylum Programme). The PNA was the first public system for the reception of asylum seekers and refugees throughout the Italian territory. The PNA instituted shared responsibilities between the Ministry of the Interior and local authorities.

Law n. 189 of 30 July 2002 institutionalized the PNA by establishing the SPRAR (Protection System for Asylum Seekers and Refugees). Subsequently, the Ministry of the Interior established a central co-ordination office and appointed the ANCI to manage it.

In 2018, the SPRAR was renamed the SIPROIMI (Protection System for Beneficiaries of International Protection and for Unaccompanied Foreign Minors) (legal decree n. 113 of 4 October 2018, enacted as Law n. 132 of 1 December 2018). The new legislation provided access to SIPROIMI's integrated reception services to holders of a residence permit for special reasons, including victims of violence, trafficking, domestic violence, labor exploitation, calamities, poor health, or for acts of particular civic value.

In 2020, the SIPROIMI was renamed the SAI (Reception and Integration System) (legal decree n. 130 of 21 October 2020, enacted as Law n.173 of 18 December 2020). The new legislation set out that access to SAI's integrated reception services could be provided to refugees, asylum seekers, unaccompanied foreign minors, and foreigners entrusted to the social services upon reaching majority age. Moreover, the SAI can also accommodate victims of disasters, migrants whose special civil value is recognized, holders of a residence permit for medical treatment, holders of a special protection residence permit (recipients of social protection, victims of domestic violence, victims of labor exploitation). The primary objective of SAI is to provide support to each individual in the reception system through an individual program designed to enable that person to regain a sense of independence and thus enjoy active participation in life in Italy in terms of employment, housing, access to local services, social interaction, and scholastic integration for minors.

2 Measuring Disability Among Migrants

In September 2020, the European Commission launched the New Pact on Migration and Asylum to much debate. The New Pact [9] does not fully consider the diversity of migrants and asylum seekers with disabilities. The EU proposal for a vulnerability assessment should be performed during the pre-entry screening process. Authorities should pay "particular attention (...) to vulnerable persons, such as (...) persons with an immediately identifiable physical or mental disability". Asking authorities to carry out examinations based on the observation of "immediately identifiable disability" ignores the complex needs related to disability and discriminates de facto people with disabilities. The proposed approach reintroduces a medical vision of disability and health, which conflicts with the United Nations Convention on the Rights of Persons with Disabilities (UNCRPD) [10] and with the standards currently used at the international level.

In the last years, many organizations have proposed different approaches to measure disability among the migrant population. In 2017, the UNHCR, together with the non-governmental organization (NGO) Humanity and Inclusion (formerly Handicap International), proposed the Vulnerability Assessment Framework (VAF) [11], which includes a short set of questions from the Washington Group on Disability Statistics (WG). In 2020, the Access for Migrants with Disabilities project funded by the European Union proposed the Needs Assessment Tool (NAT). The NAT allows both qualitative and quantitative analyses, thus reconciling the need to measure and obtain comparable data in different countries with the need to record the different experiences of migrants in a narrative dimension. The NAT includes the extended set of functioning developed by the WG. In 2021, the NGO Relief International, together with the International Centre for Evidence in Disability of the London School of Hygiene and Tropical Medicine, investigated disability among refugees in Turkey using the WG short set-enhanced tool, together with the child module of the WG and UNICEF [12]. In 2021, a group of Italian researchers at Sapienza University of Rome, together with the Italian Society of Migration Medicine and the Rehabilitation and Outcome Measures Assessment (ROMA) association investigated disability within migrant populations using the WG short set-enhanced tool. The working group also used the community-based rehabilitation (CBR) indicators developed by the World Health Organization (WHO) to explore access to healthcare, social, and employment services [13]. Preliminary results highlighted that refugees with disabilities faced challenges in each domain of the CBR matrix, namely health, education, social, employment, and empowerment domains [14].

3 Preliminary Data

Data were collected on a population within the urban area of Rome, in Lazio Region. The survey began in 2019 and was suspended due to the Covid19 emergency for which access to SPRAR centers or other migrant services were reduced/interrupted. The population consists of 40 people (14 F, 26 M) with an average age of 29.7 years (SD 8.26). NAT analysis showed that the majority of respondents (about 70%) were from the African continent (Horn of Africa or West Africa), the most frequent reasons for migration being attributable to internal unrest in the country of origin (war conflicts, persecution). More than half of respondents have no family or friend support network Also from a qualitative point of view, respondents report sleep disorders for about 50%, chronic noncommunicable diseases (~17%) and osteo-articular or nonspecific pain (10%). Half of the women surveyed were uninformed with respect to reproductive health. All women had experienced some form of violence, whether physical or sexual in nature. The main needs that emerged during the interview include employment, family reunification and obtaining personal documents. From the quantitative analysis of the NAT, the most critical areas are those related to cognition (32.5% have difficulty remembering and concentrating), emotional state (57.2% have a medium/high level of anxiety and worry, 53.8% reported feeling partly or very depressed), pain (37.5% complain of pain every day), and fatigue (27.5% experience a feeling of tiredness all or most days). From the analysis of the CBR indicators, significant issues emerged for some aspects of the five components investigated, namely: for Health, 47% are uninformed about preventive norms (exercise, balanced diet) and more than 50% complain of little involvement in decisions that affect their health; for Education, 57%, although they participate in training sessions within the centers, these do not reflect the real needs of the beneficiaries; for the Means of Livelihood component, 36 percent are unemployed, 55% of workers are unpaid or underpaid, and 27% do not have full control over their finances. The totality complain of low economic satisfaction. Finally, for the Social and Empowerment components, 58% complain of a lack of consideration at the social level, 76% are not informed about their legal rights, and 67% report that they cannot significantly influence the functioning of society. More than half of the respondents would find benefit in participating in self- and mutual-help groups, but these are not provided in shelters.

This survey, although withsome limitations-primarily related to sample size-represents a starting point for analyzing the phenomenon of disability in migrant people from a comprehensive health perspective. Precisely because Health is affected by the influence of social determinants, as emerged from this preliminary survey, the actions to be implemented should involve integrated and multi-sectoral approaches. In addition to health aspects, needs related to livelihood, social aspects and empowerment emerge strongly. For example, occupational workshops or specific trainings should be shared with the users so as to respect the expectations and needs of each one. This could lead to the development of targeted skills that can be applied in the world of work resulting in an increased possibility of earning an income. From a social point of view, several studies have shown that the migrant population has a smaller support network and that the contraction of socialization opportunities has a negative effect on quality of life. As suggested by this survey, the organization of self-help groups is desired so that moments of sharing and confrontation can be created among the migrant communities in the centers.

4 Discussion

In order to improve people's involvement in health-related decision-making processes and increase the level of awareness, it would be appropriate to organize awareness-raising activities among social-health personnel This aspect has already been widely discussed in the literature [15]. In addition, centering work on the above aspects could promote a sense of re-appropriation of one's social role; studies emphasize the role of occupational deprivation on the state of physical and psychosocial well-being in the migrant population [16]. While these represent only some initial reflections on disability and migration, the hope is that the reader will find valuable support in approaching an extremely sensitive topic to which, to date, there are few experiences and fragmentary evidence. The invitation is to be able to create a collaborative network that knows how to involve associative realities, training institutions and institutions. The issue of disability in the migrant population is gaining more and more importance on the international scene. The work of all the realities that work in this area, at the local and national level, must be systematized to create a constructive debate that, especially at this historical moment, knows how to get its proposals to the European level. Only by acting as a European Community will it be possible to unhinge a discriminatory system and ensure respect for human rights, regardless of one's legal status, disability condition or the country to which one is forced to migrate.

References

1. UNHCR (2021) UNHCR- Refugee Statistics [Internet]. 2021 [cited 2022 Feb 15]. Available from: https://www.unhcr.org/refugee-statistics/
2. World Health Organization (2011) World report on disability who [Internet]. 2011 [cited 2021 May 26]. Available from: www.who.int/about/licensing/copyright_form/en/index.html
3. Conte C (2020) What about refugees with disabilities? The interplay between eu Asylum Law and the un convention on the rights of persons with disabilities. Eur J Migr Law [Internet] 18(3):327–349, 2016 Sep 20 [cited 2022 Feb 15]. Available from: https://brill.com/view/journals/emil/18/3/article-p327_4.xml
4. Kuper H, Phyllis H (2019) The missing billion access to health services for 1 billion people with disabilities [Internet], London. [cited 26 May 2021]. Available from: https://doi.org/10.1371/journal.pone.0189996
5. United Nations (2022) THE 17 GOALS|Sustainable development [Internet]. [cited 15 Feb 2022]. Available from: https://sdgs.un.org/goals
6. UNHCR (2019) Power of inclusion mapping the protection responses for persons with disabilities among refugees in the middle east and North Africa region. 2019 Nov [cited 15 Feb 2022]; Available from: https://www.unhcr.org/tr/wp-content/uploads/sites/14/2020/10/Power-of-Inclusion.pdf
7. SAI—Sistema Accoglienza Integrazione (2022) SAI: history, objectives and characteristics | RETESAI [Internet]. [cited 15 Feb 2022]. Available from: https://www.retesai.it/english/
8. Sistema Accoglienza e Integrazione (SAI) (2021) SAI & servizio centrale | RETESAI [Internet] [cited 2021 Aug 27]. Available from: https://www.retesai.it/la-storia/
9. Gazi T (2021) The new pact on migration and asylum: supporting or constraining rights of vulnerable groups? Eur Pap J Law Integr [Internet]. 18 May 2021 [cited 2022 Feb 15] 6(1):167–175. Available from: https://www.europeanpapers.eu/en/europeanforum/new-pact-migration-asylum-supporting-or-constraining-rights-vulnerable-groups
10. United Nations D of E and SAD (2006) Convention on the rights of persons with disabilities (CRPD) | United Nations Enable [Internet]. 2006 [cited 27 Aug 2021]. Available from: https://www.un.org/development/desa/disabilities/convention-on-the-rights-of-persons-with-disabilities.html
11. Brown H, Giordano N, Maughan Ch, Wadeson A (2019) Vulnerability assessment framework

12. Polack S, Scherer N, Yonso H, Volkan S, Pivato I, Shaikhani A et al (2022) Disability among Syrian refugees living in Sultanbeyli, Istanbul: Results from a population-based survey. PLOS ONE [Internet] 16(11):e0259249, 1 Nov 2021 [cited 15 Feb 2022]. Available from: https://journals.plos.org/plosone/article?id=10.1371/journal.pone.0259249
13. Tofani M, Esposito G, Berardi A, Galeoto G, Iorio S, Marceca M (2021) Community-based rehabilitation indicators: Validation and preliminary evidence for disability in Italy. Int J Environ Res Public Health 2021, 18(21):11256 [Internet]. 26 Oct 2021 [cited 2022 Feb 15]. Available from: https://www.mdpi.com/1660-4601/18/21/11256/htm
14. Tofani M, Berardi A, Iorio S, Galeoto G, Marceca M (2022) Exploring global needs of migrants with disability within a community-based inclusive development perspective. Annali dell'Istituto Superiore di Sanità
15. Olaussen SJ, Renzaho AM (2016) Establishing components of cultural competence healthcare models to better cater for the needs of migrants with disability: a systematic review. Aust J Prim Health 22(2):100–112
16. Brown C (2008) The implications of occupational deprivation experienced by elderly female immigrants. Diversity Health Soc Care 5(1):65–69

Conclusions. From a Multidisciplinary Cultural Approach to an Integrated Organization of the City, to Build Health Capabilities

Roberto Di Monaco and Silvia Pilutti

Abstract In this short final contribution, we propose a theoretical-conceptual framework useful for understanding how the various contributions of the volume compose an organic vision of the role of multidisciplinarity and integration. They are indispensable levers for promoting health and health equity in cities. Effective concepts and practices are strongly emerging in the international literature to make the experiences and traditions of research and intervention that have been presented even more well-founded and transferable. New leadership and greater participation are required by the complexity of the problems that urban systems will have to face. Similarly, investments should increase in methodologies centred on strengthening capabilities, through the growth of social capital and empowerment. Furthermore, the importance of the cultural and organizational dimension increases, which can make integration processes dynamic and effective. Finally, recommendations are proposed, which, according to our experiences, constitute learning to be valued, to make the participation of professionals, citizens and institutional and social actors in the improvement of urban ecosystems effective and transformative.

Keywords Health equity · Capabilities · Social capital · Distributed leadership · Self-evaluation · Integrated community care

1 The Conceptual Framework of the Contextual and Multidisciplinary Strategy for Health

The framework described below is the tool used to catalogue and reorganize the findings regarding the relationship between social inequalities and health and the effectiveness of policies designed to reduce their effects in the urban context.

R. Di Monaco (✉)
University of Turin, Turin, Italy
e-mail: roberto.dimonaco@unito.it

S. Pilutti
Prospettive Ricerca Socio-Economica SAS, Turin, Italy
e-mail: silvia.pilutti@prospettivericerca.it

A. Battisti et al. (eds.), *Equity in Health and Health Promotion in Urban Areas*, Green Energy and Technology, https://doi.org/10.1007/978-3-031-16182-7_13

The framework distinguishes among the following elements:

Malfunctionings are problems associated with the difficulty of reaching ways of being and doing to which value and quality (wellbeing) are socially assigned. The framework centres on malfunctionings involving health, which are the basic object of this book, rather than on other, important, malfunctionings in the social sphere such as unemployment, school abandonment and so forth.

Resources are commodities, goods that can be used to achieve specific functionings.

Capabilities to do or to be, or in other words, the control over converting *A* into selected functionings, according to the utilization function *fi(.)*. Capability includes a component linked to the individual's abilities and one linked to his real opportunities of choice. The former increases with learning and hence with experience of real progress in exercising independence and in increasing one's store of skills (experiences, for example, that are educational, cultural, relational, professional, etc.). The latter increases when the set of actual possibilities of choice—or entitlements—available to the individual grows within a wider range of possible functionings. The amplitude of this range of actual possibilities denotes the individual's positive freedom and also enables us to distinguish between the condition of individuals whose problems are connected with similar malfunctionings (an unhealthy lifestyle, for instance) but are rooted in highly dissimilar circumstances of freedom and self-determination.

The urban context represents the multiple life environments and relational systems of which the individual is a part. The context affects the range of opportunities that are accessible to the individual's choice (social capacitation) for any given set of available individual resources, and thus makes alternatives and, consequently, functionings possible (or impossible) that the individual would not be able to reach only using his resources and/or capabilities. Above all, the context guides individuals' choices by a circumscribed range of socially structured pathways (concatenation of choices over time) which are a constraint for individuals. The way capacitation is produced (and in some cases reduced), at the social rather than individual level, generates effects of a quantitative and qualitative nature on the yields that resources have over the area, which are particularly important given that the resources for policies are limited and the mechanisms that produce risks and inequalities are in turn systemic.

Policies and interventions for increasing wellbeing can act directly on individuals' endowments (Resources, Capabilities), or problem states (functionings). However, they can affect multiple social environments (Context), increasing accessible opportunities and hence the freedom to choose desirable functionings. It is thus true that the context has a capacitating power because it can add to (or subtract from) the yield from resources by weakening (or strengthening) the negative impact of inequalities. Nevertheless, it is also true that this effect and the associated yield depend not only on the effectiveness of each policy of intervention but also on their interplay, on their level of integration and their consistency with the specific features of the territorial/social environment and the individuals populating it. The final impact, moreover, must be considered net of the unintended or adverse effects generated in the system and which may reduce the opportunities available precisely to those individuals who have the fewest resources [1].

According to this framework, then, the functioning acquired by an individual *I* depends on the choices made regarding the utilization function *fi* and the commodity vector *xi*. We can thus say that acquisitions in terms of functioning are given by *fi(c(xi))*, where c is the commodity conversion function made possible by the territorial/social environment in question. This is the crux of the framework. The utilization function *fi(.)* is in part determined by the possibility of choice, by Fi, or in other words by the possible set of utilization functions available to the individual. Likewise, *xi* is also determined partly by the limits of control a person has over goods based on income, prices, etc., thus reducing the choice of *xi* to a set of *Xi* (entitlements). However, the conversion function differs widely with context, and the yield given by the same resources changes significantly, partially offsetting or accentuating the limits of *Fi* and *Xi*. We thus propose a contextualized representation of all the functionings from which an individual can choose, which, given the circumstances and the contingencies, make up the individual's capabilities, i.e., the various groups of alternative functionings that can be acquired through the choice. As for the relationships between the variables defined in the framework, it should be emphasized that relationships must be imagined in the temporal flow. Thus, the effect at time *t*—the shortage of resources generates poor functioning in terms of health—can be followed at time $t + 1$ by—poor health generates a further reduction in the availability of resources. Consequently, the framework is capable of representing cause-effect relationships that take place over more or less lengthy periods, as well as virtuous or vicious spirals, feedback and effects of 'anticipating' future problems that entail multiple relationships concatenated in time. In particular, this property of the framework makes it possible to represent typical effects studied in life course models, i.e., of accumulation, whether transverse or longitudinal or to model events according to socially structured pathways and cultural influences which over time amplify and reinforce the impact of inequalities in resources and capabilities, partly through a gradual deterioration in health and a general consolidation in the difficulty of functioning. The framework, in any case, underscores the causal nexuses inherent to each step in the pathway, however long and uneven it may be.

As several social studies have demonstrated trajectories are not linear over time and between cohorts, not least because individuals' strategies change and the *capacitation* effects exercised by the urban context—through family resources, for instance—are modified. Accordingly, the urban context fulfils a key role from two standpoints: as regards the effects of accumulation over time of disadvantages and advantages in the individual's resources and capabilities, and as regards his function as a *social accumulator* of ongoing potential for capacitation. The gradual acquisition (or loss) of the individual's capabilities reflects a social process, centring on the interaction urban context and on the active role that the urban context makes it possible to develop. The unit of analysis to which the framework applies can thus be the individual, but also the urban or sub-urban context insofar as it is made up of a mixed collectivity populating a given environment-territory [2].

2 Multidisciplinary Approach for Urban Health Policies

About the major explanatory models for health inequalities [3, 4], the framework makes it possible to shed light on the main causal relationships.

First, the effect in the framework—shortages of resources generate poor health—has been considered as the central hypothesis of structural materialist theories—where the cause of poor health is deprivation measured on socioeconomic status, which incorporates control over resources and relationships to be used to protect oneself, or on social class, defined by the level of employment, from the standpoint of the social division of labour.

Second, effect—poor health generates a shortage of resources—is directly linked to a mechanism which is central to the theory of social selection, whereby the state of health generates an impact on social position, even though the framework does not assign its origin primarily to the individuals' bio psychic makeup, but rather to the socially correlated process of deterioration in health.

In addition, the centrality that the framework assigns to the context, as the fundamental area in which policies influence the conversion functions for the resources that individuals are able to deploy in their living environments (work, home, neighbourhood, family, school, relationships of proximity, social circles, etc.), leads to interesting interpretations regarding how we should deal with consolidated theories. This role of the context suggests that it is necessary to insert the individual analysis of the relationship between cause (social determinants) and effect (poor health) in the analysis of the set of constraints and opportunities which the context permits that particular individual, given his resources and personal capabilities.

The basic hypothesis underscored by the framework is that the *systemic qualities* of the context cannot be gauged accurately enough from the individual capabilities of the people who populate it. This realization has repercussions both on research strategies and on policy assessment.

As regards the individual-context relationship, in particular, the proposed framework acknowledges the importance of individuals' freedom to construct their well-being and social trajectories (by activating resources and the individual capabilities that characterize them), at the same time assigning importance to the social processes that take place in the contexts, which have a significant capacity to influence them through their effects on the set of constraints and opportunities that are available for choices and on the yield from resources and individual capabilities that interact with the social capabilities—learning and culture—that are typical of the context. These contextual effects act at the moment of choice, but from a temporal perspective generate effects of accumulation and structuring of social pathways, where the pathway follows trajectories whose directions are the opportunities that are actually and socially present and important in the real contexts of life.

In this light, the psycho-social theories that identify, for example, the stressful effect on work of the prolonged imbalance between the (high amounts of) effort expended and the (inadequate) compensation received, or between the (high) demands of the organization and the (inadequate) room for individual independence must be used by emphasizing the mediation performed by the organizational context, which can cause considerable variations in the relationship between individual deprivation (e.g. a job as an unskilled labourer) and prolonged stress (which is harmful to health). In this connection, we should note that there is an *objective* aspect of the cause-effect combination, as well as a *subjective* aspect which depends on the meaning that the individual assigns to his condition and the objectively sensed gap. However, the meaning assigned (for instance, when an unskilled labourer feels actively involved in doing his job well and believes that he is fairly compensated for his effort) is very much a social product, which does not characterize the individual so much as the organization's culture (or sub-culture) and hence the social micro-context in which the relationship unfolds. Consequently, the interaction of the context is decisive in analyzing the relationship of cause and effect between deprivation and health.

A similar problem of contextualization arises for the cultural-behavioural theories that focus attention on the effect that behaviour considered *normal* in certain communities, groups or relational environments has on health. Here again, the meaning socially assigned to the behaviour is very important, as is the micro-context of which it is a part. This is the most serious problem to be overcome by a policy whose goal is to change individual behaviour that can be harmful to health. And again, there may be socially structured pathways that constitute sequences of meanings that can reduce (or expand) people's freedom and change their horizon of opportunity, whatever their resources and individual capabilities may be.

The mechanisms investigated by ecological theories—which causally, and more or less directly, connect individuals' health to the characteristics of the geographical area where they live—may seem to be the case in which the importance of the context is most fully recognized. Actually, here as in the instances discussed above, there is a risk of reductionism if direct decontextualized relationships are established between elements of the context (such as the lack of green space in urban areas) and people's health. In this case, the system elements of the context that enhance it and qualify its attributes, affording real opportunities for people: even if there are green spaces such as parks in the city, for example, they could be not a real opportunity for health if people did not go there or regarded them as dangerous; conversely, if people meet friends when they go to parks, physical activity can be an indirect product of a significant system of social relationships contextualized in the park and the neighbourhood around it.

Finally, what may seem in individual pathways to be a concatenation between negative events (event A and event B) linked to cumulative individual disadvantages can be contextualized from the standpoint of the context as an absence of integration between policies that are incapable of constructing connections and pathways within people's grasp, enabling them to cope not only with event A or event B but also with their simultaneous presence and negative interaction. For example, we could mention the combination of disability and loss of work, or of leaving school and having trouble finding a job. To cope with every single disadvantage, the individual is supported by a policy, but this does not necessarily mean that a policy exists that coordinates and optimizes the impact for those who find themselves exposed to both risks. On the contrary, it may be that the two interventions interfere with each other if assistance and services for employment, or education, do not work together in constructing the intervention, the constraints and the incentives so that they are tailored to the person's needs. Thus, the opportunity of being able to access effective interventions is first of all a quality of the context, which offers people this possibility. It must be a pathway that is accessible to all those who want to make use of it, and which calls for processes of involvement and contextualized activation of the beneficiaries.

In the light of the exposed framework we would propose the following recommendations to reformulate the main indications resulting from the contributions of the book.

3 A Bottom-Up Strategy to Transfer Effective Practices

3.1 Recommendation 1—New Capabilities, Created Through Community

To promote health, people need to be able to monitor and protect their health, using their capabilities. This is an approach based on the empowerment of people, on their freedom [1]. People must be able to act with a lifestyle that is consistent with the protection of their health and must be able to make choices in their living environment that allow it, expressing their capabilities. As the example of the bicycle makes clear: to help the person move easily, it is not enough to give him a bicycle. The person must be able to use it to move and there must be paths to use it.

Many people who live in cities have insufficient personal resources and personal skills to cope with the problems that create risks for their health. Those looking only to fill their resource gap use an individualistic and passivating care approach. This type of welfare does not remove the causes that have led a person to have a high health risk. If the causes are social determinants affecting the living environment, there is the risk of treating the person but leaving him or her back in the social environment that generated the damage to health (Marmot).

Furthermore, the individual lack of resources and skills in many cases cannot be changed because it occurred in the past. For example, low education, physical disability due to illness, functional limits generated by old age, etc. Therefore, the only way in these cases would seem to be to make the urban context easier for people, activating communities, so that they become a multiplier of individual resources and a place for risk prevention. This is also the way for people to be individually and collectively protagonists in the solution of their problems, which ensures the effectiveness of the action and structural sustainability over time. Action research is the methodology that we believe represents this transformative approach to social contexts, in which institutional and social actors and people who are part of the community act together.

Since the origins of human history, communities have developed cultures and social skills to support the proper functioning of people, making use of both the ability to optimize local-specific resources and the capacity for coordination and cooperation rooted in social practices learned over time.

The activation and social use of these resources are not taken for granted but depend on the characteristics of the contexts and communities. It requires the enhancement and integration of different cultures and knowledge.

Interesting cases of community approaches and practices are described in this volume. Snakes are a threat, but some communities have learned to use them to meet their own needs, as they are available there. As proposed by João Paulo Lima Barreto, starting from the experience of the Indigence Medicine Center of Manaus-Amazonia in Brazil, there are different models and concepts for health promotion. There are different methods in the knowledge of the indigenous people, the resources of the community are different and we must always ask ourselves together with the people who belong to the community what should be used to face a problem, that is, how to do it?

Therefore, the practices are based on multicultural and multidisciplinary knowledge rooted in the histories of the communities and the innovations consist mainly in the recombination of this knowledge, integrated where necessary with new elements, for example, derived from the potential of technologies. These practices and these skills have been disrupted and sometimes wiped out with the dominant urban organization of the last century, driven by the processes of industrialization and urbanization, which has imposed standardized, depersonalized and inattentive models on pre-existing social relations and community cultures.

3.2 Recommendation 2—New Common Vision and Community Cooperation and Integration to Promote Health and Equity

Policies and services characterized by a bureaucratic culture often provide inadequate answers to address these problems. The bureaucratic culture is centralizing, it implements rigid planning of activities, guided by decisions from the top. It is based on the rigid distinction of different specializations and skills, which operate separately and are organized following vertical responsibilities, according to hierarchical-functional organizational engineering invented and applied in all organizations at the beginning of the last century. The prevalence of a hierarchical-formal logic generates a widespread de-responsibility of the people who work in the services and depersonalization of the service, which is implemented in a standardized way, without any involvement of the recipient [5].

This service culture is particularly bad in personal services that require high personalization and high-quality relationships, such as health, social and educational services. Only an overcoming of this organizational culture opens up spaces both for multicultural and multidisciplinary learning and for the integration of skills and processes. Faced with the inadequacy of services (queues, waits, poor quality, people's dissatisfaction, unequal treatment, etc.) the reaction of the bureaucracy goes in the opposite direction of what would be useful. The rigidity of the system increases, the number and rigour of the rules multiply, the powers attributed to the hierarchy are centralized with an upward shift of decisions, the sanctions are tightened, each service entrenches itself in its specialized skills and works to watertight compartments. For these reasons it is known that hierarchical-bureaucratic structures are incapable of innovation. In the volume, reference is often made to these ways of functioning that are not attentive to people and their cultures, which constitute a problem to be overcome.

Alfredo Brillembourg (founder of Urban-Think Tank Design Group 'Urban think tank: we need to reorganize the city') proposes an interesting interpretation of the limits and unexpected effects of a formal bureaucratic approach. They carried out discrete interventions on individual structures, from the vertical gym to collective housing, «but all the while, we were thinking and talking about the city, about what participatory urbanism might mean and be in the twenty-first century. The rigid separation of formal and informal, planned and ad hoc, wealth and poverty, makes no sense to us. Those distinctions are inherently unstable politically, economically, and geographically; marginalization is a social and physical phenomenon, a kind of illness afflicting the civic body».

Health promotion should adapt to the characteristics that social contexts in cities have today. These are contexts where uncertainty grows, where the speed of change makes it difficult for people and communities to adapt and find solutions simply by drawing on their own experience, as has been done for centuries in traditional communities.

Current social and market environments—called VUCA environment, Volatility, Uncertainty, Complexity, and Ambiguity [6]—are complex systems, in which continuous and dynamic relationships and interdependencies cannot be fully described, understood, or expected, as if they were single elements that add up as a whole. There are therefore emergent properties, non-linear reactions, effects that are difficult to predict, which characterize the ecosystems in which organizations operate, including those dealing with health.

Furthermore, the so-called *wicked problems* that are highly resistant to resolution are spreading. They are problems that are difficult to define, socially complex, multi-causal with many interdependencies and have no clear solution and are not the responsibility of anyone organization or government department [7].

These environments require an approach that goes beyond the linear logic of strategic planning adopted by leadership in bureaucratic systems: a top-down logic that aimed to align people's behaviour towards well-defined organizational objectives, using command and control mechanisms. The new paradigm is completely different, dominated by uncertainty and systemic complexity. In this scenario, communities and groups should be as autonomous as possible, capable of moving in unknown and changing contexts, dealing with different specializations and cultures and bringing out new ideas, strategies and anticipations. Therefore, the focus should shift from centralized control of activities to the development of interactions, which emerge and evolve at a decentralized level. These relationships require self-organized groups and people to face and overcome the challenges rooted in the ecosystems in which they operate [8, 9], such as environmental, energy and resource scarcity ones.

The point is that the protagonists should use different disciplines, tools and interpretative schemes in a contemporary and integrated way. To understand a complex natural environment, for example, one must use the telescope and the microscope at the same time: they look at different levels of the complex system, both of which are important for understanding its functioning, as are sociology, economics, urban architecture and the life sciences.

An excellent example of this perspective is the case of 'Aedification—Grands Territoires—Villes' of the École Nationale Supérieure d'Architecture de Grenoble told by Patrick Thépot, who raises the question of good living, well-being and health, based on the study the tradition of places and specific architectural proposals that analyze the environment from three different perspectives: natural, artificial and human. This approach pushes us to rethink informal building through innovative prototypes inspired by local know-how.

Also, the contribution of Jorge Mario Jáuregui (architect urbanist in Rio de Janeiro) shows that the observation of the urban environment from different perspectives is indispensable but difficult to achieve: «What we need from now on is to merge red (social justice) with green (intelligent relations with the environment) by promoting responsible public policies and mobilizing citizens, in the sense of making cities fairer, with quality public spaces and facilities, guaranteeing the enjoyment of urbanity for everyone! Uniting the space justice agenda with the economic and environmental agenda».

There are recent approaches to the organization—such as the agile organization—which consider teamwork, group heterogeneity, multiculturalism and multidisciplinarity as the conditions for being effective and innovative in complex contexts.

In the field of health promotion, the Integrated strategies of community health promotion (ISCHP) highlight the role that integration can play. The ISCHP are based on intersectoral collaborations using the *Health in All Policies* approach to addressing determinants of health. It is a logic of integrated cooperation based on a common diagnosis, which has effects on the community and consequently on health. A recent German study compared diabetes mortality in Germany with longitudinal data: a nonrandomized evaluation based on secondary county-level official data (1998–2016). In April 2019, 149 communities in Germany with ISCHP out of 401 were identified. Analyzes included 65 communities with ISCHP (IG) and 124 without ISCHP (CG). ISCHP ran for a mean of 5.6 years. The study showed that mortality responds to theoretical assumptions about the role of the community, significantly decreasing in those where integrated policies have developed. The duration of ISCHP was negatively associated with the diabetes mellitus mortality (DMM). Each year with ISCHP, the DMM reduces on average by 0.3 per 100,000 persons, decreasing to an annually DMM by 4.8 per 100,000 persons after 16 years of ISCHP

[10]. This result urges us to focus attention on the multicultural, multidisciplinary and integrated nature of the processes to be promoted.

A review conducted on 58 evaluation studies shows that interventions led by community coalitions may connect health and human service providers with ethnic and racial minority communities in ways that benefit individual health outcomes and behaviours, as well as care delivery systems. The study shows that community strategies that are not limited to generating formal coalitions but involve operators and professionals to change work processes and practices are more effective [11].

The review carried out by Nissinen, Berrios and Puska [2] on community-based noncommunicable disease interventions shows that a good understanding of the community, close collaboration with various community organizations, and full participation of the people themselves are needed. Common guidelines on the interventions must be adapted to local cultures in a flexible way [2].

The book *Implementing Health in All Policies: Adelaide 2010* [7] sustains that it is difficult to adequately document all the tangible and intangible benefits concerning health improvements that arise from the application of HiAP in communities all over the world.

This suggests the need to refine the assessment tools, which should address both short and long-term health outcomes, and the cooperation and integration requirements required of communities to generate them, which we can call intermediate outcomes [12]. It also suggests, consistently with the action research approach, to involve all actors, professionals and citizens, not only in the processes to strengthen capabilities but also in assessing that this happens in daily life.

3.3 Recommendation 3—New Distributed Leadership to Involve Bottom-Up Professionals and Citizens in Cooperative and Integrated Practices

Structural and substantial changes in the organizational approach to policies and services are necessary to promote health through cooperation and integration of cultures, disciplines and processes. New leaderships, therefore, are needed.

In the international literature in the last decade, various theories have been affirming that they answer precisely this demand for change. They radically go beyond the logic of the hierarchical manager in the bureaucratic-mechanistic organization.

The main organizational impacts of this leadership revolution appear to be the following two. First: less asymmetrical management of power and influence, to increase cooperation in work. This requires greater sharing of information, resources, autonomy and professional learning more aimed at empowering people. Second: marked structural effects of leadership on the organizational and local-territorial ecosystem, to support new multicultural, multidisciplinary and integrated cooperation processes.

Collaborative leadership and moral leadership are the most interesting evolutions of the new leadership of the last decade. These new forms of leadership are not opposite but converge and are creating a new leadership for the future that we are calling *distributed* [13]. New leadership styles that promote collaborative relationships are referred to in the literature as shared, collective, horizontal, distributed leadership [14]. The new moral styles are called ethical, authentic, servant, spiritual, humble, responsible leadership. The first three definitions are the most widespread and a recent review has analyzed their ethical foundations by identifying in the debate of moral philosophy the reasons why they can be considered fully belonging to a single moral approach to leadership [15], where the leader intends to be primarily a moral agent.

This new idea of leadership is based on solid theories and is effective according to numerous empirical research. It creates ecosystems that are increasingly rich in relationships and interdependencies, which are equipped with digital technologies and are oriented towards innovation. In these environments, the formal hierarchy takes a back seat and leaders emerge who build collaboration and empower people. Distributed leadership is innovative both because it is shared between people who cooperate, and because it is committed to multiplying itself, increasing people's responsibilities, autonomy and skills. The central question to distinguish the different leaders today is: who are you doing this for? Traditional leaders use empathy, emotional intelligence, charisma, to impose their vision, their power, their agenda on others. Servant leaders and cooperation builders use those same skills to create empowerment, to train teams, to build common and sustainable identities and meanings. The leader then becomes a social architect, educator and assistant to the people he collaborates with (Peter Senge in [16]), a builder of cooperative relationships based on the ability to respond to the differentiated needs of people [17]. Richard Kelly calls it swarm leadership, typical of the swarm of bees, distributed as it appears in nature to become the strength and intelligence of a collective-reticular subject.

It is not a downhill road, on the contrary. Research shows that organizational experiences are constantly hindered by the weight of hierarchical-bureaucratic power, which bypasses the involvement of people and the delegation of decision-making spaces, even when it is counterproductive.

The contributions of Daniela Dalessandro and Emma Capogrossi refer to the difficulties deriving from hierarchical and bureaucratic organization models, which work in watertight compartments and favour the separation between disciplines rather than a multidisciplinary approach, open to participation. Conversely, many people are also used to passivity and seek advantages in environments that do not require commitment, responsibility and participation. It is a centuries-old tradition that focuses on an individualistic conception of command, work and technology without considering the complex social rules that guide behaviour in the social environments of work and life.

3.4 Recommendation 4—New Social Mechanisms to Create Intentionally and Systematically Cooperation and Integrated Processes to Promote Health and Equity

How is it possible to increase cooperation and participation by changing processes and working practices? In a recent evaluation study of an Italian Integrated Community Care experience in the city of Trieste (Habitat Microaree Program—HMP), we measured the effectiveness of social mechanisms and their ability to create a stable social infrastructure. Based on literature data, it was assumed that social mechanisms can be determined by three characteristics, that is: considering any vulnerable individual X, the following mechanisms could elicit or amplify health-oriented behaviour: (1) strategic interdependence: when X's choices or gratifications are connected to those of other players; (2) process interdependence: when other players sequentially influence the choices of the individual X; (3) spatial-relational interdependence: when space proximity increases the number of relationships and affects the speed and direction of X's choices [18, 19]. We used these criteria in empirical research to identify and recognize social mechanisms: the qualitative analysis revealed that the work of the HMP professionals was inspired by a common vision and line of action, with the conscious and constant use of various social mechanisms. The following eight mechanisms were identified and selected, as they responded to the aforementioned empirical criteria: activation, trust, recognition, inclusion, coordination, cooperation, integration and education.

An analysis of the real-life stories verified that each of these social mechanisms created new inter-dependence between professionals, vulnerable individuals, neighbours and others within the Micro-areas. More specifically, each of these social mechanisms included the three characteristics aforementioned as definition criteria, i.e., strategic, process and spatial-relational interdependence. They generated strategic interdependence, offering new material, symbolic and gratification advantages derived from the new relationships with others. These benefits are derived from the involvement in collective processes, where individuals give gifts, exchange time and resources and together create new scenarios and alliances to face problems. In turn, the desirable and possible choice options, as well as the basic social norms which indicate appropriate behaviour within the community, were modified. Moreover, process inter-dependence was also created because collective practices are linked together, over time, due to the conditions they create, the synergies they predispose, etc. Step by step, they progressively allow experimenting with the concrete practicality of reciprocity and incremental growth in the trust. Lastly, individuals systematically exploit spatial-relational inter-dependence, creating the physical and social conditions of closeness, as well as new means of representation. This gives meaning to the new behaviours and allows for the concrete use of physical and social spaces to share experiences in person. During this phase we were able to verify that the way social mechanisms work and the new specific properties of social capital give a plausible explanation of most evident empirical phenomena (collaborative behaviour, exchange, aid, etc.) which have been narrated, observed and filmed by the actors, to tell others about the change that has taken place. These include going regularly to the collective spaces available in the Micro-area, the willingness to give and mutually help others, as well as the visible cooperation and sociability observed in these premises. This is exactly the opposite of how things were before the HMP intervention, where these areas and their inhabitants were encompassed in sentiments like diffidence and abandonment. Moreover, it came to light that the coherent application of these social mechanisms also influenced the organization of public socio-health services in two ways: (1) it engaged professionals in the continual improvement of services for vulnerable individuals, following the lean-organizational model, and (2) it allowed for progressive integration of the various processes and services supporting vulnerable individuals, in response to their needs [13].

Hence the role of public and private operators: activating social technologies that generate active and coordinated people in communities, leveraging the intrinsic motivation that drives people's direct participation. It is acting in collaboration to transform the environment that strengthens the common vision and shared meanings. It creates the city that takes care of itself, that repairs itself because citizens take care of it, through a new relationship with professionals, a new balance of power between disciplines, between people and professionals, between institutions and communities.

3.5 Recommendation 5—New Value and Measurement of the Quality and the Common Meanings of the Relationships and Exchanges in the Community

The experience of community involvement and the collaborative and integrated bottom-up transformation processes teaches two key points. First, it is necessary to identify suitable indicators to represent the change that is to be generated to verify the effectiveness of the action. Second, these indicators must be considered significant by community actors, health professionals, citizens and institutional and social actors, who must be the first to conduct observations and checks on the change [20]. The evaluation must therefore turn into self-evaluation to support and motivate the involvement and empowerment of people.

We see an important phenomenon in the experiences of Integrated Community Care: bottom-up control increases because vertical control is reduced, the capacity for coordination between professionals and citizens increases because planning and formalization from the top are reduced, people take on more responsibility because the rules for obtaining behaviours aligned with health practices are reduced and simplified.

An interesting book *Yes to the Mess. Surprising leadership lessons from jazz* by Frank J. Barrett uses the experience of the jazz band to show how involvement and improvisation, which are the basis of the best jazz performances, arise from disorder, from the ability to unlearn old practices and discover together with others. the new ones. Minimum rules and mutual listening leave room for the new. In cities, we do not yet know what exactly the best solutions will be for innovation in each place, for energy, sustainability, mobility, housing, etc. It should be the product of a collective work capable of discovering the new, as the jazz band finds new musical paths through the different creativity of its members. If everyone always plays the same thing, nothing new will ever be created.

Patrick Thépot's experience is instructive when faced with the question *how are buildings built?* This shows the need for a common path to seek new balances between different elements, between people and communities, between sun and shade, between water, humidity and dry, etc.

The activities of sharing objectives and evaluating the achievements obtained, using shared indicators, therefore constitute an essential part of the transformation processes in action research and bring together and grow different cultures, different specializations and several hypotheses about the solution, which must be measured in an empirical way regarding practicability and sustainability.

The method for guiding these measurements is important. In our practices with the communities, we have let the protagonists identify suitable indicators to measure the effective creation of social infrastructures, people's capabilities and health. The methodological support consists in guiding the search for three types of indicators: (1) process indicators, (2) intermediate impact indicators (social capital, capabilities) and (3) final impact indicators (health). In each of these three areas, according to the priorities of the community, four types of measures can be identified: (a) efficiency/cost, (b) effectiveness/quality, (c) equity, (d) systemic innovation. In the aforementioned case of evaluation of the HMP program, many of these indicators were reflected in the research and made it possible to observe the changes obtained by the intervention in capabilities, social capital and health, with a specific compensation effect of inequalities.

4 From *Social Determinants* to *Determining Societies*

The *capacitating* significance of the context, which can increase or diminish people's self-determination, freedom and self-esteem, is thus a complex property, and one which cannot readily be reduced to the sum—important though it is—of the parameters traditionally used to measure the deprivation and disadvantage of social groups or geographical areas. The book contribution proposes that there are qualities of the context that can prevent physical damage and promote people's growth. Evidence of this regards all policies and all citizens. In the virtuous cases, there is an increase in individual and collective capabilities to learn, use and combine current resources, to integrate and make the most of one's resources, family resources and social resources, to make more flexible use of one's own time and the intersection between biographies and social times, and to freely personalize structured social pathways and the shape of reproductive regimes. In these cases, moreover, there is likewise a tendency of the policy delivery systems and services to be involved in the game, showing greater capacity for personalization, integration, multi specialization and, above all, for participation in localized social learning processes. The interpretative viewpoints emphasized by our framework spotlights the importance of the cultural dimension of contexts, which can be qualified by shared values and can assign active roles to people and encourage their promotion and growth.

It is interesting to note that all the contributions contemplated major contextual dimensions, beyond an individual interpretation of people's resources and the relationship between inequalities in resources and health. The yield from economic resources can only be seen as a part of contextualized social processes. From this perspective, the determinants identified as the objects of policies in a rigid thematic distinction risk leading to partial and even misleading visions of the situation. The urban polices experience provides many examples of the risks of reductionism: reducing the speed of cars in a neighbourhood is wasted if it serves only to reduce pollution and is not used to enhance social relationships in the neighbourhood (though this also depends on how the policy is designed and implemented); an opportunity to return to work is underutilized if it only serves to generate employment income, but not to help the person grow, through the type of context the person enters, etc. Thus, only a panoramic view of the basic operating mechanisms of contexts can enable us to give a systemic, relative meaning to the many statistically significant causal relationships between determinants and health outcomes. In the same way, we must ask ourselves whether the room for improvement in policies does not lie precisely in making the most of their externalities (making them central) and in the opportunity for virtuous integration between different policies, avoiding the risk that the externalities of one will reduce or cancel out the impact of another.

Here the book provides several interesting examples: giving economic resources, in certain circumstances, can make people passive. Another relevant aspect concerns the phenomena of accumulation, which have attracted considerable attention in life course studies. From this standpoint, scrutiny of the context shows how empirical findings indicate that accumulation phenomena are processes that are not only individual but social, linked to pathways of development or deterioration over time in specific groups and communities. In this sense, the externalities of specific experiences induced or supported by policies are even more important, because they create the social construction within which certain choices and/or opportunities are possible. Accordingly, the universalistic and preventive policies must first of all address the contexts to reduce inequalities. As regards policies, this representation urges us to go beyond deterministic and materialistic views, assigning importance to the meaning that things take on in their contexts, more than to the things themselves. Contexts are not mere places or environments where policies and interventions are transmitted, and cannot be taken for granted. Therefore, it is crucial to observe the ability of policies to support the active dynamics of contexts and make them evolve so that they can create opportunities and meaning for the people involved in them. This presupposes assigning importance to their changeability and increasing the ability to represent and measure their fundamental qualities, in many social and geographical environments, both about designing policies and as regards their assessment. Investing in contexts and shifting the burden of coordinating and promoting growth to the organizations is essential because social learning and providing room for people's freedom and self-determination are prerequisites for the effectiveness of a wide range of policies.

References

1. Sen A (1986) Scelta, benessere, equità, Bologna, Il Mulino
2. Nissinen A, Berrios X, Puska P (2001) Community-based noncommunicable disease interventions: lessons from developed countries for developing ones. Bull World Health Organ 79(10):963–970. Published 1 Nov 2001
3. Costa G, Faggiano F (eds) (1994) L'equità della salute in Italia. Rapporto sulle diseguaglianze sociali in sanità. Franco Angeli, Milano
4. Costa G, Cislaghi C, Caranci N (eds) (2009) Le disuguaglianze sociali di salute. Problemi di definizione e di misura, In Salute e società, Year VIII – 1/2009
5. Laverack G (2009) Public health: power, empowerment and professional practice. Macmillan, London
6. Bennett N, Lemoine J (2014) What VUCA really means for you. Harvard Bus Rev 92(1/2)
7. Kickbusch I, Buckett K (eds) (2010) Implementing health in all policies: adelaide 2010. Department of Health, Government of South Australia
8. Birute R, Lewin R (2000) Leading at the edge: How leaders influence complex systems. Emergence 2(2):5–23
9. Russ M, Uhl-Bien M (2001) Leadership in complex organizations. Leadersh Quart 12(4):389–418
10. Röding D, Walter U, Dreier M (2021) Long-term effects of integrated strategies of community health promotion on diabetes mellitus mortality: a natural policy experiment based on aggregated longitudinal secondary data. J Urban Health 98:791–800
11. Anderson LM, Adeney KL, Shinn C, Safranek S, Buckner-Brown J, Krause LK (2015) Community coalition-driven interventions to reduce health disparities among racial and ethnic minority populations. Cochrane Database Syst Rev 2015(6) Art. No.: CD009905. https://doi.org/10.1002/14651858.CD009905.pub2
12. Di Monaco R, Pilutti S, d'Errico A, Costa G (2020) Promoting health equity through social capital in deprived communities: a natural policy experiment in Trieste, Italy. In: Social science & medicine—population health. Elsevier, vol. 12, 100677 1–11, ISSN: 2352-8273
13. Di Monaco R, Pilutti S (2021) Scommettere sulle persone. Leadership distribuita per l'organizzazione smart & green, agile, lean e 4.0. Egea Bocconi, Collana biblioteca dell'economia d'azienda, Seconda edizione, Milano, ISBN 9788823846937.
14. Zhu J, Liao Z, Yam KC, Johnson RE (2018) Shared leadership: a state-of-the-art review and future research agenda. J Organ Behav 39(7):834–852
15. Lemoine GJ, Hartnell CA, Leroy H (2019) Taking stock of moral approaches to leadership: an integrative review of ethical, authentic and servant leadership. Acad Manag 13(1):148–187
16. Quaglino GP (a cura di) (2005) Leadership: nuovi profili di leader per nuovi scenari organizzativi. Raffaello Cortina Editore, Milano
17. Barnard C (1963) Le funzioni del dirigente. Torino, Utet
18. Barbera F (2004) Meccanismi sociali. Elementi di sociologia analitica. Il Mulino, Milano
19. Hedstrom P, Swedberg R (1998) Social mechanisms: an analytical approach to social theory. Cambridge University Press
20. Zengarini N, Pilutti S, Marra M, Scavarda A, Stroscia M, Di Monaco R, Beccaria F, Costa G (2021) Focusing urban policies on health equity: the role of evidence in stakeholder engagement in an Italian urban setting. Cities & Health. https://doi.org/10.1080/23748834.2021.1886543